What is History Now?

What is History Now?

Edited by

David Cannadine

First published in hardcover 2002

First published in paperback 2004 by
PALGRAVE MACMILLAN
Houndmills, Basingstoke, Hampshire RG21 6XS and
175 Fifth Avenue, New York, N. Y. 10010
Companies and representatives throughout the world

PALGRAVE MACMILLAN is the global academic imprint of the Palgrave Macmillan division of St. Martin's Press, LLC and of Palgrave Macmillan Ltd. Macmillan® is a registered trademark in the United States, United Kingdom and other countries. Palgrave is a registered trademark in the European Union and other countries.

ISBN 0–333–98646–6 hardback
ISBN 1–4039–3336–7 paperback

This book is printed on paper suitable for recycling and made from fully managed and sustained forest sources.

A catalogue record for this book is available from the British Library.

Library of Congress Cataloging-in-Publication Data
What is history now? / edited by David Cannadine.
        p. cm.
    Includes bibliographical references and index.
    ISBN 0–333–98646–6 (cloth)
    ISBN 1–4039–3336–7 (pbk)
      1. History—Philosophy. 2. History—Historiography. 3. Historiography.
I. Cannadine, David, 1950–

    D16.8.W5 2002
    901—dc21
                                                                    2002072601

10   9   8   7   6   5   4   3   2   1
13   12   11   10   09   08   07   06   05   04

Printed and bound in Great Britain by
Antony Rowe Ltd, Chippenham and Eastbourne

Contents

Preface

The chapters gathered together in this volume, ranging widely (though not all-encompassingly) across our present-day perspectives on the past, were originally delivered as lectures at a two-day symposium, held at the Institute of Historical Research in London on 14 and 15 November 2001, to mark the fortieth anniversary of the original publication, by Macmillan, of E.H. Carr's seminal-cum-perennial *What is History?* Accordingly, my first and most grateful thanks are to the generous co-sponsors of that lively, memorable and well-attended occasion: the Master and Fellows of Trinity College, Cambridge (where Carr was for many years a Fellow), and Palgrave Macmillan (the lineal descendant of Macmillan's). I am equally indebted to each of the principal speakers, not only for performing with such vigour and elan on the day, but also for rapidly reworking their lectures for publication against a very tight deadline. As originally delivered, each lecture was followed by a respondent, and I am most grateful to Judith Herrin, Warren Boutcher, Peter Marshall, Philip Williamson, Lyndal Roper, Daniel Pick and Catherine Hall for their stimulating comments and suggestive remarks, which not only helped initiate and sustain vigorous discussion at the conference, but were also of much help to the contributors to this volume in revising their lectures for publication.

From the outset, and in conformity with the mission of the Institute of Historical Research to provide a setting where scholars from Britain and around the world may congregate and connect, confer and contend, the purpose of this gathering was threefold: to celebrate and re-evaluate Carr's original publication four decades after its first appearance; to explore and explain the many developments and astonishing diversification of history in the intervening years since Carr wrote his book; and to create a volume which might reach the sort of broad public audience for whom history rightly remains (as it should, and as it must) an essential element in educated citizenry, public culture and national life. In a conference which, for various practical reasons, could only last for two days, it was impossible to cover all the strands in Clio's widely woven raiment, and economic historians, military historians, business historians, local historians, maritime historians, historians of art, of science, of population, of the family, and of diplomacy (to name the most immediately obvious examples), may well feel themselves unreasonably neglected and unhelpfully excluded. To which the only possible reply can be that a second, complementary volume is not at all beyond the bounds of possibility.[1]

E.H. Carr's *What is History?* originated as the George Macaulay Trevelyan Lectures, delivered at Cambridge University between January and March 1961.[2] As such, they were a salute by a Fellow of Trinity to a former Master of the College who was widely regarded as the Grand Old Man of British History and the last great Whig historian. By then, Trevelyan was very much out of fashion among professional historians, and developments in the writing of history during the 1960s – many of them prefigured and foreseen by Carr – would only make this appear more so. To be sure, in describing history as a constant encounter between then and now, in which the time-bound preoccupations of the scholar needed to be recognized and appreciated, Carr was saying nothing which Trevelyan would have found exceptionable. But in urging the primacy of long-term economic and social forces, in insisting on the validity of extra-European history, in giving significant attention to sociology and causation, and in denying the importance of the individual or the unique event, Carr was advocating a very different sort of history from Trevelyan's national narratives and admiring biographies.[3]

Moreover, it was precisely this kind of history, as defined and described by Carr, which became very fashionable on the new and expanding campuses of Britain, Western Europe and North America during the 1960s and 1970s, as economic and social history (aided and abetted by the cult of quantification) threatened to marginalize traditional political history, as the preoccupation with causes and with analysis superseded the conventional interest in narrative and chronicle, and as the belief that history could help us master the present and even change the future seemed to give it a progressive public purpose that many conservative scholars detested and distrusted.[4] Chief among them was G.R. Elton, whose *The Practice of History* (Sydney: Sydney University Press 1967) was written in what even he feared was vain protest against the trends (and the trendiness) of the 1960s, and explicitly against E.H. Carr – seeking as he did to re-assert the primacy of political history and of narrative; to re-state the view that history did not help us understand the present, let alone influence the future; and to denounce the faddishness of sociology and social history, and the study of the (non-existent?) extra-European past.[5]

To be sure, a great deal of the best history accomplished during the 1960s and 1970s was of the sort that Carr encouraged and Elton disliked: works such as Lawrence Stone's *The Crisis of the Aristocracy, 1558–1641* (Oxford: Oxford University Press, 1965), J.H. Plumb's *The Growth of Political Stability in England, 1675–1725* (London: Macmillan, 1967), E.P. Thompson's *The Making of the English Working Class* (London: Victor Gollancz, 1963) and Ronald Robinson and J.A. Gallagher's *Africa and the Victorians* (London: Macmillan, 1961). Yet despite his increasingly paranoid fears, much history during the 1960s and 1970s was still being done the Elton way: it was traditional political and constitutional scholarship, deeply grounded in the archives, and conservative and empiricist in its academic values. Indeed, by the end of the 1970s, there was something of a crisis in the much-vaunted 'new' history of which *What is History?* had been in some ways the precursor: quantification did not seem to deliver as much as was hoped; sociology provided less of a help than had originally been believed; and the stress on the causal and the analytical no longer seemed so appealing. This sense of disillusion was well captured in Lawrence Stone's article on 'The Revival of Narrative', which appeared in *Past & Present* in 1979, and which might equally well have been entitled 'The Demise of Causation'.[6]

Within a year of Stone's article, the intellectual landscape was changed even more significantly, with the advent to power of Margaret Thatcher in the United Kingdom and Ronald Reagan in the United States. The fact that the 1980s also witnessed the rise of historical 'revisionism' was no coincidence: in stressing the importance and autonomy of the political past, the revisionists were deliberately rejecting the economic and social determinism fashionable in the 1960s, in the same way that Thatcher and Reagan sought to do in the political present. But for all his ardent support of the revisionist cause, this did not mean, as Geoffrey Elton hoped, that the 1980s and 1990s saw a 'return to essentials', for these decades also witnessed a profound array of other developments which changed the nature of historical enquiry in ways that Elton did not like and Carr did not foresee.[7] Among them were the revolution in IT, which transformed and democratized scholarship, and the further expansion in higher education; the shift from sociology to anthropology as the most fruitful subject from which historians were now borrowing; the influence of Michel Foucault, postmodernism and the 'linguistic turn'; the rise of women's history, gender history and cultural history, and the reconfiguration of 'imperial' history; and a broader shift away from the search for causation to the search for meaning.[8]

Many of these developments are addressed and analysed in the chapters which follow. As even its most ardent apologists admit, social history is no longer the confident, all-encompassing subject it seemed to be during the 1960s and 1970s. Instead, it has settled down to a more modest, more realistic and thus more helpful agenda – not the history of society as a whole, but the history of various aspects of society. By contrast, political history, which seemed so under 'threat' during those decades, has re-established and revived itself, not by reasserting the Eltonian claims of separateness and superiority, but by broadening its scope and embracing many of the more recent changes that have taken place in neighbouring disciplines. In the same way, 'imperial' history, which seemed so peripheral a subject in the history syllabuses of the 1960s, has now moved centre-stage, transformed and enhanced by the influence of postmodernism and post-colonial studies, and providing an essential bridge between national and global histories. In all these areas, the shift in interest from causes to meaning, from explanation to understanding, is well-marked; and as such they are all to some degree following the alternative agenda which was sketched out for historians of political thought more than thirty years ago.[9]

However, of all the historical sub-specialisms that were already in being when Carr wrote his book, it seems likely that religious history has been the most fundamentally transformed by developments since then – away from the history of theology and of the (male-dominated) institutions which proclaimed and supported it, and towards a broader concern with popular religiosity, as approached through ritual, culture and gender, which has opened up large swathes of hitherto ignored territory. Indeed, just as social history seemed poised to sweep all before it in the 1960s, now cultural history seems to be in the ascendant: partly because it has been the most receptive to the insights of anthropology; partly because it makes very large claims about the terrain of the past which it encompasses; and partly because it has benefited most from the shift in interest from explanation to understanding. Yet for many people today, both within academe and outside, the most significant development during recent decades has been the rise of women's history and gender history: the recovery of the lives and experiences of one half of the world's population, based on the recognition that gender was not merely a useful, but arguably an essential category of historical analysis and comprehension.[10]

As these chapters make vividly plain, history as practised during the first decade of the twenty-first century is going though an exceptionally vigorous, lively and innovative period. More people are writing more history than ever before, in an unprecedented range of sub-disciplinary specialisms and expositional modes. So much so, indeed, that a great deal of the history that scholars are producing now was completely unthinkable or literally unimaginable when Carr set out to describe and define the subject forty years ago. But this is not the only way in which history has expanded and developed since then, for it has extended in both scope and appeal at least as much outside the academy as it has within. The widespread pursuit of family history, the growing concern with defining and preserving the 'national heritage' and the unprecedented allure of history on television: all this betokens a burgeoning popular interest in the past as energetic and enthusiastic as that to be found within the walls of academe. History is now acclaimed as the 'new gardening' or the 'new rock and roll', and there can be no doubt that its massive potential for entertainment and recreation has not yet been fully exploited. But it is also a serious subject with a powerful public purpose.

As that caveat suggests, some words of caution are also called for. However fertile and vigorous the present historical scene, both within academe and outside, there are also criticisms and challenges. So much history is now being written that very few scholars can keep up with more than a tiny fraction of what is being published: all of us know more and more about less and less. The rise of so many new sub-specialisms threatens to produce a sort of sub-disciplinary chauvinism, where some practitioners insistently assert the primacy of their approach to the past and show little sympathy with, or knowledge of, other approaches. And far too much history today is written in dismal prose or impenetrable jargon which can only be understood by a few *aficionados* and which fails utterly to reach a broader public audience.[11] Nor is history outside universities without its problems: family history is often excessively antiquarian, devoid of any sense of the broader picture; the cult of the 'national heritage' is frequently blinded by nostalgia and distorted by snobbery; and television history, while undeniably popular and at its best quite excellent, would greatly benefit from a more searching and sustained dialogue between the people in the media and the historians who ply their trade outside. There is, then, cause for both celebration and discomfort. And perhaps for a sort of humble scepticism, too.

Today, most historians are no longer impressed by the efforts of their professional forebears, back in the 1960s and 1970s, to enumerate the causes of historical change and to offer convincing explanations as to how, why and when things happened. Yet during those two decades, this way of approaching the past seemed simultaneously innovative, exciting, plausible and relevant. Today, many of our foremost scholars claim that in moving from explanation to meaning, from causes to understanding, we have become much more sophisticated in our comprehension of the past. Perhaps this is right. Certainly, there is an impressive body of scholarship in many of history's sub-disciplines which would suggest that it is. But then again, perhaps it is not wholly right, for historians, as Carr insisted time and again, are themselves both agents and victims of the historical process. Every generation, scholars have arisen proclaiming that they have found a new key which unlocks the essence of the past in a way that no previous historical approach has ever done. Our own generation is no exception to this rule – and it will probably be no exception to this fate. For these claims have never yet stood the test of time. Twenty years from now, scholars will probably be concerned with something very different, and they will look back with bemused amazement that our generation could believe so confidently that unravelling the 'meaning' of the past was the historian's crucial and essential task.[12]

These are some of the issues raised but – rightly – not fully settled by the contributors to this book. They themselves are based on both sides of the Atlantic; they practise many, but not all, of history's varied and differing sub-specialisms; they range in their interests from the ancient world to twentieth-century Germany; and (again in a manner that would have been unimaginable forty years ago) the majority of contributors are women. When originally delivered as lectures, these chapters informed, enlightened, stimulated and provoked, and they will surely continue to do so in their final form, and also reach a much broader audience. Forty years after Carr wrote *What is History?*, the answers to that question offered here are in many ways rather different from the answers Carr provided. But not entirely. 'History', he informed us, 'is an unending dialogue between the present and the past.'[13] So, indeed, it was, then; so, indeed, it still is, now. The nature of the conversation may change, along with the subjects for discussion and the people discussing them. But the dialogue continues as, in any free society with a sense of itself existing in time and over time, it always should and always must.

In getting this multi-authored book to completion, and in seeing it through to the publisher in extra-rapid time, I am conscious of three great debts which I, as editor, particularly owe. The first is to Josie Dixon of Palgrave Macmillan, who initially conceived this project, did her utmost to make it happen, was a constant source of advice, encouragement and support throughout, and was unwavering in her determination to drive the enterprise forward to a successful outcome. The second is to Chase

Publishing Services, who have copy-edited the text with meticulous care, dealt with each of the contributors with a matchless combination of tact and firmness, checked the proofs and made the index, and generally overseen the book through its production. My third debt is to Dr Debra Birch, Head of Events and Facilities at the Institute of Historical Research, who not only planned and arranged the original conference itself – with her customary enthusiasm, dedication, efficiency, intelligence and good cheer – but also ensured that all the contributions for this book came in to length and on time. To all three of them, and also to the stimulus and example of E.H. Carr, I extend my heartfelt thanks.

David Cannadine
Norfolk
December 2001

Notes and references

1. For an earlier volume addressing similar issues, see J. Gardiner (ed.), *What is History Today?* (London: Macmillan, 1988).
2. For the background to this book, see R.J. Evans, 'Introduction' in E.H. Carr, *What is History?* (40th anniversary edition), (Basingstoke: Palgrave, 2001), pp. ix–xlvi.
3. D. Cannadine, *G.M. Trevelyan: A Life in History* (London: HarperCollins, 1992), pp. 221–2.
4. For the broader 1960s background, see D. Cannadine, 'Historians in the "Liberal Hour": Lawrence Stone and J.H. Plumb Re-Visited', *Historical Research*, (forthcoming, 2002); E.J. Hobsbawm, 'From Social History to the History of Society', *Daedalus* (Winter 1971), pp. 20–45.
5. J.P. Kenyon, *The History Men: The Historical Profession in England since the Renaissance* (London: Weidenfeld and Nicolson, 1983), pp. 278–9; R.J. Evans, 'Afterword', in G.R. Elton, *The Practice of History* (2nd edn) (Oxford: Blackwell, 2002), pp. 165–203.
6. L. Stone, 'The Revival of Narrative: Reflections on a New Old History', *Past & Present*, No. 85 (1979), pp. 3–24. See also his 'History and the Social Sciences in the Twentieth Century', in C.F. Dalzell (ed.), *The Future of History* (Nashville, TN: Vanderbilt University Press, 1977), pp. 3–42.
7. G.R. Elton, *Return to Essentials: Some Reflections on the Present State of Historical Study* (Cambridge: Cambridge University Press, 1991). Elton's title bore a close resemblance to John Major's 'Back to Basics' campaign, and met with a similar lack of success.
8. These developments are well, if varyingly, covered in J. Tosh, *The Pursuit of History* (London: Longman, 1991); R.J. Evans, *In Defence of History* (London: Granta, 1997).
9. Q.R.D. Skinner, 'Meaning and Understanding in the History of Ideas', *History and Theory*, vol. VIII (1969), pp. 3–53.
10. J. Scott, *Gender and the Politics of History* (New York: Columbia University Press, 1988).

11. K. Jenkins, *Re-thinking History* (London: Routledge, 1991); A. Munslow, *Deconstructing History* (London: Routledge, 1996).

12. Lord Dacre of Glanton (H.R. Trevor-Roper), 'The Continuity of the English Revolution', *Transactions of the Royal Historical Society*, 6th Series, vol. I (1991), p. 122.

13. E.H. Carr, *What is History?* (Harmondsworth: Penguin, 1964), p. 30.

1
Prologue: *What is History?* – Now

Richard J. Evans

I

'What is History?', asked E.H. Carr in 1961. In the course of his Trevelyan lectures, delivered in Cambridge, broadcast on BBC radio, and printed in a book that has since sold over a quarter of a million copies worldwide, Carr sought to answer this question in a number of ways. He began by making a distinction between history and chronicle. History was an attempt to understand and interpret the past, to explain the causes and origins of things in intelligible terms. Chronicle, on the other hand, was the mere cataloguing of events without any attempt to make connections between them. The chronicler was content to show that one thing followed another; the historian had to demonstrate that one thing caused another. Of course, Carr conceded, establishing that something happened was an important part of the historian's work. It was the foundation on which everything else rested. But the really important part of the historian's work lay in the edifice of explanation and interpretation which was erected on this foundation.[1]

Diligent research and factual accuracy were necessary conditions in Carr's view for becoming a historian, but they were not sufficient in themselves. For the chronicler, a fact was something that had happened in the past. But it only became a *historical* fact when it was taken up and used by a historian as part of an argument.[2] For Carr, however, historical arguments were more than simply arguments about who did what in the past, and why. Carr thought that the historian should look at the wider forces in history, at economic change, industrialization, class formation and class conflict, and so on, and in order to understand these forces the historian needed theories developed in the present, whether these were

1

Marxist ideas of one kind or another, Weberian paradigms, sociological concepts and the like. In the course of research, Carr conceded, these theories would be modified in one way or another, and might even sometimes have to be jettisoned altogether. Yet Carr insisted that the central task of the historian, with or without the help of theory, lay in discerning and interpreting patterns and regularities in the past.[3]

For Carr, the point of such a project was to assist human society in understanding the present and moulding the future. The past was only of interest insofar as it contributed to this task. There was little or no point, he thought, in explaining the past in terms of historical accident or the operation of the intentions of great men. It was not merely that the grand trends and tendencies of history brushed aside accidental events and causes, which could have no more than a short-term, partial and temporary influence on the way history moved; nor merely that men, even great men, were seldom wholly aware of why they did what they did, and almost never achieved exactly what they wanted, so that historical change often occurred in ways intended by nobody at all. More important in Carr's eyes was the point that historical causes and trends were only interesting to the *historian*, as opposed to the *chronicler*, if they could help society deal with the problems that faced it in the historian's own time.

Thus when we study the Russian Revolution, as Carr did for the last three decades or more of his long life, what should interest us – and what certainly interested Carr – is not the drama of the revolutionary conflict, the ideas and actions of the defeated forces of Tsarism, liberalism, democratic socialism, anarchism, and so on, nor even the reasons why these alternatives to Soviet communism were so easily defeated; for none of this is of any direct relevance to the problems facing society in our own time. The real focus of the historian's interest, as was the real focus of Carr's own fourteen-volume history of Soviet Russia, should instead be on how the Bolsheviks developed the ideas which they sought to put into effect once they had come to power, and how above all the idea of the planned economy came to occupy a central position in their thinking and policy.[4]

Carr took this point of view not least because he himself had a somewhat peculiar background – peculiar for a historian, that is – not in academic life but in journalism and in the civil service. Despite the fact that his book *What is History?* came to be the most widely read text on its subject amongst history students everywhere, E.H. Carr never served in a university history department or held a Chair in history at any academic institution. He studied classics, worked in the British Foreign

Office for twenty years, taught international relations and served on the staff of the London *Times* newspaper, and indeed nowadays his work in the field of international relations is probably more highly regarded than his work in the field of history.[5] This background gave Carr an instrumental view of history and its study. Like many civil servants, he was only interested in what would serve the making of policy; like many civil servants, too, he tended to dismiss as uninteresting or irrelevant people – the vast majority of people in the past – who lacked the power, the organization or the education to take part in the shaping of events. Carr, as his critics maintained, was only really interested in 'the big battalions'. He tended to identify too easily with the actions of governments and the powerful, and thought that whatever had happened was historically justified, rather as a Foreign Office mandarin had to deal with existing situations in international politics and not trouble to much about what might have been.[6]

Yet at the time he was writing, Carr struck a powerful chord with the radical student generation that was just emerging in the course of the 1960s, the baby-boom generation of the postwar years, taking advantage of the educational expansion, the growing prosperity and the general political liberalization of the decade. For many in this generation, history was exciting precisely because it offered an explanation for the present and hope for the future. Revolutions and revolutionaries, rioters and rebels, labour movements, strikes and protests, radicals and recalcitrants, fighting the encrusted orthodoxies and oppressive authoritarianism of their day, were exciting figures to rediscover and identify with in the heady atmosphere of the 1960s. They may not have been important in their own time, but they were lent significance by the influence of their ideas in the present and the promise of victory which such ideas held out for the future. Primitive rebels in pre-industrial society were interesting not because they were primitive but because they were rebels, and their rebellion pointed forward, however indistinctly, to the socialist movement that appeared in its many forms to be sweeping away the dull inequities of the postwar era in Western Europe and the US.[7]

Carr struck a chord, too, with his plea for history to be taught and studied not, as it still was in the old universities of the early 1960s, as the story of Britain and its influence in the world, but on a far wider basis, with a far greater emphasis given, for example, to the history of Russia and China, two states whose espousal of the planned economy Carr thought had much to teach the West, and beyond that the history of the 'Third World', whose liberation from colonial rule was just beginning as Carr wrote.[8] Indeed, his lectures inaugurated a lengthy and increasingly impassioned debate amongst the historians of his own university, Cambridge, which resulted some five years later in the first tentative steps towards a reform of the undergraduate history curriculum along these lines.[9] His plea for more non-British and extra-European history to be taught went along with another plea in the pages of *What is History?* for more intellectual exchange between history and sociology and for more social history to be researched, written and taught, and this, too, found favour with the student generation of the 1960s and many of the young historians of the day.[10]

Carr thought that historians were people of their own time: history was not so much a matter of what individual historians wrote about the past, as what one society found of interest in another, separated from it in time. Of course, historians had to be aware of their own biases and preconceptions so that they could rise above them; but they also had to be aware of why they were writing and how their work could be of use in their own society.[11] Young historians who took this message to heart could feel that they were doing something useful and purposeful, that their work was politically important, and that their discoveries and arguments not only reflected the concerns of the society in which they lived but also, precisely because of this, would have a real intellectual impact on it too.

This impact, Carr thought, would be all the greater because history was, in essence, a scientific rather than a literary endeavour. Its standards of proof and its procedures were not very different from those of the sciences. The historical trends and regularities which he thought were so important a part of the historian's material could be identified and pinned down with the certainty of a scientific law.[12] The objective historian was the historian who could establish such trends and then assess people, institutions and events in the past according to the contribution they made to them. History was the scientific study of the past, and its interpretation in terms of large forces and long-term developments, aided by social theory, quantification and other tools of social science and thus contributing to the creation of a firm basis of knowledge on which to take political action and political decisions in the present.[13]

II

Carr's *What is History?* was influential not least because its plea for a more scientific approach to history came at a time when the means were becoming available to fulfil it. The advent of the computer made it possible for historians to collect and analyse mass quantitative data on the past in a manner and on a scale previously undreamed of. By the middle of the 1960s, historians in a number of advanced industrial countries were proclaiming that in the future, history would be researched not by single individuals working in the style of a lone author but by groups, laboratories, organizations collaborating on large-scale projects and using all the most sophisticated tools of the advanced social sciences. Social science theories of many kinds came into vogue: some broad, like Marxism or modernization theory; some very specific and drawn from the more technical of the social sciences like demography, psephology or econometrics. Most of this social science history was designed to have a direct or indirect input into present-day decision-making as well, a further indication of how Carr's prescriptions were being fulfilled to an extent that he had probably never imagined when he wrote them.[14]

In the course of the 1960s, too, most advanced industrial societies, including Britain, undertook a vast expansion of higher education – another development for which Carr pleaded in the pages of *What is History?* New universities were founded, old ones doubled in size, polytechnics were upgraded, and the proportion of each generation that went to university increased almost exponentially. The conditions they encountered when they reached universities were among the factors that sparked the student unrest of 1968. In the longer run, however, this growth in the number of students also meant a rapid expansion of the numbers of academics employed to teach them, and this included, of course, historians. The young historians who came into the profession in the 1960s were heavily influenced by Carr, and everywhere they set to work on new projects in social history using the kind of new concepts and methods he had been advocating.[15] Broadly speaking, the liberal political and intellectual atmosphere of the 1960s continued for another decade, encouraged by the liberal and social democratic governments that came to power in countries such as Britain under Wilson and Callaghan, Germany under Brandt and Schmidt, France under Giscard d'Estaing, and, more briefly, the US under Carter. Attempts to roll the tide of liberalism back in the early 1970s, led by figures such as Heath in Britain and Nixon in the US, had ended in ignominious failure.

But at the end of the 1970s all this changed as conservative governments, often more radical than their consensual predecessors of the 1950s, took office in conditions of economic downturn caused by the oil crisis that hit the world economy in the middle of the decade. University expansion had long since ceased, and cutbacks and controls were now the order of the day. The hopes and aspirations of radical and progressive intellectuals, including historians, seemed to have been dashed. Moreover, the social science history that had achieved dominance in the 1960s had in many respects run into the sands. Quantification did not deliver the certainties it had promised. Even with the aid of the computer, the disparity between the effort put in and the results achieved was becoming painfully obvious. The new hegemony of conservatism, intellectual as well as political, cut off any chance of making the findings of radical and liberal historians relevant in policy terms.[16]

More profoundly, rapid social and economic change was undermining many of the premises on which the younger generation of historians had been operating. The decline of the old industrial working class and the emergence of a post-industrial society falsified the theoretical assumptions of Marxism, just as the growing threat of environmental degradation put a question mark behind the unthinking faith of modernization theorists in the benefits of untrammelled industrial growth. New kinds of conflict, based on gender, ethnicity, religion or sexual orientation, came to seem more urgent, and in turn demanded new kinds of historical explanation. The model of causation with which most historians had been operating, in which, however indirectly, the economy operated on society and society operated on politics, was clearly no longer adequate. Finally – and not unconnected to these other developments – the intellectual demarcation lines of the postwar era were abruptly rubbed out by the dramatic collapse of communism in the Soviet Union and Eastern Europe in 1989–90. These events destroyed not only the grand theories and teleologies which Carr had urged historians to adopt, but also any idea that history could be seen to have a single direction and purpose at all. The belief that this idea could be proven by scientific methods which delivered a demonstrably objective view of historical progress was simply refuted by events.

By the early 1990s, therefore, the intellectual world which Carr had championed was in deep crisis. In this situation, some younger historians, particularly those who were concerned with the nature of historical thought itself, began to question not only the possibility of reaching any objective interpretation or understanding of the past, but even the possibility of knowing anything for certain about the past at all. Turning away from social theory to linguistic theory, they began to argue that historians depended on texts for their knowledge of the past. In their view, texts were arbitrary assemblages of words that themselves had come into being only through an arbitrary process of human invention. Each time we read a text, therefore, we put the meaning into it ourselves. So it was with the historian also. Thus what historians wrote was their own invention and not a true or objective representation of past reality, which was in essence irrecoverable.[17]

This enabled radical historians to use history once more for political purposes, such as building the identity of a disadvantaged group by recovering, or allegedly recovering, precursors in the past. But there was nothing in this approach that would prevent right-wing groups doing the same, a problem that few radicals were prepared to admit. Moreover, there was an obvious contradiction in the position of the linguistic theorists: if all meaning was put into a text by the reader, then why should we not be able to put into their own writings any meaning we wanted to, including (to push the argument to its most absurd extreme) the view that accurate, objective and irrefutable knowledge of the past was indeed possible?[18]

For much of the 1990s, argument raged over these theories as many historians began to feel a sense of acute crisis in their profession.[19] Admitting that the social-science approach advocated by Carr had not delivered what it had promised was painful and difficult and led in some cases to nihilistic despair. To a degree, these problems were compounded by a further expansion of higher education in the early 1990s, in which the running was made mostly by applied subjects such as business studies rather than traditional academic disciplines such as history, whose practical utility in the eyes of many students was clearly minimal. Of course, there were still vastly more historians and history students around in the year 2000 than there had been forty years previously when Carr was writing, but this expansion of the profession had led to an increasing fragmentation as sub-disciplines proliferated and research and publication became ever more specialized in the quest for new historical knowledge. The damaging effects of this on history's ability to communicate with a wider audience were compounded by the emphasis of social science historians on jargon, quantification, large trends and historical averages. In much of the historical work of the 1970s and early 1980s, individual people all but disappeared from the historian's vision. The lack of human interest in a great deal of historical writing in this period did not do much to win history books a broad readership.

Among some historians, the turn to linguistic theory also failed to pay dividends in terms of readability, simply substituting one form of jargon for another.[20] Yet this kind of writing was most marked, like the ideas which underpinned it, in the field of historiography, which in the decades since Carr wrote had become a distinct sub-specialism of historical study in itself. Here a familiar process could be observed as the 1990s gave way to a new decade. The social-science historians of two or three decades before had begun by proclaiming 'traditional' history to be dead and asserting that their way of doing history rendered all others obsolete. Social history, some of them maintained, was not a branch of history, it was a whole way of doing history, a method that should and in due course would come to supersede all others. A few years later, however, this ambition had been abandoned, and instead, social historians had set themselves up as a sub-specialism within the discipline, kitted out with all the usual paraphernalia of a society, a journal and a conference network in which they could spend most of their time talking to each other instead of keeping up their seemingly hopeless campaign to convert everyone else – the political historians, economic historians, diplomatic historians, military historians and the rest – to their way of thinking.

By the early 2000s, historical theorists who had been busy proclaiming the impossibility of historical knowledge and the death of the historical profession a few years previously were doing much the same thing: organising conferences for themselves, founding a journal (*Rethinking History*) and abandoning their original crusading zeal in favour of a more comforting institutional separatism. The historical profession, after all, had not collapsed. People had not stopped writing history. Students and general readers had not stopped believing that historians were telling them some kind of truth about the past. The sense of crisis in the historical profession was passing and the debates it had generated had died down.

Yet all this had left its mark on the answer given in the early twenty-first century to the question 'what is history?'. Historians had not emerged from the battle with postmodernist ultra-scepticism entirely unchanged. Or rather, the general developments which had led to the debate about the possibility of historical knowledge in the 1990s had had their effects on the way historians thought and worked. In the first place, they had effectively destroyed the economic determinism that underlay so much of the historical writing of the 1970s and 1980s. In its place a new emphasis on cultural history had emerged, on aspects of identity, consciousness and mentality in place of social structure, social organization and the economic bases of social power.[21] The collapse of grand narratives and large teleological theories in history assisted the reinstatement of individual human beings in the historical record. Historians began writing about people again, and above all about humble, ordinary people, history's obscure, the losers and bystanders in the process of historical change. Carr would not have approved.

Nor would he have approved of the turn of historians towards the study of the irrational, the eccentric and the bizarre. He would have thought it a waste of time to study the ideas of medieval and early modern demonologists, or the strange cosmological beliefs of a humble Italian miller, or the social and spiritual life of Cathar heretics in the thirteenth century, or the fears shared by a large part of the rural population in France and other parts of Western Europe up to the middle of the 1800s and in some cases beyond.[22] Historians have not devoted their efforts to understanding these things because they think they will be useful in the framing of government policies in the present, or because they think they can contribute to the development of a particular political ideology. If there is one thing that the various exponents of this kind of cultural history share, it is evidently the belief that historical writing can enhance our appreciation of the human condition by bringing to life and explaining beliefs and cultures that are very different from our own, and so perhaps adding to the richness of human experience and understanding, and fostering tolerance of different cultures and belief systems in our own time.

Of course, the turn to cultural history does not mean that other forms of history have disappeared. History is like a palimpsest, a medieval parchment in which, as the ink of one set of writing faded, another document was written on top of it, until over the years several layers of writing accumulated, one on top of the other: so there are still diplomatic historians writing in the style and with the assumptions of many years ago, just as there are still exponents of the 'great man' theory of history, and historians who think that nothing matters except the actions of a handful of politically active people at the top. In the same way, economic and econometric historians are still plying their recondite trade in the decent obscurity of learned periodicals, conference volumes and subsidized monographs, while social historians still see no reason to disband their societies or close down their journals.[23] The chapters in this volume testify to the continued vitality of many different kinds of history, some of them unknown to Carr, or considered by him so unimportant that they were scarcely worthy of mention. Few, if any, however, have been entirely unaffected by the intellectual and cultural changes of the past decade and a half, and many – including some of those with which Carr was familiar – look very different from how they appeared in Carr's time forty years ago.

III

For the majority of younger historians, above all, the turn to cultural history has been decisive. This does not necessarily mean that they have completely rejected the theories, methods and objects of study favoured by political or social historians, but it does mean that they are viewing them and using them in a different way. This has resulted, in Britain and the US at least, in an unexpectedly broad popular appeal. Historical research, writing and teaching have not developed in the last decade or more in a cultural vacuum, and the cultural changes of the post-Cold War era have had a dramatic effect on the place of history and historians in the cultural life of post-industrial society.

Consciousness of history is all-pervasive at the start of the twenty-first century. Wherever we look, it is present. Since the late 1980s there has been a wave of public monuments and memorials to the victims of Nazi genocide during the Second World War, from the Holocaust Memorial Museum in Washington DC to the Holocaust Exhibition Wing of the Imperial War Museum in London. The construction of the new German capital of Berlin is taking as its centrepiece the memorialization of the Jewish dead. All over Europe, there have been legal actions against long-neglected war criminals, actions for the restitution of spoliated property, and campaigns (at least partially successful) for the compensation of victims such as the millions of slave labourers transported to Germany from conquered countries and forced to work there under inhuman and frequently murderous conditions. Society has recovered the public memory of the crimes of Nazism just as the last of Nazism's now-elderly former victims are fading from the scene.[24]

Literary culture has followed this recovery of memory and orientated itself increasingly towards the past. The novelists of the postwar years, such as Kingsley Amis and Iris Murdoch, wrote about contemporary society, but the best-regarded fiction of the 1990s and early 2000s most often takes the past as its setting, whether the author is Sebastian Faulks, Michael Ondaatje, Matthew Kneale, or any other; even a novel with a contemporary setting, such as Zadie Smith's deservedly successful *White Teeth*, turns out to be concerned mainly with the influence of the past on the present. These are not historical novels in the sense that their main purpose is to re-create a past world through the exercise of the fictional imagination; rather, they are novels which find it easiest to address present-day concerns by putting them in a past context.[25]

The film industry has also turned to the past for its themes. Movies such as *Enemy at the Gates*, *Pearl Harbor*, *U-571* or *Enigma*, and their small-screen counterparts in lavishly produced series such as *Band of Brothers*, testify to the movie industry's fascination with the Second World War, but other major films of the 1990s have been based on more remote historical themes, from the sinking of the *Titanic* or the contribution of *The Patriot* to the War of American Independence to the fight for freedom in medieval Scotland, the setting of *Braveheart*. *Gladiator* and *Titanic* have been among the highest-grossing movies of all time. On British television, history, as one producer is said to have announced, is 'the new gardening', replacing lifestyle programmes at the top end of the ratings. David Starkey's *The Six Wives of Henry VIII* attracted 4 million viewers for Channel 4 television, while a series of programmes on seventeenth-century England – *Plague, Fire, War and Treason* – topped this with an audience of 4.3 million. And there have been many more.[26]

Hollywood movies have scant regard for historical accuracy if it interferes with the prospects of a good profit, which is perhaps why *U-571* replaced the British submarine crew involved in the actual historical incident on which it was based with an American one, or why *Enemy at the Gates* made a probably fictional German sniper the central figure in its portrayal of the Battle of Stalingrad.[27] Nevertheless, detailed research and, above all, computer-generated imagery, allow movie directors to portray the setting for such action with an unprecedented degree of authentic-looking detail. On the small screen, the same techniques, backed by carefully prepared dramatic reconstructions, do the same. Moreover, professional historians have been involved in the preparation of these programmes to a far greater degree than used to be the case. Who would have thought, for instance, that millions of viewers would be attracted to a programme about the London Plague of 1665 based on a series of entries in a parish register, or a series in which extracts from contemporary letters and documents formed a central part, as in *The Six Wives of Henry VIII*?[28]

What is striking about these factual historical programmes is not just that they are prepared by serious historical researchers, but, far more, the fact that they are presented by particular historians who stand in front of the camera and give an avowedly personal point of view – but one that is obviously based on a deep knowledge of the subject. This is a sharp contrast to the style in which historical programmes were presented a decade or so ago, with their emphasis on authoritative and seemingly irrefutable neutrality. And it is the personal voice that counts, too, in the blockbuster history books that have achieved such extraordinary popularity in the last few years, most notably Norman Davies's *Europe: A History* (Oxford: Oxford University Press, 1996) and

The Isles (Basingstoke: Macmillan, 2000), but also many more dealing with detailed topics such as the life of Hitler[29] or the sexual antics of eighteenth-century noblewomen, the theme of both Stella Tillyard's *Aristocrats* (London: Vintage, 1993) and Amanda Foreman's *Georgiana* (London: Flamingo, 1999). Here too there is a blend of authority and documentation on the one hand, and a strong authorial voice on the other – a mix which seems to attract the public to history as never before.

To some extent, the hunger for history among the adult book-reading, television-watching, movie-going public may be a reflection of the fact that they have been starved of it through the decline of history in schools, where annual entries for the English school-leaving examination in history, the A level, declined from 47,000 to 38,500 between 1992 and 1999. The current boom in history in the media may finally be reversing this downward trend. But there are surely deeper and wider causes too. History as it is written and researched, and above all as it is presented to a popular audience, at the beginning of the twenty-first century, is about identity, about who we are and where we came from. At a time when other sources of identity such as class and region have declined, history is stepping in to fill the gap.[30]

Moreover, history is important once more in constructing national identity, and nowhere more so than in England, where the decline of the idea of British unity in the face of resurgent Welsh and Scottish nationalism on the one hand, and growing integration into Europe on the other, have left the English wondering who on earth they are. Weak tea and cricket on the village green, the characteristically nostalgic image purveyed by the former Conservative prime minister, John Major, are not potent enough to answer this question. History and the national heritage are where English people are looking instead. With the fall of communism, in addition, the negative pole against which Western democracies defined their core social and political values vanished from the scene. Socialism, too, has virtually disappeared, so that liberals and conservatives are seeking a counter-image to contrast to their own political creeds. German Nazism fulfils all these criteria only too well, which is one reason why the public memory of the Third Reich and its crimes has become central to the culture of advanced industrial societies in Europe and North America since the fall of communism.[31]

Yet the public demand for history does not stop with the Second World War. One of the most striking aspects of the current boom is the way in which it encompasses any period, any topic in history from the Vikings to the Victorians. Ancient Greece, Pharaonic Egypt, the wars of Alexander the Great and the fall of the Incas have made popular television series in

Britain just as much as the Nazis, the war between Hitler and Stalin, or the secrets of the decoding centre at Bletchley Park. The media have discovered that history is a repository of an endless quantity of human stories. The strangeness of people in the past throws our own identities in the twenty-first century into sharp relief.

But is this history as E.H. Carr defined it? Probably not, if one focuses on his belief that history is all about big forces and huge movements. Probably yes, however, if one is content with his definition of history as being about explanation and interpretation rather than simply telling a story – though even telling a story, of course, embodies a degree of interpretation simply by selecting one sequence of facts as the significant one, rather than making a different selection. History in the media and in the bookshops is of widely varying quality, of course, but the best programmes, such as Lawrence Rees's *The Nazis – A Warning from History*, manage to convey a whole series of often quite complex arguments without losing their audience. A seemingly straightforward narrative such as David Starkey's *The Six Wives of Henry VIII* carries within it a whole interpretation – sometimes implicit, sometimes explicit – about the way history works: in this case, the rather old-fashioned view that it is shaped by the whims and predicaments of powerful individuals. But the same programme also managed to get across, at a more subordinate level, another, quite different set of arguments about the nature of court society in Tudor England, the sexual mores of the high aristocracy, the role of women at the centre of power, and many other aspects of the social history of the Tudor elites.

None of this means, of course, that academic history in the narrower sense has ceased to exist. On the contrary, the current boom in popular history of all kinds rests on the foundation of detailed research, often conveyed initially in forbiddingly learned monographs, low-circulation learned journals, small conferences and specialized research seminars. The painstaking work of producing reliable scholarly editions of documents remains essential. Moreover, conveying history to a broad audience inevitably involves a degree of simplification or, in the case of Hollywood films, even downright distortion. Educational standards are nowadays generally far higher in advanced industrial or post-industrial societies than they were forty years ago. Cinema and television audiences are quite aware of the fact that a particular view is being purveyed which may be controversial or even biased, and the evidence is that a good proportion of such audiences is prompted to read serious history as a result. Just as television or cinema adaptations of a novel by Jane Austen lead to a boom in sales of her work, so a television programme such as

Band of Brothers, the dramatized story of a unit of American paratroopers from the Normandy landings in 1944 to the end of the Second World War ten months later, has brought the book on which it is based, by the academic historian Stephen Ambrose, onto the bestseller lists in the US.[32]

Historians, and above all academic historians, have been able to respond to this new boom and to take part in the current popularity of their subject to a degree that was not possible twenty years ago, when popular history was written and purveyed mainly by journalists and freelance writers, and historians like A.J.P. Taylor who reached a wider audience were rare indeed. Usually, like Taylor, or like E.H. Carr himself, they had extensive experience as journalists which enabled them to escape the confines of academia and reach out to a general readership.[33] For the majority of historians, however, the influence of the social sciences and the pursuit of the scientific ideal proclaimed by Carr erected insuperable barriers to communication beyond the profession itself. But historians did not actually want to reach a larger audience, since this smacked of vulgarity, 'dumbing down' and abandoning the cautious and scientific approach which they favoured in these years – all sins which Taylor was accused of in his day. Of course, there had always been historians whose work had been widely read – G.M. Trevelyan, for example, or, before him, Lord Macaulay. But the self-consciously literary style of history which they practised had fallen out of favour by the 1960s, and they wrote in any case for a small, highly literate and educated elite. Historians today are communicating with far larger audiences when they broadcast on radio or television, and they do so on the basis of research which owes little to the literary methods and models employed by the Whig tradition to which Macaulay and Trevelyan belonged.

What has enabled them to do this has been, ironically perhaps, the very influence of the postmodernist theories whose most extreme manifestations were causing such a sense of crisis in the historical profession in the mid-1990s. The emphasis of postmodernists on history as a form of literature, on the individuality of the historian's reading of the past and on the historian as creator of fictions rather than purveyor of objective knowledge, in the end failed to persuade historians that what they were doing was the same as what novelists and poets were engaged in. But it did have the effect in many areas of emboldening them to come out from behind the barricades of scientific objectivity and project their own voice once more. This may be ironic in view of the fact that many postmodernists have denied the existence of the authorial voice altogether, preferring to assign exclusive privilege in the creation of meaning to the reader of a text rather than its writer. But the influence of theorists such as Hayden White, who have represented and analysed historians in the same terms as they have represented and analysed novelists and fiction writers, has none the less helped to create a cultural climate in which the individual historian can adopt a strong authorial identity without in any way sacrificing history's claim to present an accurate view of the past. The transformation of historians from anonymous workers in the laboratories of historical science to bold and vivid characters purveying a particular interpretation and adopting a personal point of view is indeed symbolized by the replacement in history programmes on television from anonymous voice-over backing plainly presented archive footage and still photographs, to sharply individualized presenters accompanying dramatic reconstructions and talking to the camera in real historical settings. Without Hayden White, no David Starkey; without postmodernism, no Simon Schama.[34]

And without E.H. Carr, perhaps, none of this at all; for it was Carr above all who argued, in *What is History?*, that historians were not empty vessels through which the truth about the past was conveyed from the documents to the reader, but individuals who brought their own particular views and assumptions to their work, which had to be read with this fact in mind. Study the historian before you study the work, was Carr's advice, and he added that all historians had bees in their bonnets, and if you could not hear the buzzing when you read their work then there was something wrong either with them or with you.[35] Carr, of course, went on to argue that this buzzing was not simply caused by the historian's personal idiosyncracies, but was also a product of what one might call the hive mind: the collective discourse of the historians of a particular time and context, which in turn reflected the times in which they lived.[36] Yet he was also prepared to admit that the peculiarities of a historian's particular background, upbringing and circumstances could have an effect as well, so that his argument – perhaps the most influential of all the theses propounded in *What is History?* – made it clear that historians were not just parroting a wider social discourse when they wrote, but that they had their own individual voices as well.[37]

Carr never completely resolved the tension in his mind between his belief in the subjectivity of historians and his hope that they could rise above themselves to attain an objective view of the past that owed nothing to their particular circumstances or those of the times in which they lived. The tensions in his work between these two views mirrored perhaps a deeper tension that ran through all his work, between a realist acceptance of what was and a utopian hope that things could be entirely different.[38] One result of Carr's influence was to persuade many historians to reflect on their own biases and preconceptions, to articulate the purposes for which they wrote, and to lay bare to the reader the assumptions on which their work rested. This was a welcome development, and very helpful to the reader. But in persuading historians that they could never wholly rise above themselves, Carr also encouraged them, in the long run, to make a virtue of necessity. A genuine historian will never manipulate or distort the materials which the past has left behind and which form the basis for the historian's work;[39] but within the limits of what the sources allow there is plenty of room for differing emphases and interpretations, and Carr's influence has allowed historians to make the maximum use of it.

Notes and references

1. E.H. Carr, *What is History?* (40th anniversary edition, with a new Introduction by Richard J. Evans) (Basingstoke: Palgrave, 2001), pp. 5–6, 22–4; also E.H. Carr, 'History and Morals', *Times Literary Supplement*, 17 December 1954, distinguishing between history and chronicle.
2. Carr, *What is History?*, p. 6.
3. Ibid., pp. 47–9.
4. E.H. Carr, *A History of Soviet Russia*, Vol. I: *The Bolshevik Revolution*, I (London: Macmillan, 1950), pp. 5–6.
5. Jonathan Haslam, *The Vices of Integrity: E.H. Carr 1892–1982* (London: Verso, 1999); E.H. Carr, 'An Autobiography' (1989), in Michael Cox (ed.), *E.H. Carr: A Critical Appraisal* (Basingstoke: Palgrave, 2000), pp. xiii–xxii.
6. Haslam, *The Vices of Integrity*, p. 146; Isaiah Berlin, 'Mr Carr's Big Battalions', *New Statesman*, 5 January 1962, pp. 15–16; H.R. Trevor-Roper, 'E.H. Carr's Success Story', *Encounter*, May 1962, pp. 69–77.
7. Particularly influential here were E.J. Hobsbawm, *Primitive Rebels* (Manchester: Manchester University Press, 1958), and E.P. Thompson, *The Making of the English Working Class* (London: Victor Gollancz, 1963).
8. Carr, *What is History?*, pp. 146–7.
9. See the account of the 'discussion' in *Cambridge University Reporter* 96 (1965–66), pp. 627, 1013–29, 1292, 1591, 1830, 1852–3, and more generally in Patrick Collinson, 'Geoffrey Rudolph Elton, 1921–1994', *Proceedings of the British Academy*, Vol. 94 (1996), pp. 429–55, here pp. 448–9.
10. Carr, *What is History?*, p. 60.
11. Ibid., p. 38.
12. Ibid., pp. 51–60.
13. Ibid., pp. 60–2.
14. Keith Thomas, 'The Tools and the Job', *Times Literary Supplement*, 7 April 1966, Special Issue: 'New Ways in History'; Emmanuel Le Roy Ladurie, *The Territory of the Historian* (Chicago, IL: University of Chicago Press 1979), p. 6; R.W. Fogel and G.R. Elton, *Which Road to the Past? Two Views of History* (New Haven, CT, and London: Yale University Press, 1983).

15. Joyce Appleby, Margaret Jacob and Lynn Hunt, *Telling the Truth about History* (New York: W.W. Norton, 1994), pp. 202, 216; Peter N. Stearns, 'Coming of Age', *Journal of Social History*, Vol. 10 (1976), pp. 246–65. For a useful overview, see Georg G. Iggers, *Historiography in the Twentieth Century* (Middleton, CT: Wesleyan University Press, 1997).

16. Harvey J. Kaye, *The Powers of the Past: Reflections on the Crisis and the Promise of History* (Minneapolis, MN: University of Minnesota Press, 1991); and the introductory survey in Robert F. Berkhofer, Jr, *Beyond the Great Story: History as Text and Discourse* (Cambridge, MA: Harvard University Press, 1995).

17. For a discussion of these trends, see Richard J. Evans, *In Defence of History* (2nd edn, with a new Afterword) (London: Granta, 2001). Among many examples, see in particular Alun Munslow, *Deconstructing History* (London: Routledge, 1996) and Keith Jenkins, *Re-thinking History* (London: Routledge, 1991); more briefly, Frank Ankersmit, 'Historiography and Post-modernism', *History and Theory*, Vol. 28 (1989), pp. 137–53.

18. Christopher Norris, *Deconstruction and the Interests of Theory* (Norman, OK: University of Oklahoma Press, 1989), p. 16; Paul Boghossian, 'What the Sokal Hoax Ought to Teach Us', *Times Literary Supplement*, 13 December 1996, pp. 14–15; Alan B. Spitzer, *Historical Truth and Lies about the Past* (Chapel Hill, NC: University of North Carolina Press, 1996).

19. For references, see Richard J. Evans, *In Defence of History* (London: Granta, 1997), pp. 284–301.

20. See, for an extreme example, Sande Cohen, *Historical Culture: On the Recoding of an Academic Discipline* (Berkeley, CA: University of California Press, 1986).

21. For a critical account of this change, in the context of British labour history, see David Mayfield and Susan Thorne, 'Social History and its Discontents: Gareth Stedman Jones and the Politics of Language', *Social History*, Vol. 17 (1992), pp. 165–88.

22. Stuart Clark, *Thinking with Demons: The Idea of Witchcraft in Early Modern Europe* (Oxford: Clarendon, 1997); Carlo Ginzburg, *The Cheese and the Worms: The Cosmos of a Sixteenth-Century Miller* (Baltimore, MD: Johns Hopkins University Press, 1992); Emmanuel Le Roy Ladurie, *Montaillou* (London: Scolar Press, 1978); Jean Delumeau, *La peur en Occident (XIVe–XVIIIe siècles), une cité assiégée* (Paris: Fayard, 1978); *La péché et la peur: la culpabilisation en Occident (XIIIe–XVIIIe siècles)* (Paris: Fayard, 1983).

23. However, the British Social History Society at the beginning of the twenty-first century was actively considering changing its name to the Social and Cultural History Society.

24. Among many attempts to recount and explain this phenomenon, two of the most illuminating are Peter Novick, *The Holocaust and Collective Memory* (London: Bloomsbury, 1999) and Tony Judt, 'The Past is Another Country: Myth and Memory in Postwar Europe', in Istvan Déak, Jan T. Gross and Tony Judt (eds), *The Politics of Retribution in Europe: World War II and its Aftermath* (Princeton, NJ: Princeton University Press, 2000), pp. 293–324.

25. Kingsley Amis, *Lucky Jim* (London: Penguin, 1954) and many succeeding novels; Iris Murdoch, *Under the Net* (London: Chatto and Windus, 1994) and many more; Michael Ondaatje, *The English Patient* (London: Picador, 1992); Zadie Smith, *White Teeth* (London: Hamish Hamilton, 2000); Matthew Kneale,

English Passengers (London: Penguin, 2000); Sebastian Faulks, *Birdsong* (London: Vintage, 1993).

26. John Willis, 'Past is Perfect', *Guardian*, 29 October 2001, Media Supplement, pp. 2–3 (the author is a television executive).
27. Mark C. Carnes (ed.), *Past Imperfect: History According to the Movies* (New York: Henry Holt & Co., 1996); Richard J. Evans, 'Is This the Past as we Know it?', *Independent*, 12 March 2001, Monday review, p. 5.
28. Tristram Hunt, 'Back to the Future', *Observer*, 6 January 2002.
29. Ian Kershaw, *Hitler 1889–1936: Hubris* (New York: W.W. Norton, 1998); *Hitler 1936–1945: Nemesis* (London: Allen Lane, 2000).
30. Richard J. Evans, 'How History has become Popular Again', *New Statesman*, 12 February 2001, pp. 25–7.
31. Willis, 'Past is Perfect'; Evans, 'How History has become Popular Again'.
32. Stephen E. Ambrose, *Band of Brothers* (New York: Simon and Schuster, 1998).
33. Kathleen Burk, *Troublemaker: The Life and History of A.J.P. Taylor* (New Haven, CT, and London: Yale University Press, 2000).
34. Hayden White, *Metahistory: The Historical Imagination in Nineteenth-Century Europe* (Baltimore, MD: Johns Hopkins University Press, 1987); Simon Schama, *Citizens: A Chronicle of the French Revolution* (New York: Alfred Knopf, 1989).
35. Carr, *What is History?*, pp. 17–18.
36. Ibid., p. 38.
37. Ved Mehta, *Fly and the Fly-Bottle: Encounters with British Intellectuals* (London: Weidenfeld and Nicolson, 1963), p. 158 (interview with Carr).
38. This is a central theme of Jonathan Haslam's excellent biography, *The Vices of Integrity*.
39. For an extended discussion of such manipulation and distortion, see Richard J. Evans, *Lying About Hitler: History, Holocaust and the David Irving Trial* (New York: Basic Books, 2001).

2
What is Social History Now?[*]

Paul Cartledge

I have at the outset two confessions, or at any rate statements, to make. First, I am not myself a social historian, or perhaps it would be more accurate to say that I would not so label myself. Second, I am an ancient historian, specifically a historian of ancient Greece, and therefore belong to a happy breed not exactly notorious for its devotion to critically reflexive historiography. There are, however, exceptions; indeed, as one of them, the late Sir Moses Finley, was fond of saying, there are always exceptions.[1]

Finley was in a sense an exile, to England from the McCarthyite US; and it is almost a commonplace to observe that many of the greatest historians of Greece and Rome – Herodotus, Thucydides, Polybius and so on – were themselves also political exiles.[2] There seems to be some significant causal connection, in other words, between exile and the writing of history, and more particularly the writing of reflexive as well as merely reflective history and historiography. Finley's own practice of historiography, anyhow, was certainly influenced directly by that of another British-domiciled exile historian of the ancient world, Arnaldo Momigliano, a victim of fascist Italy's racial laws. This is how Finley began a 1968 essay on Momigliano, in characteristically polemical style:

> It is, I believe, a safe prediction that Professor Momigliano will never write a book entitled 'What is History?'

The implication of that remark, presumably, was that Momigliano should never want to write a book so titled. In any case, the implied reference to E.H. Carr's Trevelyan lectures and published book was clear enough.[3]

Carr was my starting point for obvious contingently contextual reasons.[4] I continued with Finley not only because he was an ancient historian but also because he did more than any other ancient historian during the period covered by this commemorative lecture series to integrate his (and my) special field with that of history in general. For Finley, ancient history was, first and foremost, history – and historiography; only secondarily was it ancient; and it just so happened, as it were, that he specialized in the history and historiography of the ancient, that is Graeco-Roman, world, and more particularly the world of the Greeks. I try to see things that way too.

I

So what is – or should be – social history now? I pass quickly over the pronouncement of a former British prime minister, Margaret Thatcher, who opined that there was not – and never had been – any such thing as 'society'. Even to label her a methodological individualist would be to give her too much credit.[5] I leave on one side, too, the equally dubitable, if formally cautiously expressed, remark of G.M. Trevelyan in the preface to his *English Social History*, to the effect that social history was history with the politics left out. This would be a curious enough statement in any context, but it is utterly absurd in the case of ancient Greece, where politics and the political prevailed to such an extent that what we call the 'constitution' of an ancient Greek city could be referred to without strain as its very 'life' and 'soul'. This is not a thought that would spring unbidden to many lips now when talking about the *British* constitution, perhaps.[6] Only slightly better, conversely, is Trevelyan's too generously permissive equation of the scope of social history with 'the daily life of the inhabitants of the land in past ages'.[7]

I turn instead to a witness who is every bit as distinguished and provocative as Finley, and yet another sort of exile, Eric Hobsbawm. But his testimony is not altogether encouraging, by any means. In a 1972 paper rather ominously entitled 'From Social History to the History of Society', he noted: 'A survey of social history in the past seems to show that the best practitioners have always felt uncomfortable with the term itself.' He went on to advocate the shift that his title described, away from history of individual or discrete social phenomena to history of whole societies as integrated wholes.[8] The mutations in the title of the journal originally founded in 1929 by Lucien Febvre and Marc Bloch as *Annales d'histoire économique et sociale* seem to bear out both this sense of unease with the term 'social history' and the move away from it: by 1972 it was called *Annales: Économies, Sociétés, Civilisations*; now it has become *Annales: Histoire, Sciences Sociales* – social sciences, no longer social history.[9] A similar straining to escape from the supposedly too subjective implications of a humane discipline into the comfortingly objective realm of science transpires in the latest supplement to the *International Journal of Social History*, entitled *New Methods for Social History*. This collection includes essays with titles such as 'Narrative as Data: Linguistic and Statistical Tools for the Quantitative Study of Historical Events' and 'The Logic of Qualitative Comparative Analysis', which to me carry more than just a whiff of the oxymoronic.[10]

I turn next to Adrian Wilson's 1994 collection, *Rethinking Social History*.[11] The sting of course was in the tale. One of its contributors, Keith Wrightson, observed, again somewhat discouragingly, that none of the more radical hopes of the 1960s (embodied also in Hobsbawm's piece of the early 1970s) had been realized. Instead of all historical writing becoming more sociological, more like a social science, if not actually a(nother) social science, what had in fact happened was that social history had turned into yet another specialized branch of history.[12] The result of this balkanization, as Wrightson saw it, was an ever-decreasing impact of 'social' history on other branches or specialisms, the dominant instances of which remained high political history and economic history. That observation was endorsed by one reviewer of the collection, Sir Keith Thomas, who added a fascinating parenthesis, printed as such, which I quote in full (*Times Literary Supplement* (*TLS*) 14 October 1994):

(Curiously, it was the fear of just this kind of compartmentalization which led E.P. Thompson and the present writer, quite independently of each other, to decline to support the initial formation in the 1970s of the Social History Society. As we saw it, social history was not a branch of history, like postal history or furniture history; it was a way of doing any kind of history.)

Perhaps. However, surely it was a trifle naive of him to suppose that such a 'way' of doing any kind of history could be proposed or practised without any kind of explicit and coherent theoretical structure or support? As soon as one tries to turn history into something consciously reflexive, with a methodology as well as merely a method, it seems to me that one must go that extra theoretical mile.

However that may be, the once more than merely notional empire of social history is unquestionably striking back against its latterday would-be dismantlers or occupiers. As I was compiling this chapter, for instance, the issue of the *TLS* for 21 September 2001 fell into my hands. Among the books advertised therein was a volume jointly written by Peter Burke and by Asa Briggs, entitled *A Social History of the Media*.[13] According to the enthusiastic puff provided by Anthony Smith, 'the work has the virtue of being almost an encyclopaedia'. Almost, perhaps, but yet this monograph is as nothing beside the true or at any rate *soi-disant* encyclopaedia reviewed near the beginning of the same *TLS* issue: Peter Stearns's *Encyclopedia of European Social History from 1350–2000*, published in six volumes and 3150 pages.[14]

Stearns very properly treats readers to a definition of social history, which he gives as 'changes and continuities in the experience of ordinary people'. However, as was crisply observed by the distinguished American reviewer, Stearns's encyclopaedic construction amounts in practice to an all-embracing sort of history of all kinds of people, a construction favoured by the fact (as Rabb sees it) that social history, however defined, is 'much more amorphous, much less of a discipline' than, say, philosophy; and, he continues, although 'the contributors may all regard themselves as social historians, ... it is often difficult to see what they have in common, let alone how they fit together, even within Stearns's very broad conception of the field'.[15]

So there it is – or some of it. At one pole, there are self-confessed social historians with their own journals – such as the *Journal of Social History*, the *International Review of Social History*, *Continuity and Change: A Journal of Social Structure, Law and Demography in Past Societies*, *Comparative Studies in Society and History*, and *Social History* (all UK); *Histoire Sociale/Social History* (Canada) – and now, for some of them, their own *Encyclopedia*. At the other pole, there are historians *tout court*, who believe there should be histories of whole societies or social groups (societal history?, sociological history?), or microhistory(ies) of one kind or another of social phenomena of various sorts, but not necessarily social history as such.[16] In between fall those who believe that social history is a, but no more than a, way of doing any (other) kind of history. What is the way forward – insofar, that is, as progress may be considered a legitimate goal or ambition in historiography?[17]

I propose to operate for most of the remainder of this chapter via the selective case-study approach, taking as my illustrations three recent or very recent examples of historical practice and/or historiographical theory: two American, one British, two more or less explicitly method-ological in theory, the third crucially methodological in practice. None of these, perhaps, would qualify automatically as social history without further qualification. They are chosen rather because they illustrate the limit conditions that any candidate for that in principle honorific title should in my view properly meet. But first a brief look at the temporal dimension – for here, perhaps, a crack may possibly be opened up between the social historian, on the one hand, and the historical anthropologist, at least, on the other, if not also the historical sociologist.[18]

II

Without time there is no history, but what sort of time is the time of history, and more specifically of social history?[19] One particular distinction seems to me peculiarly relevant. This is not the distinction between cyclical and linear time, endlessly discussed both as an aspect of cultural or ethnographic history and as a technical problem of historiographical chronography.[20] Nor is it the distinction between historical and mythical time – that is, the discovery both of the pastness of the past in the Renaissance (if not already in antiquity)[21] and of the finiteness of reasonably accurate human memory, going no further back than three generations, or the generation of the grandfathers of one's own contemporary adult informants.[22] I mean rather the issue of periodic rhythm and change over time.

It has very recently been asserted by Tom Gallant, a historian-archaeologist of ancient Greece turned historian-ethnographer of modern Greece, that 'Social history marches to a different chronological drummer' – different, that is, from 'its sister disciplines of political and economic history [which] lend themselves to sequential narrative analysis'.[23] As is often done in this connection, Gallant resorts for analogical illumination to the medium of photography, both moving and still: whereas the time of political and economic history is that of the sequential narrative frames of a movie, the time of social history is as he sees it 'more like a series of snapshots'. Those of you who are fans of W.G. Sebald's novels may well recall the blurred black-and-white images with which his texts are tantalizingly punctuated: surely there can be no more accurate means of recalling how it actually was (von Ranke's '*wie es eigentlich gewesen ist*')? And yet the suspicion lingers that the photos he includes not only might not be representative images but might actually be fakes.[24]

Apart from that difficulty with the photographic analogy, one might well question, I think, Gallant's bracketing of economic with political history here, since long-run economic cycles are just as much processes as the demographic, familial and other social processes that he wishes to distinguish from them. But – though he does not actually cite him –

what Gallant's language inescapably calls to my mind is rather the *Annaliste* Fernand Braudel's famous, if famously controversial, distinction of the long, the medium-term and the short '*durée*' – respectively (and somewhat artificially and crudely), the durations of social, economic and political phenomena (or in the case of the latter, as he presented them, mere epiphenomena).

This tripartite temporal model has been found widely helpful in some of the best recent historiographical practice, especially when dealing with pre-industrial, peasant societies, in which fundamental technical change in the basic agricultural toolkit and so man's impact on the environment (and vice versa) can indeed appear glacially slow and almost imperceptibly small at any one moment in time.[25] However, as I shall hope to show in the course of discussing my three examples, the model is extremely unhelpful if it leads one to suppose that social history can be history only of the *longue durée*, and that the social historian or anyone else who proposes any variety of social history or historiography must necessarily think in terms of millennia or at least centuries rather than decades or even years.

III

First, let us consider a seriously theoretical and explicitly methodological work by a classicist turned historical sociologist, W.G. Runciman. So serious is it, indeed, that it is called a 'treatise', *A Treatise on Social Theory*, and it occupies no fewer than three volumes, a total of 1170 pages in all. It has cogently been described by an acute critic as 'one of the most exotic – even flamboyant – intellectual projects of recent years'.[26] For our purposes, it is the first two volumes that are of greatest direct relevance to the issues before us, though the six-page preface of the third and final volume does most helpfully summarize not only the contents but also the driving explanatory ambition of the project as a whole. Volume I is methodological. At length, Runciman opens by distinguishing what he labels 'reportage', 'explanation', 'description' and 'evaluation'. The third volume, subtitled *Applied Social Theory*, is actually in a way less exciting than it might sound, as the method is applied only to the – admittedly complex and important – case of twentieth-century English society. Sandwiched between the first and the last volumes comes a second volume of what is labelled *Substantive Social Theory*.

Those who associate sociology irredeemably with esoteric jargon will have their worst fears – or hopes – confirmed by what Runciman self-consciously calls 'the one neologism in the whole treatise' (vol. III, p. xiii,

n. 1), namely 'systacts'. A word of impeccable Hellenic ancestry, as befits the classically trained author, this is coined to designate the 'clusters of roles' assumed by historical actors

> similarly located in a three-dimensional social space whose axes correspond to the three forms of power: the economic (hence, mode of production), the ideological (hence, mode of persuasion), and the political (hence, mode of coercion).

'The need for it', Runciman continues, 'arises because no existing sociological term, least of all "class", is at the same time specific in assigning the designated roles an ordinal ranking relative to other such clusters and neutral between the dimensions in which they are ranked.' Maybe so. Yet, notwithstanding the implication of Runciman's classically honed rhetoric, the terms 'power', 'mode of production', 'ideological' and even 'political' are all of them just as contestable as that of 'class', which term alone he places within scare quotes. One suspects that the author's allegiance to Weber in opposition to Marx may be making itself felt here either subconsciously or at least a little surreptitiously.

The same contestability applies, alas, to his distinction of 'reportage' and 'description', the main virtue of which, it seems to me, is that the terminology and intended reference are both made self-consciously explicit.[27] But do they advance understanding, let alone explanation, of significant human social phenomena of the past? Further questions are prompted by Runciman's infrastructure of terminological classification. Do we agree that societies are to be defined as so many networks of power, that is, as sets of roles whose incumbents are competitors for access to, or control of, the means of production, persuasion and coercion rather than, say, as sets of competing classes, or statuses? Are we persuaded by the overarching argument which all his individual arguments are made to subserve, namely 'the idea that social evolution is analogous but not reducible to natural selection'? It is this grand narrative that fuels Runciman's ambition to formulate a comprehensive theory of society accounting for both the sources of diversity and the constraints on it which determine its evolution (by which is meant a succession of major social changes brought about as the unpredictable, cumulative consequence of minor mutations of practice). The proof is in the eating – and that, for us, means above all in Volume II, *Substantive Social Theory*.

This is a very rich pudding indeed. I pull out, in the space available, just a single plum, a significantly but by no means entirely ancient Greek one. On Runciman's initial catalysis of power into three dimensions with respectively eight, eight and seven variants, there should be in principle and could well have been in practice some 450 possible 'types' of society to categorize and evaluate. In Runciman's own actual practice, there are but a mere dozen or so – a severe Procrusteanism that leads to some unfortunate 'lumping': for conspicuous instance, the tyranny of Peisistratus in sixth-century BCE Athens (which by our modern standards was a fairly mild, even progressive dictatorship) is lumped together with the regimes of (among others) Asoka, the Carolingian empire, Henry the Navigator, and the Tudor monarchy, all alike being categorized and classified as 'patrimonial states'. From that one would never have guessed, probably, that the Peisistratid regime had given way, or even – on some modern accounts – given rise, and by not so very many subsequent steps either, to the world's first proto-democracy, of the distinctly ancient Greek, direct variety, of course.[28]

IV

By the first word of its subtitle, 'war', my second illustration, Manus Midlarsky's *The Evolution of Inequality: War, State Survival, and Democracy in Comparative Perspective* (1999), announces a departure from the pre-occupations of Runciman. Runciman had of course mentioned war, but had dismissed it as a relevant causal variable from his evolutionary schema on the grounds that the outcome of wars 'is so often a matter of chance'. This was an odd decision in terms of Runciman's own version of his evolutionary schema, since he understands social evolution as being dependent on social selection by competition, and war is nothing if not competitive. Besides, this exclusion of 'accidents of fortune' leaves a gap to be filled, one that is especially glaring to the eyes of a historian of ancient Greece.[29] Hence my attraction, initially, to the very recent work of Midlarsky. A further initial attraction was that it has the grand ambition to explain or at least illuminate nothing less than (to quote from the blurb) 'the ultimate genesis of democracy' by way of analyses of: various forms of political violence including war and revolution; the origins and dissolution of states; and the sources of cooperation between states. Some agenda.

It is therefore the more disappointing to have to report that the author's practice falls a long way short of my hopes, at least where I am in any position to judge professionally the results. The latter in important cases seem to me either banal or demonstrably based on empirically false foundations. As an illustration of banality, I cite Midlarsky's finding of a probability of covariation between an increasing tendency to military violence in Eastern Europe and the threat to democracy there. He accounts for that finding by the greater likelihood of 'political intervention by military personnel accustomed to autocratic methods of resolving political disputes' (p. 221).[30] Suppose, however, one were to apply that assumed theorem to ancient Greece, and suppose one were to have in mind when so doing the model of military-political evolution sketched by the greatest historical sociologist of antiquity, that 'giant thinker' (as Marx accurately called him) Aristotle. According to him, political intervention by military personnel had had precisely the opposite effect of that identified by Midlarsky. It had generated the earliest form of democracy in Greece, that is, hoplite or heavy-armed infantry democracy in which preponderant political power had rested with the wealthier stratum of citizens who had formed the city's principal fighting arm, the hoplite militia. In other words, elementary comparativism would have revealed to Midlarsky that it is the nature of the army, and especially of its command structure, and the nature of the warfare practised, and the contingent context within which the political and the military factors interact, that count – those are the crucial variables in influencing or determining the political implications of military involvement in specific social situations.

I would not, however, want to end my brief discussion of *The Evolution of Inequality* on an entirely sour and disillusioned note. The long chapter entitled 'Decline and Fall of Empires and States', which manages to encompass Byzantium, China, the Maya, Israel, Judah, the Ammonites and ancient Egypt as well as ancient Rome, and the pages specifically on the rise of democracy at Athens in a chapter entitled 'Sources of Democracy' (pp. 186–9), represent an intelligent combination of reading in the best modern historical and archaeological scholarship with the application of modest middle-range theorization of the most crucial variables, namely, population density, land distribution and ideas about political entitlement (which, however, Midlarsky perhaps rather rashly and ethnocentrically calls 'rights').

V

Midlarsky dedicated his book in part to the memory of the victims of the Holocaust. My third and final illustration, I suppose the one that might most conventionally be called 'social history now', concerns precisely the causation and motivation of that catastrophe. It is the debate between two American historians, Christopher Browning and Daniel Goldhagen, over the behaviour of some supposedly 'ordinary' Germans and more particularly those composing Reserve Police Battalion 101 in Poland in 1942. Both Browning and Goldhagen agree that those involved were in some sense 'willing' executioners, but they disagree, radically, as to why they acted as such and how they were motivated so to act.

This dispute is, I think, a modern classic of social historiography for at least five reasons. First, because here are Stearns's so-called 'ordinary' people at work and at issue – with a vengeance; for, although one might well want in other contexts to question how 'ordinary' are people who choose to serve as policemen, the authoritarian nature of the Nazi state, empire and culture seems to me sufficient to justify the claim that there was nothing manifestly extraordinary in this type of social conformity.[31] Second, the dispute exemplifies one form of social history, microhistory, which is concerned to use the experience of ordinary individuals or groups of individuals as a way into understanding broader social mentalities, relationships and processes.[32] Third, it examines German anti-semitism and the role that that played in the Holocaust via one particular case history that is judged, plausibly, to have more than merely individual, or local, reference and significance. Fourth, it is also methodologically important, as a study of causation and explanation in history: why did these particular 'ordinary' Germans behave as they individually and collectively did? Fifth, it has already aroused great historiographical interest, not least from the eloquent protagonists, precisely as a case study or test case in historical interpretation.[33]

The arguments on both sides have been exceptionally well-rehearsed, and those of Goldhagen have sometimes found adherents in what might have been considered more neutrally to be unlikely quarters. Briefly, Goldhagen[34] argues that what made the difference to the behaviour of this and the other thirty-seven such Battalions at work, only one-third of whose members were party members and only one-thirtieth in the SS, was a form of anti-semitism that he classifies as 'eliminationist'; this cultural attitude, he contends, had become so deeply ingrained over the generations that by the time of the Nazi supremacy it was almost a fact of ordinary German nature. This is a form of national-social – or perhaps natural-social – history, I suppose. Browning, in sharp contrast, finds that Goldhagen's henocausal, all-purpose pseudo-explanation explains too much, and therefore nothing. It elides above all, he believes, the situational factors conspiring to manipulate the behaviour of these particular Germans in the specific circumstances of their operation in occupied Poland in 1942 – behaviour that was not in any case universal and uniform: between 10 and 20 per cent of Battalion members availed themselves of the opportunity *not* to become executioners.

The balance of authoritative weight of interpretation in this dispute seems to me, an obvious outsider, to tilt very firmly in favour of the Browning version and against that of Goldhagen. I would add only that my main reason for choosing this final illustration of social history, apart from its intrinsic methodological and cultural significance, both then and now, is that I agree with Ludmilla Jordanova on the necessity for historians to engage in and with what has been called, with some imprecision admittedly, 'public' history.[35]

VI

I conclude with some tentative overall answers to the question posed by my title. We should, I believe, resist all hegemonic disciplinary claims: claims such as that social history is the 'key' sort of history, or even *is* history, full stop. The bubble of social history, in those claimed senses, has surely (been) burst since the 1960s and 1970s and is unlikely to be inflated again.[36] But can we do without the category 'social history' altogether, on the grounds that the term is either confusing or vacuous or both? Or on the seemingly more sophisticated and reflexive grounds that, since social categories and concepts are constructed, all history – and the only proper history – is the history of ideas?

Equally surely, we cannot.[37] Pan-representationalism, as I have heard the latter approach described, is as vicious as pan-social-realist historiography. Explicit and reflexive conceptualization, on the other hand, as practised pre-eminently by Runciman, is the reverse of vicious. The term 'social history' may require prior definition, or even stipulation, but that is both possible and, arguably, necessary. For, as Richard Evans has recently reaffirmed, we continue to need social history as a kind of history or sub-species of history, specifically as a history of class, of oppression and exploitation, or – if class, oppression and exploitation are found analytically or morally objectionable terms – at all events of poverty.[38]

The poor, Jesus allegedly said, we have always with us. For Aristotle, unquestionably the greatest sociological thinker of antiquity, it was the polar antithesis of rich and poor (citizens) that best explained what he took to be the most important facet of human existence, namely politics and the political within the framework of the Greek *polis* – a framework that includes what we today would classify as society and the social.[39] Surely Jesus and Aristotle cannot both be wrong? Of course, I must at once add, the ancient Greek *polis* was but a limited range of expression of human social coexistence or solidarity.[40] Likewise, 'class' in ancient Greece cannot mean what it might or should in any contemporary

Western, post-industrial society, for example.[41] But it is hard, at any rate, to deny that these remain real issues, historiographically as well as historically speaking. I rest my case.

Notes and references

* It was an honour for me to be invited to deliver the paper on which this chapter is based, and to be invited by David Cannadine, who in addition to his many other distinctions once graced the Cambridge college to which I am myself attached, and which was also – not incidentally – the college of the late Sir Geoffrey Elton (on whom Richard Evans has many interesting things to say in his 'Afterword' to G.R. Elton, *The Practice of History* (2nd edn) (Oxford: Blackwell, 2002)). He has been an exemplary editor. Judith Herrin served as the respondent to my paper, and I am delighted that a version of her response will be published in another place. Richard Evans, likewise, very kindly offered critical observations on a draft of the spoken version.

1. Finley's historiography: M.I. Finley, *The Use and Abuse of History* (London: Chatto & Windus, 1975; revised edn, London: Hogarth Press, 1986); *Economic and Social History of Ancient Greece*, ed. B.D. Shaw and R.P. Saller (London: Chatto & Windus, 1981; Harmondsworth: Penguin, 1983); cf. 'Progress in Historiography', *Daedalus*, vol. 106 (Summer 1977), pp. 125–42. Other exceptions: C. Ampolo, *Storie greche: La formazione della moderna storiografia sugli antichi Greci* (Turin: Einaudi, 1997); A. Cameron (ed.) *History as Text: The Writing of Ancient History* (London: Routledge, 1986); P. Cartledge (ed.) *The Cambridge Illustrated History of Ancient Greece* (Cambridge: Cambridge University Press, 1997); J.T. Roberts, 'Sociology and the Classical World', *Arion* (2000); pp. 99–133; F. Hartog, 'La storiografia fra passato e presente', in S. Settis (ed.) *I Greci*, Vol. II. 2, *Storia-Cultura-Arte-Società* (Turin: Einaudi, 1997), pp. 959–81; A.D. Momigliano, *The Classical Foundations of Modern Historiography* (California and London: University of California Press, 1990), *Studies on Modern Scholarship*, ed. G.W. Bowersock and T.J. Cornell (California and London: University of California Press, 1994); N. Morley, *Writing Ancient History* (London: Duckworth, 1999) especially chapter 1 ('What is History?' Morley's negatively framed answer is that it is a way of talking about the past, that is different from myth, fiction, propaganda or science); P. Veyne, *Writing History* (Manchester: Manchester University Press, 1984) (French original, 1971).
2. Ancient historians as exiles: R. Syme, 'How Gibbon Came to History' (1977), reprinted in his *Roman Papers*, Vol. III, ed. A.R. Birley (Oxford: Oxford University Press, 1984) pp. 969–76, at 971. Syme's greatest historiographical contributions were to the understanding of Tacitus. Exile and historiography: S. Walia, *Edward Said and the Writing of History* (Duxford: Icon, 2001).
3. Finley, *Use and Abuse*, p. 75; the prediction was technically correct. Carr, however, was not cited by name here – or indeed anywhere else in Finley's voluminous writings as far as I know, despite the fact that Finley, who had been at Jesus College, Cambridge, since 1955, must have at least known of Carr and very likely attended the Trevelyan lectures in 1961. His silence was

presumably therefore a measure of his disagreement – and probably also disrespect. Finley was never a Marxist, being at best or most an anti-anti-Marxist, let alone a communist. Carr's Marxist style of historiography, coupled with what must have appeared to be his sacrificing at the altar of the Soviet monolith, would have been found rebarbative by Finley.

4. I would add that, since Carr seems to have had no formal training as a historian, I suspect his reading as a classics undergraduate at Trinity College, Cambridge, of Herodotus, Thucydides, Polybius and Tacitus (all cited, briefly, in E.H. Carr, *What is History?* (1961; 2nd edn ed. R.W. Davies, 1986; reprinted with new Afterword by R.J. Evans)) (Basingstoke: Palgrave, 2001) may have been more influential on his historiographical outlook than he might have cared to admit. See especially the fascinating anecdote mentioned by R.J. Evans, new 'Introduction' to Carr, *What is History?*, p. xi, about Herodotus' attitude to the Persian War being shaped by his personal experience of the Peloponnesian War (cf. ibid., p. 7); also ibid., p. xviii: a private letter emphasizing that the function of the historian is to explain; with Carr *What is History?*, p. 81, quoting Herodotus' Preface (contrast the view of G. Hawthorn, *Plausible Worlds: Possibility and Understanding in History and the Social Sciences* (Cambridge: Cambridge University Press, 1991) that 'cumulative and convergent certainty, not just about the workings of the world, but also about its particular contents, which we take to mark knowledge, will always elude the social sciences', which Hawthorn takes to include history; therefore, understanding not explanation must in his view be the best we can hope for). Carr's belief in historical 'regularities' (Evans in *What is History?*, pp. xii, xviii) could have come ultimately from Thucydides 1.22.4; likewise, Carr's contempt for history of the masses until at earliest the mid-nineteenth century (R.J. Evans, *In Defence of History* (London: Granta, 1997, 2001 with new Afterword), pp. 164–5; cf. below, note 31) would have been shared by his classical forerunners.

5. On the dispute between methodological individualists and methodological holists, see S. James, *The Content of Social Explanation* (Cambridge: Cambridge University Press, 1984); with James, I would give the victory to the latter; cf. C. Bird, *The Myth of Liberal Individualism* (Cambridge: Cambridge University Press, 2001).

6. On G.M. Trevelyan, *English Social History* (originally New York: Longmans, Green & Co., Inc., 1942), see especially D. Cannadine, *G.M. Trevelyan: A Life in History* (London: Penguin, 1997); cf. briefly Evans, *In Defence of History*, p. 163. On politics and the political, especially but not only in ancient Greece, see P. Cartledge, 'La Politica', in S. Settis (ed.) *I Greci*, Vol. I, *Noi e I Greci* (Turin: Einaudi, 1996), pp. 39–75.

7. I mention, but shall not discuss, the congruent opinion, expressed recently by the classically inspired literary critic Roberto Calasso, *Literature and the Gods* (London: Vintage, 2001), p. 173, in specific relation to the rise of totalitarian regimes, that 'the very notion of society has appropriated an unprecedented power, one previously the preserve of religion'. The 'daily life' genre runs the risk of being merely antiquarian; but that it need not be so is shown by, for example, R. Garland, *Daily Life of the Ancient Greeks* (Westport, CT: Greenwood Press, 1998).

8. Quotation from E.J. Hobsbawm, 'From Social History to the History of Society' (1972), reprinted in his *On History* (London: Weidenfeld & Nicolson, 1998), chapter 6, at p. 99. The desired goal, as he phrases it, should be 'the formulation of the nature and structure of societies and the mechanisms of their historic transformations (or stabilizations)' (ibid., p. 109).

9. P. Burke, *The French Historical Revolution: The* Annales *School 1929–1989* (Cambridge: Polity Press, 1990); a work to be reconsidered in the light of B. Lepetit (ed.) *Les formes de l'expérience: Une autre histoire sociale* (Paris: Albin Michel, 1995), as reviewed by G. Stedman Jones, *Annales HSS* (mars–avril 1998), pp. 383–94.

10. L.J. Griffin and M. van der Linden (eds) *New Methods for Social History* (*International Review of Social History* Supplement) (Cambridge: Cambridge University Press, 1999). The contents in full:

    L.J. Griffin & M. van der Linden 'Introduction'
    L. Isaac, L. Christiansen, J. Miller & T. Nickel 'Temporally recursive regression and social historical inquiry: an example of cross-movement militancy spillover'
    H.J. McCammon 'Using event history analysis in historical research: with illustrations from a study of the passage of women's protective legislation'
    G. Deane, E.M. Beck & S.E. Tolnay 'Incorporating space into social histories: how spatial processes operate and how we observe them'
    R. Franzosi 'Narrative as data: linguistic and statistical tools for the quantitative study of historical events'
    C.C. Ragin 'The logic of qualitative comparative analysis'
    C. Wetherell 'Historical social network analysis'
    L.J. Griffin & R.R. Korstad 'Historical inference and event-structure analysis'.

    Phraseology within the articles can be as verbally rebarbative and methodologically dubious as the articles' titles; for example, McCammon's 'The level of over-time aggregation in event history data ... ideally should be determined by the nature of the research question or by the time frame in which the event of interest occurs' (p. 35).

11. A. Wilson, *Rethinking Social History: English Society 1750–1920, and its Interpretation* (Manchester: Manchester University Press, 1994).

12. I suppose the *reductio ad absurdum* of the parcelling or compartmentalization of History was the monthly magazine *History Today*'s 'What is [social, and so on] History Today?' series of articles, edited as a book under that title by Juliet Gardiner, *What is History Today?* (London: Macmillan, 1988); see Evans, *In Defence of History*, pp. 170, 351. The contribution on social history, coincidentally by an ancient historian, was predictably jejune.

13. P. Burke and A. Briggs, *A Social History of the Media: From Gutenberg to the Internet* (Cambridge: Polity Press, 2001).

14. P. Stearns, *Encyclopedia of European Social History from 1350–2000* (six vols) (New York: Scribner's, 2001).

15. That may be an accurate and fair judgement in this particular case. But on the day I delivered the original oral version of this chapter an obituary notice appeared in the London *Times* for Peter Laslett, which began by labelling him 'the social historian' – principally, one assumes, because of Laslett's

distinguished work in the areas of demography and family history. (However, his early career, almost as distinguished, had been in the history of political thought – or 'politics, philosophy and society', as the essay collections he co-edited were entitled. He was a founder with J.G.A. Pocock of the 'Cambridge School' discussed by Annabel Brett, this volume.) Moreover, the Social History Society referred to by Sir Keith Thomas still flourishes, so one member of the audience at the *Institute of Historical Research* informed us. I add that King Alfred's College, Winchester, offers an MA in Social History (information courtesy of its Director, Dr C.M. Haydon).

16. See below, note 32.
17. Finley, 'Progress in Historiography'.
18. P. Abrams, *Historical Sociology* (London: Open Books, 1982) contended in a proto-postmodernist way that history and sociology were divided, not by logic, but only by rhetoric; history for Abrams was not just a factual presentation of the past but the social reconstruction of the past. A conventional rejoinder by Frank Parkin pontificated that 'social theory is to history as the philosophy of science is to science' (*Times Literary Supplement*, 23 July 1982, p. 801).
19. Time in history, time(s) of history: L. Jordanova, *History in Practice* (London: Edward Arnold, 2000), chapter 5; M. Pearson and M. Shanks, *Theatre/Archaeology* (London: Routledge, 2001), especially pp. 41–4.
20. A.D. Momigliano, *Time in Ancient Historiography* (*History & Theory*, Beiheft, [supplement] 1966).
21. P. Burke, *The Renaissance Sense of the Past* (London: Edward Arnold, 1969).
22. D.P. Henige, *Oral Historiography* (New York and Lagos: Longman, 1982); M. Herzfeld, *The Poetics of Manhood: Contest and Identity in a Cretan Mountain Village* (Princeton, NJ: Princeton University Press, 1985); and cf. P. Burke, *Varieties of Cultural History* (Cambridge: Polity Press, 1997), chapter 3 ('History as Social Memory' (originally 1989)); his thesis in brief is that 'all of us have access to the past (like the present) only via the categories and schemata – or as Durkheim would say, the "collective representations" – of our own culture' (ibid., pp. 45–6).
23. T.W. Gallant, *Modern Greece* (London: Edward Arnold, 2001), p. 75; chapter 5 is devoted to 'Greek Society in the Nineteenth and Early Twentieth Centuries'. For Gallant in his earlier role as ancient social and economic historian of Greece, see his *Risk and Survival in Ancient Greece: Reconstructing the Rural Domestic Economy* (Oxford: Polity Press, 1991).
24. P. Burke, *Eyewitnessing: The Uses of Images as Historical Evidence* (Ithaca, NY, and London: Cornell University Press, 2001) might be read as a cautionary manual on the fickleness of images.
25. A small illustration: E. Le Roy Ladurie, *Le Territoire de l'historien* (Paris: Gallimard, 1973), pp. 169–86 ('Événement et longue durée dans l'histoire sociale: l'exemple chouan') (English translation, 1979); cf. Burke, *The French Historical Revolution*, pp. 61–4. A typical, conservative criticism of this type of history is that, as it is concerned with structures rather than events, it cannot easily convey a sense of change over time, let alone explain it, without connecting with the established narratives of political or economic history.
26. W.G. Runciman, *A Treatise on Social Theory*, 3 Vols (Cambridge: Cambridge University Press, 1983, 1989, 1997). The quotation is from Perry Anderson,

London Review of Books, 6 July 1989, p. 6, reviewing Vol. II. But the entire work is overlooked, remarkably, by Jordanova in *History in Practice*, an otherwise excellent primer, and even by Evans in *In Defence of History*.

27. 'The need for precision in terminology is no less acute where the subject under discussion is an individual action than where it is an institution or practice' (vol. I, p. 20) nicely captures this constant preoccupation.

28. P. Cartledge, 'Democratic Politics Ancient and Modern: From Cleisthenes to Mary Robinson', *Hermathena*, vol. 166 (Summer 1999 (2000)), pp. 5–29.

29. M. Midlarsky, *The Evolution of Inequality: War, State Survival and Democracy in Comparative Perspective* (Stanford, CA: Stanford University Press; Cambridge: Cambridge University Press, 1999). War for the ancient Greeks was an *agôn*, a contest, whence we derive our word 'agony'; it was typically 'people's' warfare, if not total warfare. On ancient Greek warfare, see recently H. Van Wees (ed.) *War and Violence in Ancient Greece* (London: Duckworth, 2000); and for two very different comparativist collections, K. Raaflaub and R. Rosenstein (eds) *War and Society in the Ancient and Medieval Worlds* (Cambridge, MA: Harvard University Press, 1999); and D.R. McCann and B.S. Strauss (eds) *War and Democracy: A Comparative Study of the Korean War and the Peloponnesian War* (Armonk, NY: M.E. Sharpe, 2001).

30. Midlarsky also thinks A.C. Renfrew, 'Polity and Power: Interaction, Intensification, and Exploitation', in C. Renfrew and J.M. Wagstaff (eds) *An Island Polity: The Archaeology of Exploitation on Melos* (Cambridge: Cambridge University Press, 1982), to be worth citing on the spread of democracy in the Aegean islands under 'Ionian' influence – alas, poor Melos ... which in actual fact was an unreconstructed Dorian oligarchy.

31. As Evans, *In Defence of History*, p. 182, notes, advocates of social history such as Stearns 'claim that social history is the only approach that combines intellectual excitement with scholarly solidity'. Conversely, E.H. Carr 'clearly thought the history of ordinary people was not worth studying until they became organized in political movements and so contributed to the making of the *modern* world' (my emphasis) – a view powerfully rebutted by Evans himself (ibid., pp. 164–5).

32. G. Levi, 'On Microhistory' in P. Burke (ed.) *New Perspectives on Historical Writing* (Cambridge: Polity Press, 1991), pp. 93–113. P. Burke, *History and Social Theory* (Cambridge: Polity Press, 1993) identifies four general approaches to the conjoining of history and social theory: comparative analysis, modelling, quantitative analysis, and microhistory ('the employment of the social microscope').

33. J.C.G. Röhl, 'Ordinary Germans as Hitler's Willing Executioners? The Goldhagen Controversy' in W. Lamont (ed.) *Historical Controversies and Historians* (London: University College London Press, 1998), pp. 15–21; R. Eaglestone, *Postmodernism and Holocaust Denial* (Duxford: Icon, 2001), pp. 30–4; and above all C. Browning, 'German Memory, Judicial Interrogation and Historical Reconstruction: Writing Perpetrator History from Postwar Testimony', in S. Friedländer (ed.) *Probing the Limits of Historical Representation: Nazism and the 'Final Solution'* (Cambridge, MA: Harvard University Press, 1992), pp. 22–36, and *Ordinary Men: Reserve Police Battalion 101 and the Final Solution in Poland* (original edn 1992; new 'Afterword' 1998) (London: Penguin, 2001).

34. D. Goldhagen, *Hitler's Willing Executioners: Ordinary Germans and the Holocaust* (New York: Alfred Knopf; London: Little, Brown, 1996).

35. Jordanova, *History in Practice*, chapter 6; cf. the two concluding sentences of the personal 'Postscript': '*History in Practice* has attempted to bring some of the key issues of historical practice to a wide audience. In this respect it is a modest contribution to public history' (p. 207).

36. Perhaps the same will be said in due course for what seems to be the current contender for the Most Universal Form of History crown – cultural history (about which see Miri Rubin's contribution to this volume). See, for example, Burke, *Varieties of Cultural History*; though perhaps even he would not have anticipated D.M. Friedman, *A Mind of Its Own. A Cultural History of the Penis* (New York: The Free Press, 2001).

37. Evans, *In Defence of History*, chapter 6, 'Society and the Individual', with the bibliographical discussion at pp. 361–2, is an exemplary rejoinder.

38. Evans, *In Defence of History*, especially pp. 165–70 (different constructions of 'social history'), 183–90. Yet note his observation that 'Even in the 1990s, the view that history is essentially political history remains widespread within the profession' (p. 162). J. Arnold, *History: A Very Short Introduction* (Oxford: Oxford University Press, 2000), p. 86, gives a rather wider than Evans's – perhaps a too wide – interpretation of the scope of social history as people's 'family structures, their conduct in daily life, the way they arrange and give meaning to the social spaces around them'. J. Tosh, *The Pursuit of History: Aims, Methods and New Directions in the Study of Modern History* (2nd edn) (London: Longman, 1991) p. 96, (3rd edn, 1999), cautiously ventures that '*Social history* is less self-evident in its identity and scope than any of the categories discussed so far'; cf. ibid., pp. 209–17 (oral history). M. Bentley (ed.) *Routledge Companion to Historiography* (London: Routledge, 1997) notably has no separate entry for 'social history'.

39. Cartledge, 'La Politica'.

40. However, to call it a 'dead end', as does W.G. Runciman, 'Doomed to Extinction: The *Polis* as an Evolutionary Dead-End', in O. Murray and S. Price (eds) *The Greek City from Homer to Alexander* (Oxford: Oxford University Press, 1990), pp. 347–67, is a bit too strong; for a dead-end, the ancient Greek city had and indeed retains an awful lot of vitality, as an imagined eu-topia (place of well-faring) as well as an ou-topia (no-place): Cartledge, 'Democratic Politics Ancient and Modern'. Runciman's earlier essay, 'Origins of States: The Case of Archaic Greece', *Comparative Studies in Society and History*, vol. 24 (1982), pp. 351–77, is more successful.

41. This is notwithstanding the best efforts of G.E.M. de Ste. Croix, *The Class Struggle in the Ancient Greek World. From the Archaic Age to the Arab Conquests* (London: Duckworth, 1981) to find a definition of 'class' that would capture both ancient and modern situations and conditions with equal validity and explanatory force.

3
What is Political History Now?*

Susan Pedersen

Of all forms of historical writing, political history is surely the one that needs no justification. Since it treats questions of power and resistance, authority and legitimacy, order and obedience, not only professional historians but everyone hoping to live out their days in a modicum of peace and prosperity has a stake in such scholarship. Questions of the ways in which political systems evolve and gain legitimacy, the character and actions of their leaders, and the conditions and consequences of their breakdown are likely to remain absorbing. Debates over the character of the Nazi state or the causes of the French Revolution will never be declared decisively 'over', nor will such subjects cease to form the backbone of our undergraduate teaching syllabus anytime soon.

But when one proffers such commonsensical reassurances to today's political historians, they seem to fall rather flat. Political history, it appears, is also in a state of crisis, its practitioners circling the wagons against the assault of those former neo-Marxists and now postmodernists who are making the academy today such a disquieting place in which to live. Few might go so far as my departmental colleague William Gienapp, the distinguished historian of the early Republican Party in the United States, and declare the turn towards social history in the 1960s and 1970s to have been an unmitigated evil from which we have not recovered, but hints of defensiveness are everywhere to be found.[1] Moreover, political historians can point to grounds for such worries. In many fields, political history for some decades has had difficulties attracting able graduate students, who are understandably drawn to research areas seen to be more 'cutting edge'. At my own university, searches in the fields of

American constitutional and legal history have repeatedly come up empty-handed.

Nor is the field of modern British history, my own area of study and hence my subject here, entirely free of such trends. Take, for example, the evidence of the papers given at the North American Conference on British Studies (NACBS), the main professional meeting for scholars of Britain teaching in the United States and Canada, where over the past three years fewer than one-quarter of the panels on modern British history have fallen comfortably within the field of political history as it has been conventionally defined. Or take the submissions for the British Council Prize for the best book in British history written by a North American scholar. For two years running, most of the top contenders for this prize have been books in the field of cultural history – works like Susan Grayzel's comparative account of the uses made of the figure of the mother during the First World War in Britain and France, Michael Saler's study of Frank Pick's effort to win over the public to modernism through the buildings and decoration of the London Underground, Erika Rappaport's wonderful account of the struggle between entrepreneurial retailers and feminist reformers for the hearts and minds of late-Victorian women with time and money on their hands, or Kali Israel's clever interrogation of the multiple possible readings of the life of Emilia Dilke.[2]

Or take, finally, the case of the conference on 'Locating the Victorians' held in London last summer. What was striking here was not merely the modest place accorded to questions of politics, but also that that place existed at all only because of the conference organizers' insistence. A call for papers and for organizers which ultimately yielded some twenty-one strands on subjects ranging from 'Pain and Pleasure' to 'The Great Exhibition' initially elicited not only no offers to organize a political history 'strand' but equally no paper proposals. Only the willingness of Peter Mandler to step in and organize a day-long session on 'Liberty and Authority' saved this conference from becoming a genuine exercise in history with the politics left out.

Yet once we declare political history to be in a bad state, this contention quickly finds its rebutters. Political history, they retort, has been not so much abandoned as rediscovered and redefined. Convinced of the relevance of popular opinion and action for political outcomes, but now sceptical of a framework that would extract such opinions from a bedrock of class, erstwhile social historians have returned to the study of popular politics with new energy. Similarly, cultural historians, persuaded by Foucault's arguments about the multivalent and web-like nature of relations of power, now read public executions or election addresses, popular songs or the novels of Wilkie Collins for what such sources can reveal about the manifold ways in which authority and domination are exercised and legitimated. If only a quarter of those NACBS panels treated political history narrowly defined, probably most of the presenters at other sessions would have claimed – whatever their subject, approach or source base – to be concerned centrally with questions of authority, legitimacy and power. Against those who would see political history as under attack, our optimist might retort that, to the contrary, we are all political historians now.

This chapter examines this quarrel with particular attention to my own field of modern British history. It makes two main points. First, it argues that the perception either of crisis or of great controversy in this field is largely illusory: if anything, the theoretical and analytical trends of the past few decades have brought right-leaning 'high political' historians and left-leaning students of popular politics closer together. There is considerable common ground between post-Marxist historians' discovery of the 'relative autonomy' of the political realm and the assumptions that have always structured 'high political' history; moreover, both gender history and the 'linguistic turn' have been accommodated in ways that (however theoretically heterodox) have made our understanding of the workings of the political realm more sophisticated. But if political history is, in fact, not merely thriving but increasingly consensual, that doesn't mean that this move towards the middle hasn't brought troubles of its own. For my second point will be that, by turning its back so decisively on structural interpretation, this 'new' political history runs the risk of committing, or recommitting, what I think of as the two besetting sins of British history – the sins of parochialism and what one might call Panglossianism, of accepting the exceptional and incomparable character of British institutions and of letting our historical subjects' understanding of those institutions substitute for our own.

Whatever their weaknesses, both Marxist theory and historical comparison – two of the failed gods of the 1970s – did at least force political historians to grapple with fundamental questions of state structure and coercive power. Those approaches are now decisively out of favour; worse, because historians have moved away from both comparison and structural argument at a moment when political scientists have moved away from history altogether, the sources for renewal in this field seem worryingly absent. For reasons I will explain, not even the current 'imperial turn' is doing all that it might to push questions of governance and coercion, rather than of legitimacy and leadership, to the top of the historian's agenda. All is not well in the garden of political history, then – although I would argue that the danger comes from a different direction than the ones against which so much of the historical profession is erecting its defences.

I

In arguing for the health of political history in Britain, one has to begin by acknowledging that this field has always been, comparatively speaking, amazingly robust. The study of politics has always been the British historian's first concern. If French scholars pioneered the study of demography and rural life, and the Germans led the way in legal and ecclesiastical history, no nation rivalled Britain in the serious study of political history. Whether because Britain's modern history of unbroken parliamentarism left its historians with few cataclysmic events to attract their attention, or because Britain's political historians have been part of an 'incorporated intelligentsia' and hence prone to find the explication of their own political affiliations both fascinating and (in the strict sense) 'familiar', political history in Britain has absorbed an unusually large share of scholarly attention. Of course, much of that work falls within a genre that we might call the history of political leadership, whether it takes the form of political biography (a uniquely powerful and popular British genre) or of studies of party politics and government.

From the standpoint of other European historians, the sheer amount of that scholarship is striking. The many shelves of books analysing the emergence, composition, electoral strategies, governing practices and demise of the Liberal Party astound the historian of French radicalism (a comparably significant force), who is forced to rely on Serge Berstein's *Histoire du Parti Radical* and a few other monographs. Likewise, although Gustav Stresemann might have stood alongside Lloyd George or at least Austen Chamberlain in his influence on both national and international politics, German historians have accorded him only a fraction of the scholarly attention that their British counterparts have lavished on every utterance and action of even relatively minor early twentieth-century politicians. True, when scholars in other national fields (not to mention American graduate students entering this field) look at British political history their admiration is not always unmixed with irritation, for this is a historiography that takes its own significance as given, makes no gestures to contemporary relevance, frankly disdains the attractions of 'theory' (and, to a degree, of systematization or generalization of any kind), and implicitly proclaims that if you can't follow who the bit-players are, you shouldn't be watching the play. Yet, however interior and self-referential such a field might seem, it is, in my view, unrivalled in its scholarly standards and accomplishments. At least since Namier, political historians in Britain have assumed that one must not only understand the spoken and unspoken rules of the political game and the capacity and characters of its players but also derive and test one's understanding through unflagging archival research. If political history today has retained its standing, it is at least in part because these are its foundations.

But the second reason for its health today is that political history has not merely survived but actually profited from the recent theoretical ferments within the historical profession. Against what one might assume, the theoretical trends of the past twenty years, with which Maurice Cowling would surely have not been in sympathy, have essentially brought his opponents to his door. This may seem counter-intuitive, for the political origins and affiliations of what one might call the 'new' political history are scarcely those of the 'high politics' school, but I do think it is the case. No trend has been more marked in British history over the past twenty years than the shift away from 'class', both as a subject of study and as a foundation for explanation. That critique of class-centred interpretation has come from different directions and taken different forms, but whether scholars were motivated by the 'linguistic turn' or by a growing awareness of the significance of other bases for social identification and mobilization (such as gender), one result has been a more intense and sophisticated attention to politics. As every graduate student knows, one decisive moment in this shift came with the publication in 1983 of Gareth Stedman Jones's 'Rethinking Chartism', a piece remarkable not only for the sophisticated manner in which it replaced one comprehensive narrative (that of the emergence of 'class consciousness') with another (that of the continuity of political radicalism), but also for the wealth of debate and research it has spawned.[3]

Both Stedman Jones's rejection of an interpretive approach that would see political language as in some sense determined by, or reflective of, social conditions, and his resulting argument about the relative autonomy and longevity of a radical critique of the corrupting effects of the monopoly of political power, were taken up by a crowd of students and followers, who – from positions in Cambridge and Princeton, Liverpool and London – extended this popular politics-centred 'continuity thesis' into the late nineteenth century.[4] At the same time, and in the United States especially, historians and literary critics influenced by post-structuralist theories began to examine political debates not as descriptive of some foundational social reality but rather for what they might reveal about the strategic positions of their participants and the cultural assumptions structuring the society as a whole. Thus, for example, in Dror Wahrman's work, the appearance of an overt rhetoric about the political rights of a rising 'middle class' in the period of the French Revolution is seen to have been driven less by any actual change in class relations than by the usefulness of such arguments for particular factions at particular times; similarly, James Vernon and Patrick Joyce have treated the polyphonic world of nineteenth-century popular culture less as expressive of social interests than as an arena of discursive conflict through which particular identities and subjectivities were shaped and gained political salience.[5]

But the recruits to political history came not merely from those who exited from class analysis through the linguistic turnstile, but equally from those eager to trace the meaning of other axes of social differentiation, and particularly of gender. True, early work on gender within British history imitated rather than challenged the 'class formation' paradigm, as scholars sought to delineate the business practices, marriage choices, religious movements and trade union strategies that sustained, across class lines, a shift towards a culture of 'separate spheres'.[6] Yet no sooner had this master narrative been sketched out than it was challenged by those eager to document women's close involvement with aristocratic, radical, or even liberal politics, to show how a 'turn towards domesticity' could itself have political and electoral consequences, or to argue for the centrality of gender to national mobilization or political legitimation.[7] With social interpretations out of favour, historians of women and historians of gender made their own 'political turn', seeking to discover the elective affinities between particular gender ideals and political beliefs or forms.

Whether coming from a disillusionment with Marxist explanations or out of the intellectual ferment of feminism, then, these 'new' political historians have tended to focus on two major subjects – on the nature of the political system as expressive of relations of power, and on political culture and ideas. But these are also the two main interests of those we usually think of as 'high political' historians. 'High political' historians always treated the formal structure of politics seriously, and if most would have accepted Maurice Cowling's view of the political system of the early twentieth century as 'consist[ing] of fifty or sixty politicians in conscious tension with one another'[8] or A.B. Cooke and John Vincent's portrait of 'the politicians' world' of 1885 as 'a closed one',[9] some at least also recognized (and no one more than Cowling himself) that all politicians after 1832 lived by the word, seeking through rhetoric to foster public faith in the institutions and practices of parliamentary government in general and their own leadership in particular. As Michael Bentley perceptively noted, Cowling's own work at least 'hints' that 'lineaments exist between the overt story' of British parliamentary politics since 1867 'and the cosmologies of its actors';[10] unsurprisingly, then, Bentley and others have sought to trace those lineaments, paying as much attention to 'cosmologies', 'thought-worlds' and 'doctrines' as they have to parliamentary manoeuvres and intrigues.[11] Indeed, if there has been a discernable movement within the 'high politics' school in the last decade, it has been towards, in Jonathan Parry's words, 'a closer attention to the intellectual setting in which political activity took place'.[12] In other words, the new and intense interest in 'political culture' among historians has not been fuelled by the 'linguistic turn' alone.

What we can see developing, then, is a quite considerable common ground. I don't mean to say there are no differences between, say, Peterhouse and Princeton: intellectual heritages, methodological convictions and (often) political affiliations continue to separate the 'new political' from the 'high political' historians.[13] Nevertheless, there seems to me more than a slight affinity between the discursive approach to politics insisted upon by Gareth Stedman Jones and the high political treatment of politics as an enclosed and rule-bound game, or between (say) Eugenio Biagini's attention to the moral ideas underlying popular liberalism and (say) Parry's insistence on the central importance of religious beliefs and controversies within the party itself. Tellingly, both camps prefer to set up 'Marxist historians' or some other nefarious breed of sociological determinists as the disseminators of error against which they are bravely struggling, however vanishingly small (or, these days, non-historian in membership) this intellectual opposition might be.[14] (Indeed, Eugenio Biagini rather disarmingly admitted as much in *Liberty, Retrenchment and Reform* when he pointed out that actual 'Marxist historians' might now be rather hard to identify, although that didn't stop him from setting himself up against this particular straw man.[15])

But does this convergence matter? Have we gained anything from this rapprochement? Let me answer that question by mentioning the ways in which two subjects of sustained historical attention – the study of Gladstonian liberalism and the study of interwar politics – have been enriched and transformed. The Gladstonian Liberal Party, we all know, marched to victory on a platform of peace and free trade, fiscal retrenchment and franchise reform. Thirty years ago, when most historians (so we are told) accepted that something called the English working class had been decisively 'made' by the mid-Victorian period, its class consciousness all present and accounted for, the success of this platform seemed more puzzling; after all, Gladstonian finance was cheeseparing and Gladstonian social policy eschewed the language of class. Historians, trying to account for its success, were driven, following John Foster, to arguments about working-class false consciousness, or, following John Vincent, to arguments about organizational coalition and windy rhetorical blinds. Those making a positive case for liberalism – like Peter Clarke – were forced to overstress the socially radical aspects of an emerging 'new liberal' programme since presumably only those aspects would have been capable of holding the loyalty of a class-conscious working class.[16]

Today, however, little is left of that interpretation. If Colin Matthew alerted us to the conservative and Peelite origins of Gladstonian ideas and policies, and Boyd Hilton has stressed their evangelical foundations,[17] the 'new' historians of popular politics, freed of their earlier assumptions about the way material interest necessarily underlay political affiliation, were able to show how the political platform that emerged out of this foundation – a platform centred around religious toleration, civic action, fiscal stringency and a slow extension of political rights – could have wide popular appeal. Such a programme, after all, drew on older dissenting, radical and working-class hostility to an oppressive and patrimonial state; in Gladstone's retrenching budgets, a wide range of citizens perceived not the chance to exercise power, but rather a new and welcome lightening of power's arbitrary rule. Such an interpretation is attentive to the independent and powerful influence of inherited political understandings and idioms and does not dismiss these as 'false consciousness'; importantly, it recognizes that even the relatively humble can have what Max Weber called 'ideal' as well as material interests, and could find the party's emphasis on independence and manliness powerfully attractive. This is an explanation for the Liberal Party's long hegemony that complements rather than confounds high political accounts of the importance of parliamentary management.

Indeed, the only real weakness of this interpretation, to my mind, is the sometimes excessive claims made for its 'newness'. It was John Vincent in 1966 and not Catherine Hall in 1992 who wrote that 'the great moral idea of liberalism was manliness':

For the nineteenth-century man, the mark or note of being fully human was that he should provide for his own family, have his own religion and politics, and call no man master. It is as a mode of entry into this full humanity that the Gladstonian Liberal party most claims our respect.[18]

Vincent, cited by Jon Lawrence and Miles Taylor as the originator of a 'sociological approach' to politics that assumed a 'neat symmetry – effectively a functional relationship – between social change and party politics'[19] in fact begins his justly famous *Formation of the Liberal Party* with the statement that liberalism's popular appeal cannot be understood with reference to programme or political organization alone, but also must be sought in the realm of ideas. As they (in their more generous-spirited moments) recognize, the new political historians are still drawing on Vincent's insights even as they revise them.

The historiography of liberalism is thus one area in which this rapprochement has borne fruit, and in a second area – that of the effort to explain interwar Conservative dominance – the benefits have been even more striking. Certainly there was plenty of room for improvement. From the vantage point of the postwar Keynesian 'consensus' the dominance of Stanley Baldwin (not to mention Ramsay MacDonald) in the 1920s and 1930s seemed almost inexplicable, and those who did try to explain it tended to rely, once again, on arguments about political manipulation, 'deference' voting, or, more recently, Baldwin's adroit exploitation of a rhetoric of 'Englishness'.[20] That not simply conservatism but the deflationary, retrenching, constitutional conservatism of the Baldwin years could be positively attractive to a newly democratic (and increasingly female) electorate was almost unthinkable. Yet, as historians began to jettison assumptions about the necessary appeal of redistributive and statist policies to the working class (much less to women), the sources of conservatism's powerful cultural and ideological pull began to appear.

Here as well, 'high political' historians, historians of 'class', and even literary critics struck some common notes: witness, for example, the close attention paid by Philip Williamson, Ross McKibbin and even, from an entirely different direction, the feminist scholars Alison Light and Susan Kingsley Kent, to the ways in which a rhetoric of national reconciliation, private and civic engagement, and economic balance and probity might have been welcomed by even non-elite voters after the social and military strife of the First World War.[21] Of course, important distinctions remain, for while Williamson lays great stress on Baldwin's persuasiveness as a 'public moralist', McKibbin – true to his more 'sociological' past – points to the ways in which the Conservatives, through a politics of deflation, could themselves expand that loyal constituency of non-unionized and slightly resentful voters on which they disproportionately relied. Yet, as Williamson himself has acknowledged, there is a real affinity between these explanations.[22] Most importantly, by taking the content of Conservative rhetoric (and not just policy) seriously, and accepting the complex and often 'non-material' grounds for individual political affiliations and loyalties, these historians and literary critics have constructed a more persuasive – and, I might add, more respectful – explanation for why so many people between the wars willingly thought that a man like Stanley Baldwin could be trusted to defend their interests.

II

What, then, is political history in Britain now? It is, I hope I've shown, both flourishing and increasingly consensual. Already possessed of a strong foundation in the study of party politics and political thought, it has been enriched by new investigations into popular politics and political culture written by social historians now unpersuaded of the explanatory power of 'class'. No longer divided between those who would see politics only as a game governed by largely instrumental calculation and those who would see it as the epiphenomenal working out of social relations, historians from a variety of traditions have found in the close study of political discourse and culture considerable common ground. What we might hope is that they will, in the future, acknowledge that common ground more openly, engage more straightforwardly with one another's work, and cease to trot out the dusty figure of John Foster when searching for an exemplar of that supposedly 'dominant' school of social determinism against which they are struggling. Of course, such intellectual honesty would have its costs. For if we recognize the degree to which political historians have come to accept both the relative autonomy of politics and a method of study aimed at understanding the political ideas and culture of historical actors as they themselves saw them, we might begin to ask not only what this new consensus has given us, but also what it hasn't. I, for one, think we ought to begin to ask this question. For while I am persuaded of the merits of this new work, I remain enough of a social scientist to be conscious of what one loses by jettisoning not only class-based but also more broadly social-structural explanations. For the rest of this chapter, then, I am going to focus on what seem to me to be the worrying, if unintended, consequences of current intellectual trends.

Before I do so, however, let me pause for a brief definitional point. What do we mean by politics, and what should political history do? Let me turn briefly for help to the German sociologist Max Weber, who begins his famous essay on 'Politics as a Vocation' with a few useful pages on the core terms and concepts we must use if we intend to study politics. Weber treats politics, in essence, as those arrangements through which domination is disposed and exercised. Any adequate sociological analysis of those arrangements, he contends, must take into account the complex interactions between three factors: first, political leadership, whether by individuals or by parties; second, the structure and coercive reach of the state; and third, the nature and foundation of claims to legitimacy.[23] And an adequate political history, I would argue, would need to engage with all three aspects as well. Political processes and developments, and the ways in which in those developments are both influenced by and constrain individual men and women, can only be fully understood if one takes institutional and state structures, as well as political leadership and ideas, into account.

But here we can begin to identify a problem, for if the convergence between high political and those 'new' political historians has both revived and revised two of those aspects of political history – the study of political leaders and parties and the study of political culture and ideas – it has done little to foster (and may, in some ways, even be retarding) the serious study of what we might call governance or rule – of the structure, reach and practices of the state. This is the case, I would argue, because the methods and approaches commonly used by both 'high political' historians and 'linguistic turners' which have proved so fruitful to the study of party politics and political culture are not adequate to this latter set of problems. As I have shown, both groups now pay close attention to the language of politics, whether at the elite or popular level, on the assumption that through such a hermeneutic, thick-descriptive approach we can recapture the political beliefs and actions of historical actors, *as they themselves would have understood them*; likewise, both pay close attention to the cultural traditions and inherited understandings that structure those practices and beliefs. And again, as I've argued, those methods and approaches have paid off: there is no question but that we can better explain political beliefs and loyalties in this way than by assuming they reflect purely instrumental calculations or by reading them off of social relations.

The problem is that these approaches do relatively little to help us understand the nature and reach of state institutions, and – insofar as they persuade us to take our subjects' carefully reconstructed understandings of their political surroundings as in some analytical sense 'accurate' – might even lead us astray. For the structure, reach, and practices of the state are best studied not through 'thick description' but with some effort at abstraction, not diachronically but synchronically and comparatively. Questions of 'meaning' are not unimportant here, but they are *less* important, for when we study (say) incarceration or education or conscription, what we wish to know is not just how those systems were understood by their subjects and whether they were seen as legitimate (although we do wish to know that), but also whether and how they made those subjects (and those states) law-abiding, learned or victorious. The 'test' of state institutions is, after all, not how well they accord with historic understandings but rather how well they stand up against other states in the critical and competitive arenas of production, reproduction and war. When studying the state, then, one must always proceed with a global context and structured comparison at least implicitly in mind.

But here, again, we face a problem, for when it comes to comparative and global analysis, British historians do not have particularly powerful intellectual traditions (unless one were to count the traditions of open immigration and Anglo-American exchange) on which to draw. Rather, they both reflect and suffer from the dominant traditions of British intellectual life more generally. Comparison came naturally to German and Japanese politicians and industrialists as they sought to build up their economies and empires, to French statesmen casting anxious glances across the Rhine, and to Russian intellectuals weighing the relative values of Slavophilism and a turn to the West. Except at rare moments and among restricted circles, however, it did not come naturally to the British (or, for that matter, to the Chinese), who were always more likely to think historically than comparatively, and to judge their political institutions either against some idealized version of their own past, or against classical examples. British historians, moreover, have followed their lead, generally eschewing comparative analysis and preferring instead to trace the development of political practices and institutions over time. Small wonder, then, that the best structural accounts of Britain's political institutions, from Lewis Namier's *Structure of Politics* to Samuel Beer's *Treasury Control*, have tended to be written by immigrants, outsiders, or transplants to the United States, for whom Britain's rather peculiar political institutions (and, still more, their capacity to win consent and foster stability and prosperity) seemed less than self-evident and worthy of investigation.[24]

Let me try to make these points about the costs of a 'political turn' without an accompanying interest in cross-national comparison clearer by discussing briefly three separate historiographies: those of early-modern political corruption, of welfare state formation, and of wartime and postwar consumption policies. 'Old corruption' is, of course, a nineteenth-century term of abuse for eighteenth-century political practices – and it remained, as Stedman Jones and others have pointed out, central to the radical analysis of the British state until at least mid-century. As an entry point into the mindset of British radicalism, the concept of 'old corruption' bears (and has profited from) a great deal of recent attention: the problem arises when historians begin (as E.P. Thompson urged) to treat it as 'a ... serious term of political analysis', a concept in some way accurately descriptive of the workings of the eighteenth-century state.[25] For while the eighteenth-century state was indeed patrimonial and patronage-ridden, it was also, as John Brewer and Thomas Ertman have pointed out, in comparative terms highly efficient. Not only was it able to extract a strikingly large proportion of GNP to sustain the functions of the state (and pre-eminently to sustain its wars), but the collection and dispersal of these funds was never (as it was in France) actually delegated to parasitic private interests. Indeed, insofar as such funds were amassed through self-assessed taxes and a publicly held debt, it seems clear that, in some important ways, the state was not simply (comparatively speaking) relatively 'clean' but was perceived to be clean (and hence creditworthy) by a fairly wide section of the populace.[26] That that same populace may have deployed a fiercely critical language of 'old corruption' in order both to check any tendencies towards graft and to insist on their own political claims should not surprise us, but nor should it lead us to equate Henry Fox with the Farmers General or even Walpole's parliament with the Spanish Cortes. If we do so, not only the operation of the state in this era but equally Britain's quite surprising military performance becomes incomprehensible. In studying state development, then, some attention to the structure and performance of the political competition – by which I mean other eighteenth-century states and not oppositional parliamentary factions – is essential and has already proven fruitful.

And the same point can be made for the study of the state in the twentieth century, although here it is the state's capacity to 'foster life' through social and population policies and not simply its ability to wage war that draws our attention.[27] Yet, in this field as well, British historians have been less inclined than those in other countries to think comparatively. When I first began working on the British welfare state, I was struck by the degree to which standard works in the field tended to focus very largely on national developments across time – on, say, the relationship between Victorian poor relief and interwar unemployment policy – rather than on the impact of international counter-examples or such external 'shocks to the system' as economic crisis and world war.[28] In this, they were only following their subjects' lead: the architects of the British welfare state tended to argue for their programmes historically rather than comparatively, by invoking the evils of the past needing redress rather than the pressure of competitors across the water.[29] And this did make for a kind of myopia. For, viewed comparatively, what is striking about British social policy is the degree to which it has been, well into the last decades of the twentieth century, a kind of gendered labour policy in disguise, with health, anti-poverty and child welfare measures all held hostage to a concerted effort to sustain the fiction of a male-breadwinner norm.

Britain thus addressed the social problems that arose from the interwar global economic crisis largely through unemployment benefits (which, although chastised for stinginess, were markedly more generous than similar policies elsewhere) rather than through the family policies adopted in a number of other countries.[30] Yet so accustomed were politicians, British citizens and (later) historians to these traditions that the peculiar and non-normative nature of British developments was lost to view. Popular understandings of the institutions of the welfare state, in other words, however critically important to the social history and party politics of the period, do not give us a very good analytical understanding of these states; nor do they tell us how well or badly they did in meeting goals that those governments and populaces may have themselves identified. Only comparison can answer that question, and if historians feel any responsibility to make public debates about political choices more realistic and better informed they will make more of an effort to 'think comparatively'.

Finally, consider the interesting question of the political consequences of consumption policies in Britain during and after the Second World War. Here, historians attuned to the ways in which gender identities can be shaped and mobilized have had a particularly valuable impact. Fifteen years ago, in her influential work on the making of postwar subjectivities, *Landscape for a Good Woman*, Carolyn Steedman movingly recounted how the postwar Labour government's insistence that free milk for schoolchildren take precedence over fancy frocks for women both heartened her young self and alienated her tired, glamour-starved mother – and recent, more systematic research has built upon her insight.[31] Thus, in a new prize-winning book on the workings of the rationing system from the Second World War until its final abolition under the Tories, Ina Zweiniger-Bargielowska demonstrates that such consumption policies both burdened women in particular and ultimately alienated them: to put it most crudely, the Labour government paid at the polls for its inability to understand why, after almost a dozen years, women's patience with utility fabrics and margarine might be running thin.[32] Here again, then, an attention to gender and an awareness of the ways in which subjective desires may confound or transgress the prescriptions of 'class' has provided us with a more persuasive and respectful explanation for particular political choices.

And yet, this new work has its limitations. For if a close attention to differential gender effects and popular experiences illuminates electoral outcomes, it is less helpful when we seek to evaluate these programmes' wider social, and in this case even military, significance. For the test of wartime and postwar consumption policies is surely not only how well they lived up to their own rhetorical justifications (whether socialist or market-orientated), nor even how well they meshed with particular party strategies, but equally how comparatively well they sustained civilian health and productivity – and, by extension, the capacity and stability of the state itself – in a period of sustained military and economic competition. Bluntly, before Labour could win the 1945 election, Britain had to win the war. Consumption policies played a part in the latter as well as the former victory, but just what that part was can only really be understood when British policies and achievements are weighed against those of other belligerent countries, especially Germany. A full account of the effects of rationing and austerity should surely thus include a comparative dimension, but thus far military and economic historians have been more likely than political or gender historians to move in this direction.[33]

III

I have spent some time on these three separate subjects of study in order to show how a comparative focus, or simply some attention to the web of global economic and political relations in which all nations are caught, can not only deepen our understanding of the nature and workings of political institutions and practices but also might even act as a check on some distortions or weaknesses to which both 'high political' history and the 'new' political history might be prone. Yet, in making the case for comparison, I am quite aware that I am running against the current historical tide. Comparative history was born of the political optimism of the 1960s and 1970s and of the engagement of historians with social science methods – and both that optimistic moment and those alliances are decisively over. In an era of relative cultural pessimism, historians have been more concerned with meaning than causation and have found literary critics and anthropologists more congenial companions than political scientists. And the latter have certainly returned the cold shoulder, jettisoning historical approaches for formal modelling, quantification and theories of rational choice. Not only is interest in comparative history low, but the sources for its revival seem worryingly weak.

But what, one might ask, about the current interest in empire in British history – an interest particularly marked in the United States, where scholars of Britain have responded to declining enrolments and a shift in student interests by retooling wholesale as imperial historians? If comparative history is on the wane, at least the current preoccupation with Britain's imperial involvements must be challenging any 'little Englandist' proclivities, forcing us to consider that Britain's governing ideals and institutions may have been forged in Cape Town and Calcutta as well as in Liverpool or London, and hence to begin to work out an analytical framework capable of incorporating developments in both locales. And indeed, I would agree that this is the area in which structural interpretation and an attention to political culture have come together: albeit in very different ways, C.A. Bayly's *Imperial Meridian*, Peter Cain and Anthony Hopkins's *British Imperialism* and Mrinalini Sinha's *Colonial Masculinity* can all be read as attempts to place domestic and imperial developments in the same analytical frame.[34]

Again, however, both institutional and intellectual pressures – from the traditional practice of treating domestic and imperial history as separate fields of study to the post-Saidian propensity to treat literary texts and cultural artefacts (rather than political developments and practices) as the critical bearers of imperialism – militate against such integration. In a series of important articles, Sinha – although herself in many ways a child of the Saidian moment – has worried about just this problem. Recent scholars influenced by the 'imperial turn', she points out, have certainly put questions of imperialism back at the centre of British and Indian national histories; what they have not really done is to 'bring the metropole and colony together' into a unified analytical frame.[35] For all its problems, the Marxist and structuralist scholarship of the 1970s, which tended to locate power either in the coercive apparatus of the state or in global economic relations, was sometimes better at grappling with the character and limits of rule than are the current culturalist interpretations. The fact that an older imperial history now often dismissed as 'traditional' has retained that concern with social structures and economic relations is all to the good; this focus should be sustained and elaborated, and not derided.

This chapter began as an encomium, and I fear it has turned into a jeremiad. This was not my intent, for what are now called 'sociological' or 'deterministic' approaches, when applied to the political beliefs and affiliations of actually existing human beings, did tend to be unsophisticated and unrevealing; if leadership and culture are our main preoccupations, we are better for their demise. But structural analysis was and is necessary for some things, and pre-eminently for the study of the practices and institutions of rule, practices and institutions which are not always well-understood either by the governors or the governed, and which either may be resistant to change or may change in unintended and unexpected directions. If British political historians were to ask more routinely how global conditions, state structures and competition between states may have affected their particular story, or were to locate those stories in a comparative or imperial frame, we might be able to preserve the gains made by the recent 'political turn' without foundering on the twin shoals of parochialism and Panglossianism. This is a matter of some urgency. Today, when the relationship between national political cultures and global relations of power is particularly fraught and hard to understand, I think I am justified in saying that we need this kind of political history, *now*.

Notes and references

*   I wish to thank Thomas Ertman, Peter Mandler, Robert Travers, and especially Philip Williamson for their helpful comments on this chapter, and Jeremy Knowles for trying to ameliorate the conditions under which it was written.

1. William Gienapp, 'The Myth of Class in Jacksonian America', *Journal of Policy History*, vol. 6, no. 2 (1994), pp. 232–9, 277–81.
2. Susan R. Grayzel, *Women's Identities at War: Gender, Motherhood, and Politics in Britain and France during the First World War* (Chapel Hill: University of North Carolina Press, 1999); Michael T. Saler, *The Avant-Garde in Interwar England: Medieval Modernism and the London Underground* (New York: Oxford University Press, 1999); Erika Rappaport, *Shopping for Pleasure: Women in the Making of London's West End* (Princeton, NJ: Princeton University Press, 2000); Kali Israel, *Names and Stories: Emilia Dilke and Victorian Culture* (New York: Oxford University Press, 1999).
3. Gareth Stedman Jones, 'Rethinking Chartism', in his *Languages of Class: Studies in English Working Class History, 1832–1982* (Cambridge: Cambridge University Press, 1983), pp. 90–178.
4. For one important statement of this thesis, see Eugenio Biagini and Alastair Reid, 'Currents of radicalism, 1850–1914', introduction to their *Currents of*

Radicalism: Popular Radicalism, Organised Labour and Party Politics in Britain, 1850–1914 (Cambridge: Cambridge University Press, 1991), pp. 1–19; also, among other works, Miles Taylor, *The Decline of British Radicalism, 1847–1860* (Oxford: Clarendon Press, 1995); Jon Lawrence, *Speaking for the People: Party, Language and Popular Politics in England, 1867–1914* (Cambridge: Cambridge University Press, 1998); Eugenio Biagini, *Liberty, Retrenchment and Reform: Popular Liberalism in the Age of Gladstone, 1860–1880* (Cambridge: Cambridge University Press, 1992).

5. Dror Wahrman, *Imagining the Middle Class: The Political Representation of Class in Britain, c. 1780–1840* (Cambridge: Cambridge University Press, 1995); Patrick Joyce, *Visions of the People: Industrial England and the Question of Class, 1840–1914* (Cambridge: Cambridge University Press, 1991); James Vernon, *Politics and the People: A Study in English Political Culture, c. 1815–1867* (Cambridge: Cambridge University Press, 1993).

6. The landmark work being Leonore Davidoff and Catherine Hall, *Family Fortunes: Men and Women of the English Middle Class, 1780–1850* (Chicago, IL: University of Chicago Press, 1987). Anna Clark and Sonya Rose both extended this approach, more or less uncritically, to the working class: see Anna Clark, *The Struggle for the Breeches: Gender and the Making of the British Working Class* (Berkeley: University of California Press, 1995); Sonya Rose, *Limited Livelihoods: Gender and Class in Nineteenth-Century England* (Berkeley: University of California Press, 1992).

7. This historiography is far too extensive to summarize here. One particularly fine early study of women's involvement in radical politics is Barbara Taylor, *Eve and the New Jerusalem: Socialism and Feminism in the Nineteenth Century* (New York: Pantheon Books, 1983); on aristocratic women, see K.D. Reynolds, *Aristocratic Women and Political Society in Victorian Britain* (Oxford: Clarendon Press, 1998). The suffrage and feminist movements have their own very large literatures, but women's involvement in the realm of formal politics has been less well studied. For women in local government, the gold standard remains Patricia Hollis, *Ladies Elect: Women in English Local Government, 1865–1914* (Oxford: Clarendon Press, 1987), but there is also a burgeoning literature on women in twentieth-century parliamentary and international politics. 'Gendered' interpretations of British national politics remain exceptional, but for the period of the First World War, see Susan Grayzel, *Women's Identities at War*, and Susan Kingsley Kent, *Making Peace: The Reconstruction of Gender in Interwar Britain* (Princeton, NJ: Princeton University Press, 1993).

8. Maurice Cowling, *The Impact of Labour, 1920–1924: The Beginning of Modern British Politics* (Cambridge: Cambridge University Press, 1971), p. 3.

9. 'It was closed to those outside, in terms of direct access and influence: it was closed also in that politicians were bound to see more significance in the definite structure of relationships at Westminster, than in their contacts with the world outside.' Cooke and Vincent, *The Governing Passion: Cabinet Government and Party Politics in Britain, 1885–86* (Brighton: Harvester Press, 1974), p. 21.

10. Michael Bentley, 'Politics, Doctrine, and Thought', in Michael Bentley and John Stevenson (eds), *High and Low Politics in Modern Britain* (Oxford: Clarendon Press, 1983), p. 130.

11. See, notably, the *festschrift* edited by Michael Bentley, *Public and Private Doctrine: Essays in British History presented to Maurice Cowling* (Cambridge: Cambridge University Press, 1993), and Bentley's exemplary, almost anthropological, *Lord Salisbury's World: Conservative Environments in Late-Victorian Britain* (Cambridge: Cambridge University Press, 2001).

12. Jonathan Parry, *Democracy and Religion: Gladstone and the Liberal Party, 1867–1875* (Cambridge: Cambridge University Press, 1986), p. 3.

13. Probably the major difference being the 'new' political historians' continued, probing engagement with both Marxism and linguistic theory. In a recent essay, for example, Stedman Jones defends his claim that 'politics occurs wholly within discourse' while also offering a trenchant critique of Foucault's genealogy of modernity as a 'bleak dystopian inversion of liberal optimism' whose appeal can only be explained in light of the twentieth century's horrors. See Gareth Stedman Jones, 'Anglo-Marxism, Neo-Marxism and the Discursive Approach to History', in Alf Lüdtke (ed.), *Was bliebt von marxistichen Perspektiven in der Geschichtsforschung?* (Göttingen: Max-Planck-Institut für Geschichte/Wallstein Verlag, 1997), especially pp. 194, 197, 205.

14. Biagini and Reid, in *Currents of Radicalism*, insist that the Marxist interpretation of politics as a direct expression of class interests has been 'surprisingly dominant' (p. 3); similarly, Miles Taylor claims – citing two accounts – that 'many studies' of mid-Victorian politics 'routinely' assume clearly distinct class-based strategies (*The Decline of British Radicalism*, p. 3). Jonathan Parry, more realistically, admits that political historians have been warning of 'the perils involved in attempting to explain political activity in "class" terms' since the 1960s (Parry, *Democracy and Religion*, pp. 1–2).

15. Biagini, *Liberty, Retrenchment and Reform*, pp. 6–7.

16. John Foster, *Class Struggle and the Industrial Revolution: Early Industrial Capitalism in Three English Towns* (London: Weidenfeld and Nicolson, 1974); John Vincent, *The Formation of the Liberal Party, 1857–1868* (London: Constable, 1966); Peter Clarke, *Lancashire and the New Liberalism* (Cambridge: Cambridge University Press, 1971).

17. H.C.G. Matthew, *Gladstone, 1809–1874* (Oxford: Clarendon Press, 1986), especially chapter 5; Boyd Hilton, *The Age of Atonement: The Influence of Evangelicalism on Social and Economic Thought, 1785–1865* (Oxford: Clarendon Press, 1988), chapter 9. Two excellent summary statements of this new narrative of liberalism's birth are Peter Mandler, *The Strange Birth of Liberal England: Conservative Origins of the Laissez-Faire State, 1780–1860*, Harvard University Center for European Studies Working Paper Series No. 19 (Cambridge, Mass., 1989); Pat Thane, 'Government and Society in England and Wales, 1750–1914', in F.M.L. Thompson (ed.) *The Cambridge Social History of Britain, 1750–1950*, vol. 1, *Social Agencies and Institutions* (Cambridge: Cambridge University Press, 1990), pp. 1–61.

18. Vincent, *The Formation of the Liberal Party*, pp. xiv, xiii. Catherine Hall would agree, but would not conflate masculinity with 'full humanity' in this way: see her 'Competing Masculinities: Thomas Carlyle, John Start Mill and the case of Governor Eyre', in her *White, Male and Middle Class: Explorations in Feminism and History* (London: Routledge, 1992), pp. 255–95.

19. Jon Lawrence and Miles Taylor, 'Introduction: Electoral Sociology and the Historians', in Jon Lawrence and Miles Taylor (eds), *Party, State and Society: Electoral Behaviour in Britain since 1820* (Aldershot: Scolar Press, 1997), p. 2.

20. For the latter, see especially, Bill Schwarz, 'The Language of Constitutionalism: Baldwinite Conservatism', in his *Formations of Nation and People* (London: Routledge, 1984), pp. 1–18.

21. Philip Williamson, *Stanley Baldwin: Conservative Leadership and National Values* (Cambridge: Cambridge University Press, 1999); Ross McKibbin, 'Class and Conventional Wisdom: The Conservative Party and the "Public" in Inter-war Britain', in his *Ideologies of Class: Social Relations in Britain, 1880–1950* (Oxford: Clarendon Press, 1990), pp. 259–93; Susan Kent, *Making Peace*; Alison Light, *Forever England: Femininity, Literature and Conservatism Between the Wars* (London: Routledge, 1991).

22. Williamson, *Stanley Baldwin*, pp. 350–7.

23. Max Weber, 'Politics as a Vocation', in H.H. Gerth and C. Wright Mills (eds), *From Max Weber: Essays in Sociology* (New York: Oxford University Press, 1946), pp. 77–9.

24. Lewis B. Namier, *The Structure of Politics at the Accession of George III* (London: Macmillan, 1929); Samuel H. Beer, *Treasury Control: The Co-ordination of Financial and Economic Policy in Great Britain* (Oxford: Clarendon Press, 1956).

25. E.P. Thompson, 'Eighteenth-Century English Society: Class Struggle Without Class?', *Social History*, vol. 3 (1978), p. 141, quoted in Philip Harling, *The Waning of 'Old Corruption': The Politics of Economical Reform in Britain, 1779–1846* (Oxford: Clarendon Press, 1996).

26. John Brewer, *The Sinews of Power: War, Money and the English State, 1688–1783* (New York: Alfred Knopf, 1988); Thomas C. Ertman, *Birth of the Leviathan: Building States and Regimes in Medieval and Early Modern Europe* (Cambridge: Cambridge University Press, 1997).

27. I'm drawing on Michel Foucault's rough distinction here: see his *History of Sexuality*, vol. 1, *An Introduction* (New York: Vintage, 1980), part 5.

28. See, for example, Maurice Bruce, *The Coming of the Welfare State* (London: B.T. Batsford, 1961); Derek Fraser, *The Evolution of the British Welfare State* (1973) (2nd edn, London: Macmillan, 1984). By contrast, Pat Thane explicitly acknowledges the global context within which social policy developments occur by including (as Brewer did) comparative sections in her study, *The Foundations of the Welfare State* (London: Longman, 1982).

29. The classic example being, of course, T.H. Marshall's famous 1949 lecture, 'Citizenship and Social Class', reprinted in his *Class, Citizenship and Social Development* (Garden City, NY: Doubleday, 1964), pp. 71–134.

30. For which, see my earlier study, *Family, Dependence, and the Origins of the Welfare State: Britain and France, 1914–1945* (Cambridge: Cambridge University Press, 1993).

31. Carolyn Kay Steedman, *Landscape for a Good Woman: A Story of Two Lives* (1986) (reprinted, New Brunswick, NJ: Rutgers University Press, 1987), especially pp. 29–30, 121–4.

32. Ina Zweiniger-Bargielowska, *Austerity in Britain: Rationing, Consumption and Controls, 1939–1955* (Oxford: Oxford University Press, 2000).

33. See, especially, R.J. Overy, *War and Economy in the Third Reich* (Oxford: Clarendon Press, 1994), particularly chapter 9.

34. C.A. Bayly, *Imperial Meridian: The British Empire and the World, 1780–1830* (London: Longman, 1989); P.J. Cain and A.G. Hopkins, *British Imperialism*, 2 vols (London: Longman, 1993); Mrinalini Sinha, *Colonial Masculinity: The 'Manly Englishman' and the 'Effeminate Bengali' in the Late Nineteenth Century* (Manchester: Manchester University Press, 1995).
35. Mrinalini Sinha, 'Britishness, Clubbability, and the Colonial Public Sphere: The Genealogy of an Imperial Institution in Colonial India', *Journal of British Studies*, vol. 40 (October 2001), especially pp. 491, 521.

4
What is Religious History Now?

Olwen Hufton

As an undergraduate at London University, religious history was largely political history – indeed, looking back, what was offered for the early modern period of British history in the late 1950s could have been termed the Gospel of Sir Geoffrey Elton. What was offered for Europe was very much religion and political outcomes – *cuius regio eius religio* – seasoned with words such as transubstantiation and iconoclasm to convey the content of faith and strife. Certain key facts remain engraved upon my mind from that experience, such as a lecture by Renier intended to impress upon the undergraduate mind that only one in ten people of the Netherlands were Calvinist at the time of the Dutch revolt. I am perhaps exaggerating somewhat as to the limitations of the package. I remember, without precise reference as to the content, some very elegant Lambeth Palace lectures by Dom David Knowles on English monasticism and realising that on exam papers religion and the rise of capitalism was a proverbial chestnut. Weber and Tawney and the confessional character of economic change must certainly have figured.

I was politely interested but not fired. For me what was interesting as I embarked on my postgraduate career was what was going on across the Channel in the form of the *Annales* approach, and I was also drawn by work on both sides of that water inspired by a Marxist problematic. As far as the second approach is concerned, I have always thought that for me the questions it generated were more important than the overarching interpretation. History from below became an important and challenging preoccupation in the 1960s and 1970s and that was emphatically where I stood. Both the *Annales* school and the questions generated by Marxism were at that time locked into the 'material' and *malgré* Lucien Febvre highly resistant to a *mentalités* approach. However, horizons were broadening, and part of that broadening experience for me was a new kind of religious history.

My road to Damascus opened up in the early 1960s when, as a graduate student engaged in writing the history of a Normandy town and its sociopolitical experience during the Revolution (a town where I had spent some time at convent school), I began work in the departmental archives of the Calvados. Around the table were perhaps a dozen old gentlemen: some in religious habits; some wearing dog collars. They were part of a now-vanished world, a doomed constituency of scholarly regular and secular clerics writing in their declining years a history of their order from cartulary and land register, or one of the fate of those imprisoned or exiled during the Revolution. I can still visualize the scene. They commanded in terms of numbers and time the production of a religious history from the inside. It was not exactly a neutral history in terms of emphasis and some of it was overtly hagiographic. But as one who has spent some time recently with the massive volumes of the *Archivium Historicum Societatis Iesu* can attest, there was some magnificent work of retrieval which was heavily document-based. Moreover, historians such as Schurhammer, Rahner, Tacchi Venturi, have not been replaced as the West has largely rejected the religious vocation.

I came to the Calvados from Paris, where I had attended a very left-wing seminar of French revolutionary history, and made aware of a reading of religious history from the outside. This came in two forms. First, there was the republican tradition formally articulated by Michelet and, second, the Marxist approach adopted by a long line of historians from Aulard to Mathiez. These two strands came together to provide a dominant narrative of religious history from outside. For both French republican and Marxist, religion was anathema and Church and state were polarized forces competing for the commitment of the people. Such an approach saw the people as dupes, done to rather than doing. Religion, as seen from these viewpoints, was the opium of the people. The victory of state over Church, of modernity over secularization, after a long and bitter confrontation in France, was presented as largely achieved without their collusion. More precisely, this ineluctable triumph was impeded by the resistance of the ignorant peasant. In the end the victory was that of reason or, put another way, the victory of the state over the Church.

On the one side, then, there was the insider activity and, on the other, the outside, an overarching political interpretation. What was about to happen was something which markedly changed the face of religion in history. This was the entry of a hitherto largely missing presence, a religious history from the point of view of the consumer (alias the congregation). This widening of the framework of reference, if not the only change, I would suggest was the dominant one, transforming the writing of the religious history of Western civilization in the twentieth century. It moved the writing of religious history away from the subject of the establishment, clerical, lay and male, downmarket. It also interfaced with other historical concerns which marked the period and from which it became indistinguishable in some cases. Religion by the 1980s was interpreted as an intrinsic part of culture and a producer of culture. Women and men were seen as made, not born, and in that shaping process in the West, religious belief lay at the centre of this process of manufacture.

I

The chronology of the shift in focus of interest from ecclesiastical hierarchy and high politics to the congregation and 'popular' religion cannot be fully precise. The first leap, and the one I shall initially consider, was perhaps the major force projecting the change of vision from priest to flock. It came from within Catholic society itself and originated in France. This force was to catapult the writing of religious history into the realms of something understandable to the *Annalistes*, because it was at once *histoire sérielle* (history which could be counted and therefore rested on a serial base) but also *histoire des mentalités*. In a wider world context – although the French were leaders in some part of this field as well – there was another development; one perhaps more enticing for English and American scholars because it did not presuppose a twenty-year stint in the departmental archives to produce a *doctorat ès lettres*. This development carried a branch of historical studies into the realms of human emotion, the factors affecting those emotions and the motors of change. One is tempted to summarize the metamorphosis by saying that Lawrence Stone was at work on the family.[1]

I want for a moment to hold these two developments apart and to concentrate on the first. Amongst the clerics around the table of the departmental archives of the Calvados was the Abbé Berthelot du Chesnay, younger than the others, a teacher and a dynamic scholar. He was interested in what I was doing, as I was in his work on the seventeenth-century cleric and educational reformer Jean Eudes. One day he lent me the works of a religious sociologist, Gabriel Le Bras. The concern of Le Bras from the 1930s had been to explain a number of problems yet more apparent in the postwar world in France. One was popular religious slippage – the flock was leaving, but doing so more conspicuously in some places than in others. Another was a crisis in religious vocations, of which the most serious manifestation was a lack of parochial clergy, but also of nuns who were teachers of the next generation. (In fact the exodus of nuns was only just beginning as the postwar world had seen a mini-boom in women's vocations.)

As Le Bras saw it in the 1950s, the first step in working on these problems was to understand them. He sought in history, geography and sociology keys to the movement of rejection of the Catholic faith. In *Etudes de sociologie religieuse*[2] he proposed a methodology – one which threw the ball into the realms of history and *histoire sérielle*, at that – which, if followed, would permit the construction of a map or maps charting the incidence of slippage at particular times. The sources for this aspect of the enquiry would be visitation registers. The visitation register was the result of a periodic enquiry by the bishop, or a delegated substitute, of the religious state of a parish(es). The parochial picture could be related to a diocesan picture in turn a sub-section of a broader provincial picture. The end product of the cumulated fruits of such records would be a religious geography, something dear to *nous des Annales* and nothing short of a marriage of *histoire sérielle* and *mentalités*. Second, the entry registers of aspirants to the priesthood could be addressed (also by reference to serial categorization); the incidence, family status and educational levels could be examined, and where and when the falling off occurred could be charted. In short, one could have a map that related to any period from the sixteenth century (visitation became more common after the bishops' roles were changed by the Council of Trent) to modern times, and a series of maps which located at what point slippage became visible.

The exercise demanded certain decisions related to the limits of quantification. First, according to what criteria could religious commitment and conformity be measured? Le Bras's yardstick was determined in part by the sort of questions the visiting bishops asked of the parish priest upon whom they descended. They recorded practice according to certain criteria. This made possible the categorization of degrees of commitment and lack of commitment. The first category was that of *croyant/pratiquant* – meaning those baptized, married and dying, fortified by the rites of the Church, as well as observing the Lenten confession and Communion and putting in weekly attendance at Mass on Sundays and on fête days. The second category was that of *conformisme saisonnière*, by which was meant someone who might perform Easter obligations and would adhere to rites of passage, marrying in the Church and having his children baptized, but perhaps not bothering with regular Sunday practice or extreme unction. The third category was that of those indifferent to religious practice.

At risk of oversimplifying what was a gargantuan task, which only a Frenchman would undertake in pursuit of knowledge, Le Bras's work revealed a *pratiquant* west and east and certain fervent areas where Catholic and Protestant were geographically juxtaposed. In the mid-1950s certain cities and the impious Ile de France, Bouches du Rhône, the city of Troyes, and so on, stood out as those marked by the most precocious slippage.

Perhaps most importantly, the point of most slippage was pushed largely into the late nineteenth century and even into the twentieth century, to World War One or even the Second World War and its aftermath. It demonstrated the following characteristics. First, generally, but with some exceptions, the outward flow occurred in big cities before small towns and in small towns before villages. Men followed the exodus before women, though big-city women left before village men. *Le dimorphisme sessuel* became a part of a working vocabulary of analysis. In short, a good twenty years before other branches of history dealt in gender, and *avant le mot* Le Bras embraced the concept. He also postulated reasons for the earlier slippage of men; for example, periods of military service, or a tavern-based sociability which presented a competing sociability pattern.

Furthermore, his work showed that on the eve of the French Revolution there was scarcely a village in France where *non pratiquants* exceeded 8 per cent of the adult male population, and they were concentrated in certain jobs associated with the drinks trade or barges, or they were itinerant pedlars. Intellectuals never dent statistics. In fact, looking at this work one could say one sees no evidence whatsoever of dechristianization or the effects of the Enlightenment before the 1790s. The Revolution disrupted regular practice and placed the pious in a hostile relationship with the republican state, but on the whole the early nineteenth-century Church was capable of recapturing the majority of its adherents.

Where there was slippage, there was a crisis of vocations, but the fall in numbers for the priesthood was most marked in affluent cities and amongst the bourgeoisie. The Church, stripped of its land and its hierarchy, now paid modest salaries and was a less attractive prospect for substantial families. There may have been other reasons. I think it was the Abbé Berthelot du Chesnay who gave me the idea that when mothers stopped directing the feet of the son they did not want to lose to another woman towards the Church and perpetual celibacy, a crisis of vocations became inevitable. Italian historians of the twentieth century posit that the crisis occurred in vocations when rural families perceived that having a priest in the family no longer meant a rise in status for them. The numbers of women entering active religious orders peaked in 1947 and thereafter declined rapidly. For the Church this was near-fatal. The women's orders had survived the separation of Church and state (1905) and the dissolution of the teaching orders and had staged a significant comeback, particularly in primary and girls' education. The drying up of the supply of nuns cut off the primary agencies of socialization.

It is worth beginning with Le Bras because religious history was never the same again. *Histoire sérielle* had intruded into *mentalités*: the congregation were centre-stage. Separate regional studies, such as those by Gérard Cholvy for the diocese of Montpellier,[3] introduced the confrontation between left-wing politics and religion into the equation. Others, such as the study of the diocese of La Rochelle, a stronghold of Protestantism, introduced confrontational religious traditions as agencies in the perpetuation of commitment of both parties.[4]

'How could religiosity be tested and understood?' This question posed by Le Bras with regard to the congregation thus far had been addressed solely through conformity and practice. Could there be other pointers to test faith and the phenomenon of slippage? The answer was to be 'Yes', but I must put the question on hold because other aspects of historical concern were about to intrude on the development.

The interest in family history and the history of relationships, emotions and later sexuality grew conspicuously from the late 1960s with the work of historians such as Lawrence Stone,[5] Philippe Ariès[6] and Jean Louis Flandrin,[7] who had many followers. The aim of the new family history was to detect changes in the comportment of the Western family. The new family history drew in part on demographic data, *histoire sérielle*, but far more on predicative literature itself designed to instruct the faithful in Christian behaviour. This literature, which poured from the early printing presses, was severe. It placed duty to God above the love of man or woman and interpreted the child as the font of sin to be disciplined into the right behaviour. Parents were warned against emotional investment in a baby or child and were urged to see a divine purpose to infantile loss. It sought to put the Church, as purveyor of Christian doctrine, in control of sexuality. Jean Louis Flandrin dunked his readers in the grim confessional literature which forbade all sexual behaviour not directed to legitimate procreation. This gloomy picture softened, according to Lawrence Stone, in the eighteenth century (argued to be 'the century of the child'), with secularization, national peace and consumerism.

I do not need to argue a case against constructing history on the sands of predication, but the preoccupation with family history and household history introduced a consideration of the interface between religion and behaviour. It emphasized that in the religious reform movements of the sixteenth century, and with new weapons of persuasion in print and tract, the control of sexuality by the Church was firmly on the agenda. Developments in demographic history confirmed the success of the reform movements to get marriage into Church (and hence to control it), and progressively – for it took a century or more – these movements produced the exceptionally low levels of illegitimacy (under 1 per cent of births) remarkable in seventeenth-century Western Europe. True, these levels rose again in the eighteenth century amongst the labouring classes of the towns. However, the seventeenth-century record seemed to confirm the existence of the truly holy household – a triumph, in the words of Dylan Thomas, for having '*Thou shalt not ...*' on the wall. Family history had led a movement away from analysing and commenting upon the process of control by both Church and state, or the pursuit of orthodoxy in home and community, and also away from the concern with statistics alone. The qualitative material of predication and selected sampling of data, rather than the remorseless gathering of numbers, became more common.

II

A concern with religion as an agency of social control in the home and the wider community became a strong theme in historiography throughout the West from the 1970s, and indeed it remains so.[8] Definitions of how orthodoxy was achieved through the confessional, the Inquisition, catechetical instruction and the humiliation of offenders in the community have informed some of the best historical writing of the late twentieth century.[9] Such works have examined the lines between coercion to achieved conformity – as, for example, evinced in the Inquisition or in the new emphasis on the purgatorial threat – and hope: the promise of salvation for those who obeyed the rules. From amongst the abundant literature I shall elect three works, all French, but all translated into many European languages, and each one vitally important in shaping the field of study.

The first addressed the uncomfortable question, 'At what point in time can one count a population Christianized?'. It was a study by Emmanuel Le Roy Ladurie, *Montaillou: Cathars and Catholics in a French Village 1294–1324*[10] and predominantly based on a fourteenth-century visitation record of an area in the Pyrenees which had experienced the Cathars. It sought to convey the moral state of a remote area which had embraced heresy in the thirteenth century. The work was very readable and rather disturbing. It was also slightly deceptive in that it picked out all the juiciest stories of an entire diocese and concentrated them in a single village. Some of these were very spicy, such as the testimony of a woman that it was acceptable, and did not incur the imputation of sin, to copulate with a priest (as well as her husband) simply because he was a priest. There was also ignorance of the Lord's Prayer and the Commandments, and a general inability to bless oneself properly, and so on. In short, the effective content of religious doctrine was very weak. That is to say, by a generous extention, this study permitted the formulation of a thesis that Europe was not effectively Christianized before the Reformation and the Catholic reform. There is a voice of resistance to this grand theory, but it still commands wide consensus.

The second example is taken from the works of Jean Delumeau, author of many studies on religion.[11] The work I think his most influential work, though perhaps not his best, is *Sin and Fear* (1983). His earliest work on sixteenth-century Rome has classic status and is an *Annaliste* approach to the socio-economic and political institutional structures of the celestial city. His text on the two Reformations, translated in 1977, is still perhaps the best general interpretation of the period. *Sin and Fear*, in contrast, is one of *parti pris*, and occasionally somewhat rambling. None the less, it has been very influential. It is based largely on sermons, confessional manuals and other literature and addresses the relationship between confessor and spiritual child. It poses the question, 'How did the sixteenth-century Church [and, he broaches, both the Catholic and Protestant reforms] manage to "convert" a population lacking in orthodox knowledge?' The (oversimple) answer is through a development of notions of sin and evil (witches and fornicators) and fear. Even the clearly blameless were prompted to mortify the flesh and, through fear of a panoply of punishments both in the here and now and in the hereafter, they dwelt in constant disquiet. The wages of sin are death. In this way, Delumeau argued, the two confessions succeeded in implanting obedience to their teaching. In short, social control for Delumeau was enforced conformity to one or the other confession through fear and the development of institutions such as the confessional box and confessional practice, as well as the Inquisition. The case had been urged before, but in less harrowing form. Morality ('Thou shalt not ...') was imposed through paralysingly terrible concepts of Purgatory and the everlasting bonfires of hell.

The history of Purgatory was one of a space between death and eternal life where the sinner was tormented until purged (hence the term) and able to find peace. Purgatory was essentially a *promotion catholique* because Protestant reformers considered it to have inadequate scriptural backing. It was firmly rejected by Luther and indeed all Protestant theologians, who were, none the less, hardliners on the sin front and protagonists of the torments of hell. Purgatory had been commercialized at two levels in the late Middle Ages: first, by the sale of Indulgences granting respite from its worst torments and, second, by the purchase of Masses for the repose of the faithful departed, with the friars to the forefront in performing the latter. The Councils of Trent reaffirmed the purgatorial space, and hence belief in Purgatory was seen as a fundamental distinction between Catholic and Protestant belief. At Trent it was made clear that the critical factor determining how long one spent in this terrible place was confession, contrition and the amendment of one's ways, and the Catholic death must be accompanied by a final clearing of conscience. But provisions for mitigating the horrendous possibilities of the purgatorial space – prayers, good works, and so on – remained. Delumeau's work on sin and fear was concerned to make the latter emotion virtually the only motor of religious conformity. Notions of hope or of the attainment of grace or solace in a hard world – or indeed of any kind of comfort – had no space. In my view, though I admire the richness of Delumeau's work and the questions he asked, this is where he was guilty of some distortion. Nevertheless, he made a powerful contribution to the evolving historiographical death industry.

For Delumeau, the early modern period was about the imposition of fear of nonconformity and the structures of control enforced by Church teaching. If Stone and Flandrin were gloomy in their accounts of human relationships as a result of the impact of the Reformation and Catholic reform teaching, Delumeau's accounts of rituals of collective mortification and individual penance have a searing effect. Nevertheless, his thesis cannot be entirely rejected and indeed, in one form or another, even current Catholic historiography admits to the strong element of fear revealed in the effort to missionize the masses. Moreover, in the medium run of three centuries it succeeded in enforcing religious and moral conformity on the masses. Reformation and Catholic reform are widely acknowledged to represent the triumph of Lent. The belief in evil (stronger, perhaps, than a belief in good) which manifested itself in the trials of witches; the frequent examination of conscience and the acceptance of penance; the apprehension in particular of sexual pleasure, and shame at the failure to conform to the criteria demanded in scriptural injunction, all endorse Delumeau's thesis. However, he certainly leaves to one side more positive aspects of change.

The third work of my election, a massive French *doctorat ès lettres* – one cited by far more people than have actually read it – is Michel Vovelle's *Piété baroque et déchristianisation*.[12] Vovelle (a congenial Marxist and first-rate scholar) drew on literally thousands of Provençal wills (this was another work of *histoire sérielle)* in furtherance of a quest for the onset of dechristianization or signs of secularization. He elected to define a Catholic by how he or she provided for death. His work was an exceptionally rich study of *ars moriendi*. It drew upon the iconography of the tomb or funeral monument and it sought to analyse and quantify the formal introductory preamble to thousands of wills. These wills were categorized according to town, country, gender, and so on.

The preamble contained instructions for the funeral of the deceased in terms of processions (usually with a token number of paupers to follow the hearse) and donations to charity on the day of the event, as well as provision for Masses for the repose of the soul in Purgatory, over a considerable chronological span. He did not offer samples of his sources, but aimed to be exhaustive. Re-reading Vovelle is to be aware of the extent to which the vanished state *doctorat ès lettres* moved historical knowledge forward. He demonstrated first the stylistic collapse of the baroque tomb in the eighteenth century; the simplification of the funeral procession and, amongst male urban elites, a reduction in the number of Masses for the repose of the soul by the 1770s. These trends he saw as prefiguring dechristianization/secularization and as effectively marking the onset of a decline in the belief in Purgatory. He also detected a slight decline in sums made available in the preamble of the will to charitable causes. The extent of Vovelle's work was breathtaking, and it was selectively copied on a relatively small scale (a few hundred cases rather than thousands) to see if the trends he suggested had more general application. Work on Paris by a collective initiative organized by Pierre Chaunu[13] suggested that the capital was perhaps a little more precocious than Provence.

Vovelle's interpretation was more coincident with an earlier view of the impact of Enlightenment thought on social behaviour. In fact, it offers little to challenge the Le Bras picture of conformity since what we may be looking at is no more than a change in artistic styles in which classical influence triumphed over the florid baroque. The Catholic Enlightenment itself sought to simplify ceremonials. The decline in charitable giving detected by Vovelle to the hospitals of Provence was confirmed by Daniel Roche for pre-revolutionary Paris. However, Vovelle himself noted that donations were increasingly made to women's religious orders with a social vocation, but that since these had not existed at the beginning of his study, he had not incorporated them into his analysis. What Vovelle did demonstrate was that change was visible only in the practices of male elites.

Vovelle made an examination of the rise and fall of the rituals surrounding death a major preoccupation. Some went further. Sam Cohn, in *Death and Property in Siena, 1205–1800: Strategies for the Afterlife*[14] criticized Vovelle's practice of using only the preamble to the will, wherein a mere fraction of the total estate is distributed, because it obscured the number of testators who made major gifts or turned charitable institutions into the *erede universalis*. In this view, Vovelle obscured the real worth of gifts to assistance. Cohn raised the interesting question of defining changing priorities of charitable giving within a long chronological span of wills. He discerned, for example, that in fifteenth-century Siena, the favoured recipient of bequests was the nunnery, but this changed in the sixteenth and seventeenth centuries to donations to dowry funds to help young girls to marry. (One reason for this, in my view, could be a wide repugnance for the new harshness of claustration imposed by the Councils of Trent.)

Whatever the reservations one makes about Vovelle's magisterial thesis, he came perhaps as near as possible to charting the waxing and waning of Purgatory. Moreover, although there have been more modest works in terms of numbers of wills examined and the sampling of specific groups and chronological specificity, no one has approached his work with the same geographical breadth and chronological span. None the less, selective sampling for Madrid in the sixteenth century by Carlos Eire has conveyed with particular intensity and a wealth of detail the Spanish apprehension of the afterlife.[15]

III

On a different note, developments in family history and the linguistic turn generated a concern with autobiographies, letters and diaries (ego documents) – the diary first marketed as a vehicle for the keeping of a spiritual record. In addition, confessors, confronted with a pious woman committed to good works and of a spiritual bent, urged her to write down her religious experiences for discussion. In the majority of cases, such women had some education. A harsh reading of this practice might be that the confessor hoped he had someone special on his hands which would establish him as the spiritual guide of a future saint or mystic. A kinder reading might be that he was intent upon discussing the importance of her thoughts or alleged experiences. In this kind of writing there is much less gloom and much more hope than one finds in the literature of predication. Indeed, Italian women historians[16] see this kind of exercise as an initial step in women appropriating to themselves some kind of *autoconscienza*; that is, learning to think abstractly and to find value in their own thoughts.

The relationship between history and literature raised questions of literacy and the differences between regions and countries. The dominant genre of publication which issued from the presses of both confessions was religious. The people of Europe became 'the people of the book'. The differential records of Protestant and Catholic areas were highlighted with the English and the Dutch and some German states outpacing the Catholic record in respect of the ability to read. Margaret Spufford demonstrated how female literacy in East Anglian villages grew out of community Bible-reading.[17] The perceived lag, however, between Protestant and Catholic literacy prompted the question as to why such a lag existed. In fact, whys started to multiply exponentially in the late 1960s and 1970s.

One important development multiplying the questions was that of women's and gender history and the related concern with 'the cultural'. Family history had drawn heavily upon predication, but gender history went further to explore the cultural factors which shaped women and men. 'Women and men are made, not born', so what made them? It was difficult for the European historian, let alone the anthropologist or sociologist or the historian of the Middle East or Asia, not to start with religion as the dominant cultural referent. The emphasis given by the reform movements to Bible knowledge or to catechetical instruction which manifested itself in the predicative literature that poured from the presses, was only one aspect of the presence of scriptural models in social development. The Adam and Eve story, which made woman the temptress and the gullible, more sinful sex, opened the discourse. In Genesis, to be confirmed by St Paul, women were constrained to sit in silence in church, to be under the dominance of man, and to suffer pain in childbirth. This text even in the twelfth century led to debates among Churchmen as to whether women had souls.

Fortunately, that issue was decided in the affirmative. The Eve legend lay behind a reading of women as the inferior sex. The seeping of differential responsibility into law codes, the double standards of male and female chastity, the proclivity to regard women as potentially the agents of the devil, certainly had to be factored into the package of disabilities facing women. Religion was part of the cultural tangle of restraints and liabilities within which a female child had to negotiate an existence. Genesis, Timothy 11(4) and the Good Housewife of Proverbs 31 became part of the documents' course for a history of women. Moreover, the convent, as religious institution, provided a 'mop-up' function for the victims of dynastic ambition in many European countries; notably perhaps, Italy, where the dowry system restricted the number of girls per household who might marry. One in three or one in five patrician girls originating in major Italian cities in the early modern period were destined for the cloister. How did they feel about it? How did they fill their time? What was this female space about? In the late twentieth century much wordage was dedicated to the history of the nun, and excitement grew as individual women in religion were identified as the first women writers, painters and musicians to whom names could be given – Hildegarde of Bingen, Suor Juana of Mexico City, Plautilla Nelli of Florence. Another question was broached: was the book-lined cell a room of one's own? The weight of the emergent evidence was that it offered some possibilities, particularly for literary study, but that it was in fact a highly mediated space, and the strict enclosure enforced for some years after Trent cut off needful outside contact.

The study of tertiaries and mystics grew in volume and a contradiction was addressed. Why did a religion which seemed to offer women only second-class participation prove attractive to them? The answers to such a question proved diverse. Studies appeared on 'Holy Anorexia',[18] the condition of women in search of mystical experience through food deprivation – even Teresa of Avila recognized them as a distinct category – so as to gain esteem in the population. Some, particularly American historians, explained this phenomenon in terms of empowerment within a society that offered few alternatives. But there were other explanations for the appeal of religion to women. One productive line of enquiry made religion part of the business of solace insofar as it permitted the construction of a relationship between women suffering in society and saints to whom certain experiences were attributed. To this day, if one stands in front of the shrine of St Rita of Cascia and reads the *ex votos*, one is aware of the relationship between suffering and solace. Still outstripping even the Virgin in popularity, St Rita, in popular though not official recognition, has been the saint of the battered wife.[19] Christian Europe is also spattered with shrines for the solicitations of the barren. Women took their stillborn babies to the *sanctuaires à répit* and prayed for a miracle that would resuscitate them so that they could be baptized and their little spirits would not have to wander in limbo.[20] What is at stake here? Is it fear? Is it sorrow and the desire to do one's best? The history of motherhood and the history of manifestations of religiosity are obviously related.

Italian women historians were quick to appropriate the notion that religion in the home is a maternal concern. Children learn their prayers, and how to bless themselves, from their mothers; the cooking and preparation for religious feasts is done by the mothers, and so on. In short, and one could spend a long time on this theme, what women's and gender history did for religion was to splinter the congregation more distinctly than Le Bras and Vovelle had done, into male and female and to suggest differing reasons for commitment, different modes of participation. The development of a history of masculinities and a concern with homosexuality also in due course intruded, here proffering different motives for abandoning religious commitment.

The splintering did not stop there. Perhaps even prefiguring the concern with gender was the concern with class and the notion of elite and popular cultures. The history of witchcraft persecutions was long posited as a moment, historically speaking, when there was consonance between the two. This consonance was ruptured with the doubts of elites who began to resist the denunciations coming from below. The history of the persecutions and local concepts of evil and its omnipresence in the world at large have given us a lot to think about vis-à-vis popular credence. Are notions of good and evil dependent on each other?[21] Why were more women than men denounced as witches, and why were other women so prominent amongst those who denounced them?

The history of the religion of the people was also informed by the examination of popular devotions, pilgrimages, altarpieces, *ex votos*, lawsuits, the contents of churches, practices. Le Bras himself had urged that pilgrimages were worth examining to this end, but it was perhaps not until the mid-1990s that a systematic assessment of the shifting fashions of pilgrimage sites and the changes in the constituencies of the pilgrims themselves was made. Similarly, art historians examined the content of churches and the particular significance of certain artefacts such as the prone parturient virgins of the Massif Central, worn smooth by parish women who made a tisane from scraping the stone to encourage conception. An examination of the contents of English parish churches provided the raw material for Eamonn Duffy's study *The Stripping of the Altars*,[22] which argued for the vibrancy of English religious life when the Reformation intruded. All these ways of approaching manifestations of religiosity clearly advance understanding of what religion meant for the masses and could doubtless be carried much further.

A valorization of this kind of material gained momentum with the anthropological drift of history in the late 1970s.[23] The close pursuit of symbols and rituals as a means of decoding the dynamic and thought structures of entire societies gave a new prominence to certain aspects of religious practice. Such studies focused upon the ceremonies of city, church and court life, processions, pilgrimages, and rites, the ceremonies that marked the passage of an individual through the various phases of the lifecycle, such as baptism, which marked social entry into a community, located one in a set of kin and gave wider support through godparents; marriage, the institution the Church strove for two centuries to control so as to regulate and legitimize certain sexual relations, but also a ceremony which marked the transference of a woman from the authority of one man to another and the creation of a new unit in the story of the community. Transcending both these was death – or rather the rites surrounding it. However, as in the case of baptism and marriage, perhaps what we are looking at in these participatory rituals is part of the business of belonging, of being an insider and of staking a claim.

IV

Associated with this awareness of religion as an attribute of belonging was another 'buzz' concern of twentieth-century historiography, that of 'identity' formation. Although I have been firmly told on many occasions that identity is a creation of modernity, I refuse to believe it. Amongst the cultural baggage of European populations, religious confession and practice was imbibed with mothers' milk, and difference as among confessions marked off one population from another. Early modern religious history, using the vocabulary of the French school, posits *frontières de catholicité*, areas where Catholic and Protestant lived in uneasy proximity to each other. Such areas were critical heartlands of witch hunts and denunciations.

Mixed communities of Jews and Gentiles, Catholics and Protestants, Protestants and versions of Protestantism, even when they were not involved in actual conflict, were conscious of difference and demarcated each other quite closely. Separate schooling and separate sources of poor relief were associated with religious difference. Certain jobs were associated with Jewishness – for example the second-hand clothes trade in sixteenth-century Venice and nineteenth-century Vienna. Eating habits were preserved and demarcated one religion from another. In a novel of 1528, Delgado, a syphilitic priest, described Lozana, a conversa (one whose Jewish ancestors had converted to Christianity) and prostitute who had fled from Spain when the persecutions began and plied her trade in sixteenth-century Rome. She knew nothing of Jewish ritual or beliefs but she never ate pork sausages. Ways of cooking and cleaning vessels betrayed the hidden Jew. Nineteenth- and twentieth-century nationalism embraced religious difference, as in the mixed communities of Ireland, or in Poland resisting Russianization. The notion of difference, called more elegantly 'otherness' or 'alterity', has become a major analytical tool in cultural studies.

Indeed, the question of religious history and identity definition has surfaced as a key issue even without Holocaust studies and Islam. It has often been an important constituent of microhistorical writing, the reading of a culture through an incident or a lawsuit. The model and most successful of these works was Carlo Ginzburg's, *The Cheese and the Worms* (1992). The incidents, intended to locate an event in a carefully constructed particular cultural milieu and timeframe, are encapsulated in an individual lawsuit or a temporally circumscribed journal, or an event such as a carnival which eventuated in a riot between two religious groups, or a dossier to endorse an application for sainthood. The religious commitment and definitions described are seen as a critical cultural keys to understanding an entire society.

The balancing of notions of difference in the juxtaposition of two religions with contrasting codes of belief has been fundamental to the understanding of the cultural encounters of Europeans as they expanded in Asia and the Americas. I have recently been immersed in some of the literature of the sixteenth-century Jesuit missions with a view to understanding how they were financed. However, one does not get very far without an awareness of how the missionaries viewed the societies they encountered, and for this reason works such as Schurhammer's *Francis Xavier*[25] have been exploited for purposes far beyond the author's original intent. I regard Spence's *Memory Palace of Matteo Ricci*[26] as one of the most engaging works I read in the last decades of the twentieth century. Its aim is to demonstrate the means by which an Italian of great learning and astuteness confronted a civilization which was not Christian, but nevertheless one for which he had great respect. Indeed, of all the civilizations he encountered, the Chinese culture was the only one he was prepared to put on a level with the Catholic cultures of Europe. Not only did he write the most influential commentary on the civilization of China, which transformed European thinking about that continent, but he also sought to persuade Chinese mandarin society (the Jesuits began at the top because they had no doubt whatsoever that if the top was not in agreement the effort was wasted) to accept Christianity by comparing common elements in the religion and moral values of Confucianism and by demonstrating European scientific knowledge. His courting of the mandarin class through the teaching of mnemonics as an aid to examination learning and his use of the visual as a teaching tool served to emphasize cultural difference.

Amongst the five didactic prints Ricci had at his disposal, two – the *piscatio* (fishing for men) and the supper at Emmaeus (hospitality and commemoration) – found an easy reception with the Chinese. But that of the Virgin and Child, and still more that of the Crucifixion, proved problematic. The Virgin was a puzzle since she gave the impression that the central figure of Christianity was a woman. The Crucifixion was a non-starter. This was a punishment reserved in China for the lowest of the low. How could one initiate the promotion of a religion through a spectacle which generated contempt? This confrontation of cultures on issues at the heart of Christian practice permits a very immediate appreciation of difference.

The carrying of Ricci's book in a Latin translation to Europe is one of my present concerns because the bearer, Father Trigault, was engaged in a largely fundraising mission on behalf of the Chinese enterprise and Ricci's text was integral to the generation of enthusiasm and therefore money for the mission. Trigault's actual journey to Rome, which was across land in an attempt to find a way to avoid having to travel out on Portuguese ships, being subjected to racial scrutiny by the Portuguese and told who he could take and who he could not, is exciting enough. But my concern has been with how he found a publisher to provide him with 200 free copies to give to potential donors at court and how he solicited gifts, and of what type; both to impress the Chinese ruling class with the advanced technology of Western civilization and to reward helpers. The clocks, mirrors, scientific instruments, as well as money and men to staff the missions and academic works to sustain them, were critical to the enterprise. Ricci's book was pruned somewhat in Trigault's translation to make China more acceptable to Europeans. What was omitted on themes of sex and violence becomes as important to the understanding of cultural difference as what was included. The work became a bestseller, so the publisher did not lose on providing the free copies.

It could be said very fairly that I have not addressed religious history *tout court*, and indeed from the very beginning I have stressed my intent to pursue religion as part of the issue rather than as something in itself. I am well aware that there is a classical religious history of the sort that the occupants of Chairs or posts in the subject pursue. The study of individual churchmen and of national churches, of monastic and conventual development and theological complexities have proceeded apace, but some of these new perceptions have also embraced approaches developed outside the field. The network analysis introduced by Wolfgang Reinhard[27] into papal finances, for example, has been one aspect of major developments in recent years in the history of the papacy. In Italy some truly novel work on the uses and intent of ceremonials by the Renaissance and baroque papacy has been provided by Maria Antonietta Visceglia.[28] Her work demonstrates how the imperial legacy is copied to create a linkage between the Pope and the Roman emperors who triumphed over Europe. Renata Ago has looked at career building within the papal court by particular families.[29] The papal court in the sixteenth century was the most considerable dispatcher and receiver of ambassadors, and Ago's work has included a consideration of the structures of proceeding to obtain cardinalates and thereafter ambassadorial posts and benefices in this period. She has examined the family strategies (the *giochi di squadra*, or team games) involving women and men, the parents and families of the aspirant; each parent representing in their person two family lines and playing different parts. The women were involved at the beginning informally, through dinner parties which seated influential people together and thus permitted the airing of notions and, above all, their letter-writing to relatives and contacts – a female pursuit – able to forward the cause of the chosen family member. High-born women travelled to marry and then became inveterate letter-writers, which enabled them to develop influential connections. When the matter was known to be aired and received favourably, the men – usually including the head of house – stepped in to finish the business without risk of loss of honour through rebuttal.

Through Ago we know the content of an ambassadorial bag of a cardinal travelling from Rome to Paris: the silk flowers produced by nuns to be given to helpful women, the valuable ornaments in gold bought by the male members of the family to be given by the ambassador to the

French King, and the crystal vases (bought by the women) and bathroom ornaments for Italian women who married into the French court or even for the Queen herself. In short, the functioning of an institution, the court, is examined through family history and material culture, through networking and the gift economy.

V

Finally, I would conclude with an observation which bears some relationship to Le Bras and where I began. It has been said that Europe was not effectively Christianized *en masse* until the eighteenth century, at the moment when the first intellectuals were fighting their war with the very notion of God. Amongst issues which have marked religious history in recent years has been the theme of secularization – how the West stepped out of the corset of a belief in absolute truths and the comfort or liability of the hereafter and committed itself to tolerance of the tolerant and intolerance of the intolerant, and hence moved into 'modernity'. These processes have often been seen as much more complete and smooth than they actually were, and there is now a very determined effort to push them forward into the twentieth century. The eighteenth-century Enlightenment indeed produced some critical voices which challenged the Roman Catholic Church in particular for its intolerance and superstitious practices as well as its unfair share of landed wealth and privilege. Yet such criticism was concentrated in the pens of the very few. Indeed, the German and Scottish Enlightenments were deeply religious and one really had to go to Paris to wage war on God, as did d'Holbach and Helvétius. Even then, one had to choose the right salon in which to do so. The French Revolution and the Counter Revolution demonstrated the folly of trying to unravel the religious commitments of the past for the vast majority of the population.

In examining these resistances, the notion that religion draws its primary intensity from fear of Purgatory looks very weak. At the height of the Terror, clandestine Masses were held without a priest by a parish content with an officiating schoolmaster who knew the liturgy. Communion, confession and the last rites proved quite difficult to re-establish after the Concordat among a population that was prepared to fight for the ringing of bells and the repositioning of familiar images.[30] The community practices of religion were shown to be the most valorized element. Progress towards 'free thinking' in the nineteenth century was very patchy and divided according to where one lived, in which town or country, and whether one was male or female. There were 220,000 nuns in France in the 1870s largely propping up educational and welfare services. The Lourdes phenomenon, as Ruth Harris has recently demonstrated so evocatively,[31] the Marpingen visions[32] and the children of Fatima generated in the second half of the nineteenth century, expressions of (female-led) popular fervour which were redolent of the Middle Ages.

If intellectual elites moved towards secularization through logic and rational philosophy, such motives were not popular inducements. Urbanization and industrialization might have been accelerating factors from the mid-nineteenth century, but one can exaggerate the pace of any such exodus from conventional practice. Studies of northern English industrial towns show how nonconformity continued to dominate the cultural lives of the majority of the population.[33] Holocaust studies presently draw upon the persistence of confessional intensity in Germany in the mid-twentieth century. In much of Catholic Europe women clung to the traditional faith longer than men. What finally prompted them to leave? There is probably no single answer. However, for Catholics, increasingly from the 1920s, the Church's hardline stance on contraception can be seen to have posed problems for the conformist believer. In 1995, Martine Sevregand published two works, *L'amour en toute lettre* and *Les enfants du Bon Dieu*, which, very coolly and dispassionately, allowing the documents to speak for themselves, analysed a cache of letters to a priest who ran an advice column in a Catholic periodical.

The attention the works secured revealed how severed the contemporary world of the 1990s was from that of the 1920s. The studies captured the agony of couples – the grandparents of the present generation of twenty-somethings, perhaps – who wished to conform to Church teaching but who had a superfluity of children they could ill afford or whose birth had menaced the life of the mother and left her debilitated. In France, government policy was itself pronatalist until the 1970s and it was the abandonment by the state of such policies which made birth control available. This gave women more choice and control over their bodies, and perhaps amongst the many helped to accelerate changes which left the Church isolated as the sole protagonist of the former status quo. In short, multiple factors need consideration in assessing secularization and modernity, and a more nuanced record which takes account of many cultural factors.

In the twenty-first century we still live with the Ulster problem, a cultural divide which originated in religious factors, and one magnificently depicted by Marianne Elliott's recent study.[34] Moreover, other topical issues have exposed gaping chasms between the secularized West and Islam. As we look forward further into the twenty-first century the political history of our pluralist societies looks set to be much concerned with the religious. Moreover, historians, who are usually children of their times in the questions they set themselves, will doubtless continue the process of dissolving the old boundaries of historical enquiry so as to integrate religion as a category of analysis.

Notes

1. L. Stone, *The Family, Sex and Marriage in England 1570–1640* (abridged version, London, 1979).
2. G. Le Bras, *Etudes de sociologie religieuse*, vol. I, *Sociologie de la pratique religieuse dans les compagnes françaises* (Paris, 1955).
3. G. Cholvy, *Histoire du diocèse de Montpellier* (Paris, 1976).
4. L. Pérouas, *Le diocèse de la Rochelle 1648–1724. Sociologie et pastorale* (Paris, 1964).
5. L. Stone, *The Family, Sex and Marriage in England* (1979).
6. P. Ariès, *Centuries of Childhood: A Social History of Family Life* (New York, 1962).
7. J.L. Flandrin, *Families in Former Times: Kinship, Household and Sexuality* (Cambridge, 1979).
8. R. Po-Chia Hsia, *Social Discipline in the Reformation: Central Europe, 1550–1700* (London, 1989); *The World of Catholic Renewal 1540–1700* (Cambridge, 1998).
9. H. Schilling, 'Chiese confessionali e disciplinamento sociale. Un bilancio provvisoria della ricerca storica', in P. Prodi (ed.), *Disciplino dell'anima, disciplina del corpo e disciplina della società tra medievo e età moderna* (Bologna, 1994), pp. 125–60; A. Prosperi, *Tribunali della coscienza: Inquisitori, confessori, missionari* (Turin, 1996).
10. E. Le Roy Ladurie, *Montaillou: Cathars and Catholics in a French Village 1294–1324* (London, 1980).
11. J. Delumeau, *La Vie économique et sociale de Rome dans la seconde moitié du XVIe siècle*, 2 vols (Paris, 1957–59); *Catholicism between Luther and Voltaire* (Cambridge, 1977); *Sin and Fear: The Emergence of a Western Guilt Culture* (New York, 1990) (first published in French, 1983); *Rassurer et protéger. Le sentiment de securité dans l'Occident d'autrefois* (Paris, 1989).
12. M. Vovelle, *Piété baroque et déchristianisation en Provence 1750–1820* (Paris, 1973).
13. P. Chaunu, *La Mort à Paris XV1, XV11et XV111 siècles* (Paris, 1978).
14. S.K. Cohn, *Death and Property in Siena, 1205–1800: Strategies for the Afterlife* (Baltimore, 1988).
15. C. Eire, *From Madrid to Purgatory: The Art and Craft of Dying in Sixteenth Century Spain* (Cambridge, 1995).
16. L. Scarrafia and G. Zarri, (eds), *Women and Faith* (Cambridge, MA, 1999).
17. M. Spufford, *Contrasting Communities: English Villagers in the 16th and 17th Centuries* (Cambridge, 1974).
18. C.W. Bynum, *Holy Feast and Holy Fast: The Religious Significance of Food to Medieval Women* (Berkeley, 1987); R. Bell, *Holy Anorexia* (Chicago, 1995).

19. L. Scarrafia, *La santa degli impossibili. Vicende e significati della devozione a Santa Rita* (Turin, 1990).
20. O. Hufton, *The Prospect Before Her: A History of Women in Western Europe 1500–1800* (London, 1995).
21. L. Roper, *Oedipus and the Devil: Witchcraft, Sexuality and Religion in Early Modern Europe* (London, 1994).
22. E. Duffy, *The Stripping of the Altars: Traditional Religion in England 1400–1580* (London, 1992).
23. C. Geerz, *The Interpretation of Cultures* (New York, 1973).
24. C. Ginzburg, *The Cheese and the Worms* (London, 1992).
25. G. Schurhammer, *Francis Xavier: His Life and Times*, 4 vols (Rome, 1982).
26. J. Spence, *The Memory Palace of Matteo Ricci* (New York, 1984).
27. W. Reinhard, *Papstfinanz und Nepotismus unter Paul V (1605–1621)* (Stuttgart, 1974).
28. M.A. Visceglia, 'Ceremoniale romani: il ritorno e la trasfigurazione dei trionfi antichi', in L. Fiorini and A. Prosperi (eds), *Roma la città del papa* (Turin, 2000).
29. R. Ago, *Carriere e clientele nella Roma barocca* (Rome, 1990).
30. O. Hufton, *Women and the Limits of Citizenship in the French Revolution* (Toronto, 1992), chapters 2 and 3.
31. R. Harris, *Lourdes: Body and Spirit in the Secular Age* (London, 1999).
32. D. Blackbourn, *The Marpingen Visions: Rationalism, Religion and the Rise of Modern Germany* (London, 1995).
33. S.J.D. Green, *Religion in the Age of Decline: Organisation and Experience in Industrial Yorkshire, 1870–1920* (Cambridge, 1996); J. Morris, *Religion and Urban Change: Croydon, 1840–1914* (London, 1992).
34. M. Elliott, *The Catholics of Ulster: A History* (London, 2000).

Further reading

Baroja, J.C., *Las formas complejas de la vida religiosa. Religión, sociedad, y carácter en las España de los siglos XV1 y XV11* (Madrid, 1978).
Bell, R., *Saints and Society. The Two Worlds of Western Christendom* (Chicago, 1982).
Berthelot du Chesnay, *Les missions de Saint Jean d'Eudes* (Paris, 1967).
Burke, P., 'How to be a Counter-Reformation saint', in K. von Greyerrs (ed.), *Religion and Society in Early Modern Europe 1500–1800* (London, 1984), pp. 71–83.
Châtellier, L., *Tradition chrétienne et renouveau catholique dans le cadre de l'ancien diocèse de Strasbourg (1650–1770)* (Paris, 1981).
Cholvy, G. with Hilaire, Y., *Histoire religeuse de la France contemporaine* (Toulouse, 1989).
Christian, W.A., *Local Religion in Sixteenth Century Spain* (Princeton, 1981).
Cousin, B., *Le miracle et le quotidien. Les ex voto provençaux. Images d'une société* (Aix en Provence, 1983).
Gentilcore, D., 'Adapt Yourself to the People's Capabilities: Methods and Impact in the Kingdom of Naples, 1600–1800', *Journal of Ecclesiastical History*, vol. 45 (1994), pp. 269–96.
Hufton, O., *Bayeux in the Late Eighteenth Century* (Oxford, 1967).
Hufton, O., 'The French Church', in W.J. Callahan and D. Higgs (eds), *Church and Society in Catholic Europe in the Eighteenth Century* (Cambridge, 1979), pp. 13–33.

Hufton, O., 'The Reconstruction of a Church 1796–1801', in G. Lewis and C. Lucas (eds), *Beyond the Terror* (Cambridge, 1981), pp. 21–53.

Hufton, O., 'Whatever Happened to the History of the Nun?', (Royal Holloway College Hayes Robinson Lecture, 2000).

Langlois, C., *Le catholicisme au féminin: Les congrégations à supérieure générale au X1Xe siècle* (Paris, 1984).

Le Bras, G., *Etudes de sociologie religieuse*, vol. II, *De la morphologie à la typologie* (Paris, 1956).

MacCulloch, D., *Thomas Cranmer: A Life* (London and New Haven, 1998).

Peris, N., 'La religion populaire, mythes et réalités. L'exemple de la France sous l'ancien régime', *Colloques Internationaux du Centre National de la Recherche Scientifique* (Paris, 1979), pp. 221–8.

Prodi, P., *Lo sviluppo dell'assolutismo nello Stato Pontificio.1, La monarchia papale e gli organi centrali di governo* (Bologna, 1968).

Prodi, P., *The Papal Prince: One Body and Two Souls. The Papal Monarchy in Early Modern Europe* (Cambridge, 1987).

Quéniart, J., *Les hommes, l'eglise et Dieu dans la France du XV111 siècle* (Paris, 1978).

Rahner, H., *Ignatius Loyola: Letters to Women* (London, 1967).

Rahner, H., *Ignatius the Theologian* (London, 1968).

Safley, T.M., *Let No Man Put Asunder: The Control of Marriage in the German Southwest. A Comparative Study 1550–60* (Kirksville, 1984).

Scattigno, A., 'Jeanne de Chantal: la fondatrice', in G. Calvi (ed.), *Barocco al femminile* (Rome, 1991).

Schmitt, T.J., *L'Organisation ecclésiastiique et la pratique religieuse dans l'archidiaconé d'Autun* (Autun, 1957).

Schultze, W., 'Il concetto di "disciplinamento sociale" nel prima età moderna', *Annali dell'Istituto italo-germanico di Trento* vol. 18, pp. 371–411.

Scribner, R.W., 'Ritual and Popular Religion at the time of the Reformation', *Journal of Ecclesiastical History*, vol. 35 (1984), pp. 49–77.

Tacchi-Venturi, P., *Storia della compagnia di Gesù in Italia*, 3 vols (Rome, 1922–38).

Venard, M., *Réforme protestante, réforme catholique dans la province d'Avignon au XVIe siècle* (Paris, 1993).

Vovelle, M., *Religion et Révolution. La déchristianisation de l'an 11* (Paris, 1976).

Vovelle, M., *La Révolution contre l'Eglise: De la raison à l'Etre Suprême* (Paris, 1989).

Zarri, G., 'From Prophecy to Discipline 1450–1650', in L. Scaraffia and G. Zarri (eds), *Women and Faith* (Cambridge, MA, 1999).

5
What is Cultural History Now?[*]

Miri Rubin

In his book *Culture: The Anthropologists' Account*, Adam Kuper advises us to avoid altogether the use of that 'hyper-referential word', 'culture'.[1] It has come to denote too much and thus came to mean too little. The same might be said of the use of 'cultural history', which may cover quite traditional histories of artistic and intellectual production as well as something different, called by some the 'new cultural history'.[2] For while shame-faced political, hard-nosed demographic, forbidding diplomatic, and chapped-skinned imperial historians were left out of all the good historical party-lists in the 1970s and 1980s, they are now back on them, invited as experts on political rituals, Cold War culture, cultural encounters. The same can be said of the histories of medicine, science and law – spheres which were marginal to the first wave of the 'new' history in the 1960s and 1970s – but have been remade as exciting new areas by those able to probe their 'cultural' making.

I

If the 'cultural turn' can now affect all types of history, it is not evenly spread over periods. Just as social history was most fully embraced by historians of the eighteenth and nineteenth centuries, inspired by work on crowd behaviour or moral economy, first highlighting class, and later gender, the cultural turn has been most prominent in the works of historians of the late medieval and early modern periods – hardly as unknowable and irrelevant as E.H. Carr had them – at least until recently. In these periods of seemingly such uneven cultural production, within powerful religious cultures that perpetuated the dichotomy of Latin/vernacular, priesthood/laity, Christian/other, there was most reason to place the process of cultural production under the microscope. It is here that Menocchio's autodidacticism became a privileged emblem, where we learned about the invention of rituals of misrule, the undermining of theology by 'vernacular theology',[3] of popular religious cults – even that of a dog[4] – the elaborate ceremonial of honour and shame, the use and abuse of images. The realization that texts are perhaps the least straightforward of sources comes easily to those operating in periods of low literacy, within religious cultures that invest cultic meaning in the book.

The encounter between the historian – product of an unenchanted world – and religious cultures humbles and encourages the search for equivalents or analogies elsewhere. As we will see, 'elsewhere' has often been found in anthropological studies, in the problems of textuality and in the fruitful juxtaposition of different types of genre and matter: prayer and altarpiece, coronation slippers and royal law, community and its environment. Lessons and tasks have been learnt here and then applied elsewhere.[5] And it is hardly surprising that the 'cultural turn' has spread, for what it highlights and treats as fundamental to human interaction are the conditions of communication, the terms of representation, the interaction between structures of meaning – narratives, discourses – and the ways in which individuals and groups use them and thus express themselves.

Like all good ideas the basic point is simple. The cultural turn asks not only 'How it really was' but rather 'How was it for him, or her, or them?' To dare to ask such questions, and provide answers while meeting E.H. Carr's 'standard of significance', is, of course, the challenge. Meeting it has been facilitated by the recognition, which E.H. Carr willingly acknowledged, that history is bound to reflect our historic moment and life experiences. Thus the *Bildung* of the historian is achieved not only by way of an anointment with the dust of the archives, but through the mobilization of an informed subjectivity, human and intellectual capacities for categorization, system building and empathy. Bringing to the traces of the past wishes, pain, hope and desire is now acknowledged as not only a useful but a necessary part of human reflection and learning about the past. A new type of historiography – self-reflective and conversational – has come into being, and with it an exploration of that which has for too long been left unsaid.

All this might seem a strange outcome from the preoccupation with culture which for large parts of the twentieth century owed so much to the contributions of French history-writing. For French reflection on the social can be notoriously impersonalizing; a lot of it aims at system building, it has been strongly structuralist in its analyses, it favours abstraction, and it revels in the convergence of models and in discerning long-term trends. In the postwar world the historians appointed by the state to the Sixth Section of the Ecole Pratique des Hautes Etudes were making a new history of Europe. This vision owed a great deal to a previous generation of historians, like Marc Bloch and Lucien Febvre who, in the aftermath of the First World War, and inspired by American vision and funding, tried to create a new type of history, about people, about rhythms of life, work, death, a collaborative history which would be worked out in historians' workshops, international meetings, where erstwhile foes would meet as professional friends. Although Febvre and Bloch failed to mobilize the doyen of European historians – the Belgian Henri Pirenne – they set up a French operation based in Paris, the *Annales d'histoire économique et sociale*, which unlike Bloch survived the Second World War; it launched into the world post-1945 with enthusiasm and a re-enforced set of objectives.[6]

This was to be history which would not fall prey to nationalist, militarist, divisive, regional identity, but would rather uncover long-term, slow-moving and deep structures which were European rather than French or German or Italian. Their history was to touch multitudes rather than elites, and incorporated the scientific tools of economics, demography and a venerable French-style geography. In every way this was to move from *événement* to *structure*, from *histoire toute courte* to *histoire-problème*.[7] Such a history was none the less to be seamless in its unfolding; as Braudel saw it, *histoire totale*, into which different spheres of action are always interlocked, inseparable. Only the knowing historian can tell the whole tale in a prose which is as suggestive as it is informative and precise. A hectic engagement with the re-creation of systems of the past through series of statistical data over long periods followed – *l'histoire sérielle*[8] – of trade and demography, of food production, and reproduction, childhood and work unto death.[9]

Soon they were grasping for ideas commensurate with the demographic rhythms and the agrarian patterns. What were the mental structures which corresponded to those of agriculture and kinship? What were the representations and rituals which underpinned lordship? These too were bound to be slow-moving, shared over large European territories transcending the blips of wars and invasions and conquests. These were the *mentalités*, the *representations collectives* about death, childhood, sexuality, kinship, purgatory and the hereafter.[10] And so from *c*.1968

Annalistes were heavily involved in the excavation of genealogies of ideas for Europeans of the past. Their neighbours in the Maison des Sciences de l'Homme were anthropologists such as Claude Lévi-Strauss and his disciples, sociolinguists such as Emile Benveniste, and later philosophers such as Jacques Derrida and social theorists such as Pierre Bourdieu. Although most *Annalistes* denied a Marxist position, they were none the less indebted to a vision of culture as operating from within social relations and relations of production, either to promote or retard 'modernization'. The history of reading, of revolution, of Purgatory or of the family was being produced by French scholars whose works were soon translated into English and Italian and Spanish, and who by the 1970s were being invited to teach and interact at American universities. The blend of materiality and ideas was a heady one, and to it was about to be added another voice, that of the maverick, ever-disturbing and ever-elusive philosopher/historian/archaeologist, Michel Foucault.

II

What Foucault has bequeathed to historians is a history embodied. He has opened our eyes to bodies 'in hospitals, in clinics, in asylums and in prisons',[11] in embodied states of being; bodies as the vehicle for pain and for pleasure. For Foucault these bodies, considered marginal or aberrant by their own societies, were signs of the powers which were operating on all, through fear, through the control and shaping of knowledge, through the representation of convention as nature and through the confusion of myth and essence. This control applied to all, not only to those who ended up on gallows or in prisons. Foucault's impact has been not so much in the implications of his history of power as in the attention to the body. Seized of this embodied realization, historians, who know rich sources, found bodies: at play, in ritual, at prayer, at work, in pain.[12]

With Foucault the system building, structuring, moment came to an end, left almost beyond repair. For was model building, Foucauldian discourse formation, not the very essence of the operation of power, the subject which intellectuals and activists must try to unmask and demystify? He bequeathed not a thoery, but some insights and a method, that of 'vigorous genealogy'. For the historian this means a not unfamiliar search for influence, convergence and contiguity. The results have varied in significance but have produced exercises in the unravelling of myths and reflections on the making of 'common knowledge'. Did we not all learn that the right to deflower a servile maiden on her marriage night was the essence of overbearing masculinist feudal privilege? Yet now we know that the *'droit de cuissage'* began as a sixteenth-century jurists' joke, and was remade as an anti-clerical fantasy by polemicists in the nineteenth century.[13] Was cannibalism not a practice which defined non-European otherness? – only since it was invented by Columbus and gained depth and meaning within the eucharistic polemics of the sixteenth and seventeenth centuries.[14]

In other words, particularly relevant to our discussion here, meaning is always made out of pre-existing words and within language. The historian must trace the trails of meaning as these lead us to patterns of influence and power, habits of use and trails of access. When the new feast of the Eucharist – Corpus Christi – was founded in early fourteenth-century Europe, the language of majesty, which attached to the rituals around Christ's body in France, inspired processional rituals which used elements of royal iconography – the Eucharist as king, the eucharistic procession as royal entry. When it reached Peru in the sixteenth century, it was understood through the imagery of the sun deity and processions were planned to culminate at sunrise on a mountain-top.[15] By tracing the symbol as embedded in different contexts the possiblity for comparison arises, as between cosmologies, ideas about space and sacrality.[16]

The Foucauldian moment emphasized the operation of power as the intellectual prey; and it reverberated in the movements of liberation and self-expression of the 1970s and 1980s: feminism, civil rights movements, gay liberation, environmental movements, anti-colonial campaigns. The political work of struggle for rights necessitated a historical engagement with the genealogies of oppression: feminists wanted a women's history, African-Americans wanted a black history, newly created states and regions in revolt created their own histories. In almost all these cases the story of oppression was related to cultural representations of biological difference: women's oppression was based on an interpretation of biological difference, African-Americans were marked by racial stereotyping. Furthermore, cultural packages kept oppression in place through the rituals of state or the rhythms of separate spheres of gender. The story of oppression seemed to be a cultural story, probably most famously encapsulated for the colonial encounter in Edward Said's *Orientalism*.[17] Culture was the site where relations of power could very readily be discerned.

Crucial to the making of 'the cultural turn' have been the wider effects of feminist interests and aspirations. Multifarious, and many-mooded, differing between generations as well as by the period or place studied, feminist historians, still mainly women, have promoted the understanding of 'culture' just as they had extended the understanding of what constitutes 'society' in the 1970s. For one of the central concepts of feminist enquiry – gender – claims that men and women are not born but made. They are made within webs of representation, exhortation and example, between ideas and practices, by and within embodied persons. Within these webs it is possible to work towards the mapping of structures of oppression, inequality, disenfranchisement, low expectations and limited access to education, but it is also possible to identify resistance, creativity and the appropriation of meaning. Ideas about gender organized whole areas of cultural production: when, early in his career, Chaucer decided to translate that greatest of medieval vernacular poems, the *Roman de la rose*, he abridged and expunged whole sections, those which were considered to be the most misogynistic and hateful even by contemporaries.[18] Clearly what went down well with a French readership was not suited to the ears and tastes of English courtiers, or merchants and their wives and daughters. Gender language was used differently to mean different things in social and linguistic European regions.

Attending to gender has taught historians to read symbols in clusters of meaning, in contexts of use, in cases of meaningful practice, through texts and artefacts of varying genres and texture. Caroline Bynum has explored the uses of central Christian symbols – Crucifixion, Eucharist – by religious females, modes which she sees as expressive and enriching.[19] To say 'female' was to invoke a cluster of meanings.[20] To call Richard II effeminate in 1399 was to raise a whole range of criticisms about the effectiveness of his rule, his bellicosity, his reason, morality and reliability. To call Jews effeminate was to dismiss their authority to read and interpret scripture; to suggest that they read through the flesh, not through the spirit. The clusters of association here draw some insight from psychoanalytic practice, and reading a text culturally is something like the interpretation of dreams. In reading sources 'culturally' we are able to assemble a whole range of related ones – visual, textual, musical – and through their superimposition, as if through a prism, to gain a point of fresh focus and insight.

As in the acquisition of any language, encountering and learning to use materials in differing idioms and genres is hard work, but it extends our understanding and leads historians to sources written, memorized, sung, sculpted and prayed. Some historians even tried to engage in something akin to 'observation' by various imaginative ploys: Carlo Ginzburg by re-creating the worlds of the mill in the Friulese village which Menocchio inhabited over 400 years ago; Natalie Davis by accepting the challenge of re-creating the *mis-en-scène* for a cinematic version of the events surrounding the sixteenth-century deception of Martin Guerre;[21] and more recently Ruth Harris by submitting herself to the ordeal of pilgrimage to Lourdes, and encountering the limits of what her body and mind could bear.[22]

III

To achieve an understanding of public events and collective experiences rich with symbolic meaning, historians have turned to anthropology. The romance of history and anthropology has nourished the 'cultural turn'. Historians in this key fruitfully pretend to be entering into a conversation with the people of the past. Just as anthropologists did their fieldwork by probing and interpreting systems of meaning, aiming at learning the culture as a language, so historians have attempted to work on historical traces towards the remaking of past worlds. Like anthropologists, historians have granted special importance to those dense occasions of symbolic poignancy – rituals – in which communities not only acted but re-enacted their myths of origins and their complex affinities with deities, rulers and each other. Following the structuralism of Lévi-Strauss and the Anglophone brands developed by Mary Douglas and Victor Turner,[23] historians expected to find meaningful binary packages, demarcations of the sacred and the profane, the pure and the polluted, but were ultimately drawn to the messy terrain between each pair. They later came to probe the delineations of gender within the ritual field.[24] Above all, under the influence of Clifford Geertz, the ritual became a point of departure for investigations into all areas of life: work, kinship, religion and rule. Although ritual could not always be explained, it could be interpreted by a careful unfolding which has come to be known as 'thick description'. Geertz's method has probably found its most ardent users, its most committed followers, among historians;[25] partly because it seems like no method at all, but more like a gentle exercise in common sense, written with elegance, and always embedded in a broad historical context – sounding very much like good history.

Ritual encapsulates the fundamental explanatory conundrums of any approach to human behaviour, for in order to work it must be rule-bound and a fair degree of shared knowledge must be contained within it: and yet it is open to rearrangements, redesign and interpretation by every ritual actor and observer. For ritual to work in the manner suggested by Durkheim, individuals must be absorbed into its meanings and physical demands, so as to create within the sweating, dancing, chanting or kneeling subjects, that effervescent state of receptivity which in turn produces the outcome: a deeper commitment to, and facility with, the moral narratives and norms of that society.

With the advent of the Foucauldian moment, with the unveiling of the work of social order by a feminist critique, with the growing emphasis on subject positions within social relations, the ritual conceived as shared event, as social glue, evident and powerful in its imprint and meaning, was subjected to a multitude of critiques. From the Carnival at Romans to the Notting Hill Carnival, ritual is full of indeterminacy; it is essentially performative, as Mikhail Bakhtin (1895–1975) helped historians to realize. It is amenable to lapses, repression, and even to simple forgetfulness; it sometimes even rains on the parade.[26] Evidently, ritual can take unexpected turns, spectacularly in Romans in 1579–80, when it turned into a bloodbath as notables killed craftsmen, marking a dramatic reorientation of the dynamics of the French Wars of Religion.[27] Less famous is the disorder of a parish Mass, the contradiction of the coronation of an infant such as Edward VI, or the more mundane private reservation maintained by a Huguenot during a Catholic ritual in seventeenth-century France.[28] The ritual process, seen by sociologists in the early twentieth century as an occasion for the enhancement of all that was consensual and reaffirming of social and moral order, might be observed differently. Inasmuch as ritual condenses complex social relations and ideas – in space and time – it might offer distorting, less acceptable versions of life, more apt to irritate and induce discontent.

IV

Despite the growing number of puffs by historians from the 1960s onward – like those of Keith Thomas and Natalie Davis – anthropologists by the 1980s were undergoing their own type of crisis, visible in seminal rethinking of their aims and in a questioning of 'ethnographic authority'. Some of the works of the great founding mothers and fathers of the discipline were exposed as the products of colonial enterprise, or naive fantasies of disenchanted members of societies of plenty. The very notion of coming to know a different society, the belief that good-will, a strong constitution and anti-malaria pills were all that were needed to survive the ordeal and to coax people to reveal themselves to the ethnographer's gaze, was treated as risible, and worse. The collection of essays edited by James Clifford and George E. Marcus in 1982, *Writing Culture*, claimed even more. In a comparative analysis of Emmanuel Le Roy Ladurie's *Montaillou* and E.E. Evans-Pritchard's *The Nuer*, Renato Rosaldo likened the ethnographer to an inquisitor. Texts of ethnography were deconstructed by fellow ethnographers, as Vincent Crapanzano shows in his article in that volume in an analysis of ethnographic rhetoric and the modes by which ethnographers try to make their analyses persuasive.[29]

Ethnography and anthropology were thus being undone through the lessons of post-colonial criticism, feminism and the challenges of deconstructive readings. The result has been a partial withdrawal by anthropologists from terrains with colonial pasts, and a redoubling of efforts to understand the diversities and the ills of Western societies: this has resulted in works such as Tanya Luhrmann's study of American psychiatry, Ray Raphael's study of coming of age in contemporary US, or Claudine Fabre-Vassas's book on the cultural uses of the pig in contemporary south-west France which reveals layers of anti-semitic sensibility.[30] Historians have generally not wanted to hear this very telling debate. But they should, because problems about communication, about understanding other cultures and the terms of encounter with them, are crucial to historians of sixteenth-century Europe as they are to the ethnographer in tribal Latin America. We are engaged in both cases in eliciting meaning from traces and self-description, through a multitude of interrelated artefacts and statements, rituals, writings and sayings. Our projects are very similar indeed.[31] The crisis of ethnography has ways of hurting historians too.[32]

Like ethnographers, historians have all too readily accepted that some people will be naive informants, eager to play with the kindly adult probing their games. An example will serve well: an often repeated story recounts the experience of the Puritan John Shaw as he travelled in Westmorland in 1644 in search of persons to improve through biblical instruction. One of the old men he met and examined had a vague knowledge of Jesus Christ: was he not that man he had seen once in a play 'on a tree, and blood ran down'?[33] Shock, horror, the Puritan's fantasy of godlessness – not only a man who knew little, but a man whose scant knowledge was learned from the idolatrous spectacle of religious drama. But should we take the informant as a willing and innocent bystander who answers questions when asked, and produces an unsullied truth? May he not be a teller of tales too, and an underminer of pompous pretence, a joker at the expense of the man in black from other parts? Might he not resent the intrusive suggestion that people in Westmorland were too ignorant in 1644 to know their saviour? To allow the subjects of our – ethnographers and historians alike – enquiry to talk is to recognize the possibility of a variety of intentions in them, capacities which only protracted exchange and contextual cross-reference may sometimes be able to identify and locate.[34]

Probably the best exponent of this position is someone hard to classify as either anthropologist or historian, Marshall Sahlins. Sahlins has interpreted some seminal moments of cultural encounter, most famously the voyages and ultimate death of Captain Cook in the Pacific. His studies have followed individuals within challenging cultural contexts – persons out of place, one might say. In the improbability and the uncharted nature of such situations a drama of human existence is amplified, and it is this. We are all heirs to heritages which we call culture – language, habits, myths of origins – and yet we are also the very particular and utterly unique instantiators, users of that inheritance. Just like Captain Cook was faced by, and posed to the Hawaiians, a riddle for interpretation, so we are all to a lesser or greater extent placed in extraordinary positions in our lifetimes. Formed by the anti-Vietnam movement as a teacher-activist, Sahlins observed the soldier in Vietnam and the student on the campus, faced with moral dilemmas which are the products of economy and politics, and which call for very practical decisions about personal conduct. Each, like the members of the Reserve Police Battalion 101, uses the inheritance of language and narrative to determine good from evil and find his or her way in it all. This is Sahlins's approach to historical interpretation: we begin with our endowment – culture – and yet life creates occasions when we must act, can act, with that material in new and unique ways. Here is the return of the individual, an individual caught in webs of significance which have been inherited, but from which he makes new meanings, she forges new ways.[35] And when the individual is concerned, then psyche and emotion are at stake too; a history of emotions is now being considered by historians, tentatively, and with some degree of bemused self-awareness.[36]

V

The search for voice within the structures of language has animated scholars in the humanities in the last twenty years from various and convergent directions. There has been the search for 'unofficial' scripts of events, developed in the study of peasant societies[37] and in subaltern studies among historians of the Indian sub-continent,[38] in the work of feminist historians, in working-class histories seeking agency and voice. For medieval and early modern Europe, new historicism has seen a coming together of historians and literary scholars in an attempt to 'feel the real' through a textual analysis of non-canonical texts, side by side with material traces of daily life. Stephen Greenblatt, like a seasoned ethnographer, and inspired by Clifford Geertz's uses of the mundane and of 'common sense', has demonstrated the insights resulting from reading artefacts as texts, and putting (pitting?) genre against genre – drama, sermon and image, for example.[39]

This move has liberated historians and emboldened the literary scholar: Paul Strohm's *England's Empty Throne* displays the usefulness of a literary-critical approach to work on documents of English constitutional history: chronicles, statutes of parliament and ordinances reveal the work of genre and the political purpose that went into the crafting of legitimacy, voices planted in the written record like so much of what we have come to know as spin, all in support of the claim of a usurper-king Henry IV and his heir.[40] Such an approach also reveals that texts can tell things they were never meant to tell; they can inform despite the efforts of their author – fairly uncontroversial – but also impart knowledge of which the author, maker, painter, was never aware. As Paul Strohm suggests, we can know things about Chaucer that 'Chaucer never knew about himself':[41] he could not control the emergence of his unconscious in the text, he could not know of unfolding historical events into which his text was born, he could not fully anticipate the reception by the reader on reading him, or the changes in this reception over time. There is a lot we can know about his *oeuvre* which he could not know – but which he would have been rather interested to know, given the chance.

The 'cultural turn' is served by a hybrid of critical strategies which illuminate modes of communication, the circulation of ideas and practices and the agency of the individual, and which always attend to meaning. It is best when practised with an awareness of the intellectual roots of its concepts and procedures, alert to the allure of its rhetoric. To deal with culture is thus to deal by definition with the mixing of categories, for it is the system of meanings which makes order, ranks priority and suggests useful connections between things – real, felt and imagined. Bread is good to eat; bread is also a good gift to give, and it is an excellent thing when consecrated into God's body. It always looks the same, but it becomes different things according to the contexts of *use*; use and practice are the ways in which we gain entry into the world of meanings of those among whom we have never lived.[42] Some of this work may be chronicling and describing the trails of meaning – a historical ethnography and genealogy. Another part of this work is to understand why and how and wherefore the meanings have attached, and thus to appreciate and spot those instances when the meaning is newly articulated, questioned, revealed or reinvested with meaning. And these questions attach to all areas of life – something many commentators have missed. The 'cultural turn' contributes to the explanation and understanding of work, economics and politics.[43] No area of experience – personal and collective – is beyond its use.

Notes and references

* I am grateful to my friends Christopher Clark, David Feldman, Eric Foner, Adam I.P. Smith, Naomi Tadmor and Miles Taylor for helpful conversations, and to Peter Burke and Gareth Stedman Jones for reading and commenting on this chapter.

1. Cambridge, MA: Harvard University Press, 2000, p. x. On the term see William H. Sewell, 'The Concept(s) of Culture', in Victoria E. Bonnell and Lynn Hunt (eds), *Beyond the Cultural Turn: New Directions in the Study of Society and Culture* (Berkeley, CA: University of California Press, 1999), pp. 35–61.

2. Lynn Hunt (ed.), *The New Cultural History* (Berkeley, CA: University of California Press, 1989); Bonnell and Hunt, *Beyond the Cultural Turn*.

3. Nicholas Watson, 'The Politics of Middle English Writing', in Jocelyn Wogan-Browne, Nicholas Watson, Andrew Taylor and Ruth Evans (eds), *The Idea of the Vernacular: An Anthology of Middle English Literary Theory, 1280–1520* (University Park, PA: Penn State Press, 1999), pp. 331–52.

4. Jean-Claude Schmitt, *The Holy Greyhound: Guinefort, Healer of Children since the Thirteenth Century*, trans. Martin Thom (Cambridge: Cambridge University Press, 1982) (*Le saint lévrier: Guinefort, guérisseur d'enfants depuis le XIIIe siècle* (Paris: Flammarion, 1979)).

5. For some examples of influential theoretical reflection by medievalists and early modernists see Gabrielle M. Spiegel, *The Past as Text: The Theory and Practice of Medieval Historiography* (Baltimore, MD: Johns Hopkins University Press, 1997); Brian Stock, *Listening for the Texts: On the Uses of the Past* (Baltimore, MD: Johns Hopkins University Press, 1990); and the recent Paul Strohm, *Theory and the Pre-modern Text* (Minneapolis, MN: University of Minnesota Press, 2000). On the uses of psychoanalysis: Lyndal Roper, *Oedipus and the Devil: Witchcraft, Sexuality and Religion in Early Modern Europe* (London: Routledge, 1994).

6. On the *Annales* vision and institutional context see Carole Fink, *Marc Bloch: A Life in History* (Cambridge: Cambridge University Press, 1989), pp. 128–65; see also Peter Schöttler (ed.), *Marc Bloch: Historiker und Widerstand-Kämpfer* (Frankfurt and New York: Campus, 1999).

7. This is not to say that others had not sought this turn before: see Lord Acton's Inaugural Lecture of June 1895 which called to 'study problems in preference to periods', John Edward Emerich Acton, 'The Study of History', in John Neville Figgis and Reginald Vere Laurence (eds), *Lectures on Modern History* (London: Macmillan, 1906), p. 24.

8. The most ambitious is Emmanuel Le Roy Ladurie, *The peasants of Languedoc*, trans. John Day (Urbana, IL: University of Illinois Press, 1976) (*Les Paysans de Languedoc*, 2 vols (Paris: SEVPEN, 1966)); and for a critique see Jean-Yves Grenier, in Bernard Lepetit (ed.), *Les Formes de l'experience: une autre histoire*

sociale (Paris: Albin Michel, 1995), pp. 227–8; for a comment on this re-evaluation see G. Stedman Jones, 'Une autre histoire sociale? (note critique)', *Annales HSS*, vol. LIII (1998), pp. 383–94.

9. Philippe Carrard, *Poetics of the New History: French Historical Discourse from Braudel to Chartier* (Baltimore, MD: Johns Hopkins University Press, 1992); Trajan Stoianovich, *French Historical Method: The Annales Paradigm* (Ithaca, NY, and London: Cornell University Press, 1976); Peter Burke, *The French Historical Revolution: The Annales School 1929–1989* (Cambridge: Polity Press, 1990). For a critique by historians associated with *Annales* see *Les formes de l'experience*. On the reception of *Annales* historiography see articles by Vauchez, Oexle, Little, Simons, Rucquoi, Klaniczay and Gurevich in Miri Rubin (ed.), *The Work of Jacques Le Goff and the Challenges of Medieval History* (Woodbridge: Boydell, 1997), pp. 71–141, 223–48.

10. On the genealogy of *mentalité* and related concepts see Peter Burke, 'Strengths and Weaknesses of the History of Mentalities', in *Varieties of Cultural History* (Cambridge: Polity Press, 1997), pp. 162–82; Stoianovich, *French Historical Method*, pp. 120–1.

11. Patricia O'Brien, 'Michel Foucault's history of culture', in Lynn Hunt (ed.), *The New Cultural History* (Berkeley, CA: University of California Press, 1989), p. 34.

12. On the body and its products as metaphors for the spiritual state see Piroska Nagy, *Le Don des larmes au moyen âge* (Paris: Albin Michel, 2000); Jean-Claude Schmitt, *La Raison des gestes* (Paris: Gallimard, 1990); Alain Boureau, *Le simple corps du roi: l'impossible sacralité des souverains français XVe-XVIIIe* (Paris: Editions de Paris, 1988); Laura Kendrick, *Animating the Letter: the Figurative Embodiment of Writing from Late Antiquity to the Renaissance* (Columbus, OH: Ohio State University Press, 1999).

13. Alain Boureau, *The Lord's First Night: The Myth of the Droit de Cuissage*, trans. Lydia G. Cochrane (Chicago, IL: University of Chicago Press 1998) (*Le Droit de cuissage: la fabrication d'un mythe XIIe-XXe* (Paris: Albin Michel, 1995)).

14. Frank Lestrignant, *Cannibalism: The Discovery and Representation of the Cannibal from Columbus to Jules Verne*, trans. Rosemary Morris (Cambridge: Polity Press, 1997); *Une saint horreur; ou le voyage en eucharistie, XVIe-XVIII siècles* (Paris: Presses Universitaires de France, 1996).

15. Antoinette Molinié, 'D'un village de La Mancha à un glacier des Andes. Deux célébrations "sauvages" du Corps de Dieu', in Antoinette Molinié (ed.), *Le Corps de Dieu en Fêtes* (Paris: Cerf, 1996), pp. 223–53.

16. A related debate is that on popular culture. For one of many such debates see Lawrence W. Levine, 'The Folklore of Industrial Society: Popular Culture and its Audiences', *American Historical Review*, vol. XCVII (1992), pp. 1369–99, and the related comments by Robin D.G. Kelley, Natalie Zemon Davis and T.J. Jackson Lears, ibid., pp. 1400–30.

17. Edward W. Said, *Orientalism* (New York: Pantheon, 1978).

18. See David Wallace, 'Chaucer and the European Rose', *Studies in the Age of Chaucer* vol. I (1984), pp. 61–7.

19. Caroline W. Bynum, *Holy Feast and Holy Fast: The Religious Signifcance of Food to Medieval Women* (Berkeley, CA: University of California Press, 1987).

20. Joan Wallach Scott, *Gender and the Politics of History* (New York: Columbia University Press, 1988).

21. For an exchange about her work on the Martin Guerre case see Robert Findlay, 'The Refashioning of Martin Guerre' and Natalie Z. Davis, '"On the lame"', *American Historical Review*, vol. XCIII (1988), pp. 553–71, 572–603.

22. Ruth Harris, *Lourdes: Body and Spirit in a Secular Age* (London: Penguin, 1999).

23. On Mary Douglas's impact on cultural studies see Sonya O. Rose, 'Cultural Analysis and Moral Discourses: Episodes, Continuities, and Transformations', in Bonnell and Hunt (eds), *Beyond the Cultural Turn*, pp. 217–38, at 220–5.

24. A. Kuper, 'Culture, Identity and the Project of Cosmopolitan Anthropology', in *Among the Anthropologists: History and Context in Anthropology* (London and New Brunswick, NJ: Athlone Press, 1999), pp. 26–58, at p. 37.

25. See Robert Darnton's 'Workers Revolt: The Great Cat Massacre of Rue Saint-Séverin', in *The Great Cat Massacre and Other Episodes in French Cultural History* (London: Allen Lane, 1984), pp. 75–104; Roger Chartier, 'Texts, symbols, and Frenchness', *Journal of Modern History*, vol. LVII (1985), pp. 682–95 and Dominick La Capra, 'Chartier, Darnton, and the Great Symbol Massacre', *Journal of Modern History*, vol. LX (1988), pp. 95–112. For a more recent evaluation of Geertz's contribution see the articles in Sherry B. Ortner (ed.), *The Fate of 'Culture': Geertz and Beyond* (Berkeley, CA: University of California Press, 1999).

26. For an ethnographically grounded theory of 'loose' ritual see Caroline Humphrey and James Laidlaw, *The Archetypal Actions of Ritual: A Theory of Ritual Illustrated by the Jain Rite of Worship* (Oxford: Clarendon, 1994).

27. Emmanuel Le Roy Ladurie, *Carnival: A People's Uprising at Romans, 1579–80*, trans. Mary Feeney (London: Scolar Press, 1980).

28. See for example Roger Mettam, 'Dissemblers, Dissenters, Guerrillas: The Huguenots in France after 1685', *Historical Research* (2002) (forthcoming).

29. Renato Rosaldo, 'From the Door of his Tent: The Fieldworker and the Inquisitor', and Vincent Crapanzano, 'Hermes' Dilemma: The Masking of Subversion in Ethnographic Description', in James Clifford and George E. Marcus (eds), *Writing Culture: The Poetics and Politics of Ethnography* (Berkeley, CA: University of California Press, 1982), pp. 77–97 and pp. 51–76, respectively. See also James Clifford *The Predicament of Culture: Twentieth-Century Ethnography, Literature, and Art* (Cambridge, MA: Harvard University Press, 1988).

30. Tanya M. Luhrmann, *Of Two Minds: The Growing Disorder in American Psychiatry* (New York: Alfred Knopf, 2000); Ray Raphael, *The Men from the Boys: Rites of Passage in Male America* (Lincoln, NB: University of Nebraska Press, 1988); Claudine Fabre-Vassas, *The Singular Beast: Jews, Christians, and the Pig*, trans. Carol Volk (New York: Columbia University Press, 1997) (*La bête singulière: les juifs, les chrétiens, et le cochon* (Paris: Gallimard, 1994)).

31. On ethnographic practice (white ethnographers and black 'informants') see Robin D.G. Kelley, *Yo' Mama's Disfunktional! Fighting the Cultural Wars in Urban America* (Boston, MA: Beacon Press, 1997), pp. 17–23.

32. For Clifford Geertz's view of the current diversity of 'fieldwork' see his *Available Light: Anthropological Reflections on Philosophical Topics* (Princeton, NJ: Princeton University Press, 2000), chapter V, pp. 89–142.

33. *Memoirs of the Life of Dr John Shaw*, Surtees Society, no. 65.

34. On manipulation of encounters across cultural and ethnic lines see Robin G.D. Kelley, *Race Rebels: Culture, Poetics, and the Black Working Class* (New

York: The Free Press, 1994), p. 22, on the 'cult of true sambohood'. And on the perception of ethnographic interrogation held by an 'informant': 'I think this anthropology is just another way to call me a nigger', in John Langton Gwaltney, *Drylongso: A Self-Portrait of Black America* (New York: Random House, 1980), p. xix; for *Drylongso* as an attempt at a different type of cultural record, see pp. xxii–xxx. On the problem of 'historical' subjects without a voice see Jacques Rancière, *The Nights of Labour: The Workers' Dream in Nineteenth-Century France*, trans. John Drury (Philadelphia, PA: Temple University Press, 1989) (*La nuit des proletaires* (Paris: Hachette, 1981)).

35. See the collected essays in Marshall Sahlins, *Culture in Practice: Selected Essays* (New York: Zone Books, 2000); *How 'Natives' Think, about Captain Cook, for Example* (Chicago, IL, and London: University of Chicago Press, 1995), which is an answer to Gananath Obeyesekereh, *The Apotheosis of Captain Cook: European Mythmaking in the Pacific* (Princeton, NJ: Princeton University Press, 1992).

36. See for example Barbara H. Rosenwein (ed.), *Anger's Past: The Social Histories of an Emotion in the Middle Ages* (Ithaca, NY: Cornell University Press, 1998). For a pioneering collection see Hans Medick and David W. Sabean (eds), *Interest and Emotion: Essays on the Study of Family and Kinship* (Cambridge: Cambridge University Press, 1984).

37. James C. Scott, *Domination and the Arts of Resistance: Hidden Transcripts* (New Haven, CT: Yale University Press, 1990); Sherry B. Ortner, 'Resistance and the Problem of Ethnographic Refusal', *Comparative Studies in Society and History*, vol. XXXVII (1995), pp. 173–93.

38. Rosalind O'Hanlon (trans. and ed.), *A Comparison between Women and Men: Tarabai Shinde and the Critique of Gender Relations in Colonial India* (Madras: Oxford University Press, 1994).

39. Catherine Gallagher and Stephen Greenblatt (eds), *Practicing New Historicism* (Chicago, IL: University of Chicago Press, 2000), Introduction on pp. 1–19; see also Stephen Greenblatt, 'The Touch of the Real', in Ortner, *The Fate of Culture*, pp. 14–29.

40. Paul Strohm, *England's Empty Throne: Usurpation and the Language of Legitimation, 1399–1422* (New Haven, CN: Yale University Press, 1998).

41. Paul Strohm, 'Chaucer's Lollard Joke: History, and the Textual Unconscious', *Studies in the Age of Chaucer*, vol. XVII (1995), pp. 34–42.

42. Roger Chartier, 'Culture as Appropriation: Popular Cultural Uses in Early Modern France', in S.L. Kaplan (ed.), *Understanding Popular Culture: Europe from the Middle Ages to the Nineteenth Century New Babylon: Studies in the Social Sciences 40* (Berlin and New York: Mouton, 1984), pp. 229–53.

43. This possibility was hinted at in John Toews, 'Intellectual History after the Linguistic Turn: The Autonomy of Meaning and Irreducibility of Experience', *American Historical Review*, vol. XCII (1987), pp. 879–907, at pp. 882–3.

6
What is Gender History Now?*

Alice Kessler-Harris

I begin at the beginning – the very beginning. Carr precedes his text with an epigram from Jane Austen's *Northanger Abbey*. The quotation is from the novel's heroine, Catherine Morland, who is responding to a challenge about why she does not read history: 'I often think it odd that it should be so dull for a great deal of it must be invention.'[1] Carr hopes of course to make the point that invention is the heart of the historian's project. But I'm not the first person to point out that Catherine Morland wants to say something more.[2] Here's the sentence in its entirety. 'The quarrels of popes and kings,' says Miss Morland, 'with wars or pestilences in every page; the men all so good for nothing, and hardly any women at all – it is very tiresome: and yet I often think it odd that it should be so dull for a great deal of it must be invention.'

What turns history into a 'torment' for little girls and boys,[3] as Catherine Morland later describes it, is the lack of realistic motive, its absence starkly rendered by the invisibility of women in the inventions (or interventions) of historians. Carr may well have understood the hidden text, though he did not cite it. It's not surprising, given what we now know of Carr's personal biography, including his apparently shameless exploitation of at least one wife as a researcher, that Carr overlooked the women.[4] Still, he might well have concurred that in the absence of women, the men appear as good for nothing, their actions reduced to quarrels based on ignoble self-interest. It's not too great a stretch to imagine that if Carr were alive today, he would recognize that his arguments made room for a gendered perspective – one that invokes the social relations of the sexes – as a source of change and, yes, power.

Indeed, *What is History?* lends itself to an argument for gender as a way of seeing without which we deprive ourselves of an important analytic tool and handicap ourselves with partial blindness. In that respect it is quite different from the other categories represented in this volume. While cultural, political and religious history can be construed broadly enough to incorporate great portions of the historical narrative, gender is both informed by and enriches every branch of the historical enterprise, providing the kind of synthetic framework we have recently lacked.

I

My argument is predicated on a reading of Carr that is forty years old and originates in the United States. My generation of graduate students in the US cut their teeth on E.H. Carr. For many of us who were in training in the 1960s, Carr offered a way out of the empirically based objectivism that had been the hallmark of historical studies till then, attacking full throttle its claims to truth. In the postmodern world, my defence will seem somewhat old-fashioned, as will my argument that a gendered history appropriately extends Carr's paradigm, for my defence is rooted not in the theoretical abstractions of language and the nature of experience, but in the traditional phraseology of power and politics. What we liked about Carr in the US of the 1960s was that, unlike R.G. Collingwood, who came perilously close to mounting the relativist barricade, Carr thought there was something to objectivity. His mission was not to persuade us to eschew facts, nor to denigrate their material reality, but to treat them with a sceptical eye; to recognize, as he put it, that 'by and large the historian will get the kinds of facts he wants'. Facts, he told us, in a memorable passage, were not like fish on a fishmonger's slab – but like fish swimming about in the ocean.[5] In that vein, objectivity could be measured not by whether a historian 'gets his facts right, but by whether he chooses the right facts'.[6]

By what standards would he measure those choices? We resonated to the voice that acknowledged the complexity of decision-making. In Carr's view, choices would be made by individuals who necessarily operated in the context of their times. The objective historian had both the respon-sibility and the capacity to recognize and to rise above 'the limited vision of his own situation in society and in history'.[7] The historian's bias, he told our eager ears, would be 'judged by the hypotheses he adopts'.[8] Carr's argument for a history steeped in the values and standpoints (yes, he used that word even then) of the historian with self-knowledge gave heart to the first generation of what in the US is often called radical history. His willingness to label as parochial the writing of a history centred in Britain and written through Western eyes opened the shutters that restricted our vision, revealing some of the canonical texts as the products of particular social perspectives. His identification of modern history as the moment when 'more and more people emerge into social and political consciousness'[9] legitimized our search for the voices of immigrants, outsiders, women and blacks. My generation – anti-war activists, critics of authority, rebels of all kinds – responded to his call for self-examination. For some of us (I think it fair to say that most American history graduate students in the 1960s were unfamiliar with Marx) reading Carr was our first encounter with a serious alternative framework.

My early acquaintance with Carr wasn't about gender. I don't think I then noticed how resolutely he separated the moral and the private from the public, and refused to see the political meanings of the sexual; how determinedly he locked himself into a position that identified personal decisions with the realm of private morality and therefore no business of the historian.[10] All the while I was reading Carr, I was writing a dissertation about New York's immigrant labour movement in the 1890s. Believing that labour was about men, I systematically discarded any information about women that I came across. But Carr nevertheless legitimized projects like mine, which were then attempting to understand axes of power anew. *What is History?* encouraged us to renegotiate and honour our social identities as historians – recognizing in them the location from which we began to think. This was no small matter in the US where a new generation of historians faced the hostility of a profession deeply committed to its own standards of truth. In his often quoted 1963 presidential address to the American Historical Association, the distinguished colonialist Carl Bridenbaugh warned his professional colleagues that the future of the field lay in the hands of young faculty and apprentices who were the 'products of lower-middle class or foreign origins', and whose 'emotions not infrequently get in the way of historical reconstructions'.[11] In that context it isn't surprising that we cheered Carr's acknowledgement of the value-laden ground on which all history was written.

To a generation embroiled in a war in Vietnam and in winning civil rights for African-Americans, Carr's contention that history constituted a dialogue of the past, not with the present, but with the future came as something of a relief. It destroyed illusions about the interpretations of our predecessors and offered persuasive ammunition against accusations of present-mindedness and politicization. We had seen how unselfconscious claims to a value-free history lulled entire generations of Americans into wiping out the presence of Native Americans and Spanish settlers. Such claims cloaked the search for empire in the language of manifest destiny, encouraging historians to attribute all manner of acts (Western expansion, the civil war, economic imperialism) to a search for more perfect liberty at home and abroad. They allowed us to locate explanation in sectional struggles (the South versus the North, the frontier versus settled areas, or business versus reformers) instead of urging us to look further for root causes. As we sought a more critical vision, notions of class re-entered our vocabularies and a future less constrained by competitive individualism began to influence our interpretations of the meanings of hegemonic ideologies. Such responses to attacks on a value-free history were neither simple nor predictable. For example, some historians, influenced by the egalitarian hopes of the 1960s civil rights movement, turned to Southern patriarchal culture to explain slave culture; others turned to slave resistance.[12] Still, imagining the future as part of a continuing historical trajectory opened the possibility of examining the changing content of previously empty boxes (or sacks) labelled freedom, equality and liberty. But freedom for whom? Carr granted permission to ask.

Some of us (I count myself here) used the invitation to explore the history of workers and immigrant groups on their own terms. But it took a women's movement to alter our collective national goals sufficiently to include women among those for whom the future offered the promise of access to previously denied goals like equality, liberty and individual satisfaction. In light of that opportunity, historians of women have fished in some sections of the historical pond previously overlooked: they have amassed enough facts to render the promised dialogue long overdue. Our generation of historians knows much more abut women than our predecessors did. But that of course is not enough. If we choose to write about women (or, for that matter, about men as men) we recognize that men and women acknowledge and act on their gendered identities. We recover, recuperate and celebrate women and men for a purpose. If we choose to write out of a larger politics that imagines a more inclusionary polity – indeed out of a feminist politics – then that is exactly in line with what Carr envisioned. And when we move a step beyond inclusion to fragment the idea of 'women' into its multiple and sometimes contesting parts, we are not fragmenting history but opening the possibility for creating a larger explanatory pallette. We need the data we have recovered – but recovery marks only one phase of an enduring historical quest. The second and perhaps more enduring phase is to ensure that these facts achieve significance, filling up the empty sacks of those whose work seems far afield from women's history. This is the work of gender.

In the past three decades, historians of all kinds, like historians of women, have begun to incorporate the new facts to see if they add up to anything. As the chapters in this volume make clear, gendered questions abound, invading every sphere of political, social and economic history. They illuminate the workings of everyday politics; the ability of nations to engage the loyalty of their citizens, and the effect of racial strife on economic outcomes. We can no longer pretend to understand any historical moment (industrialization, urbanization, a strike won or lost, a sexual revolution) without including gender in the calculus of causes and explanations.

With the help of our newly caught fish/facts, and in dialogue with them, historians have created a new interpretive stance that enriches our view of the past, enabling us to construct a fuller portrait of historical change and to comprehend it more completely. Employing a complicated notion of gender, imbricated with race and class, historians have revealed it as an important axis of power. To be sure, historians of gender have taken two sometimes inconsistent views of power. On the one hand, historians have insisted that attention to gender fosters a new approach to the meaning of power, rooting it not in a hierarchy that extends from top to bottom but rather in many different places. This group has utilized the insights of Michel Foucault to insist that power is exercised from multiple, diffuse and quotidian locations.[13] Their search for the influence of gender particularly reveals the impact of masculinity and ideas about manhood in sustaining the actions of union leaders, ordinary workers and family heads. At the same time, historians of women have claimed that gender is capable of shaping and restraining the coercive power of the state and its capacity to achieve and maintain economic domination. This is illustrated, for example, by the now widely accepted notion that the early twentieth-century welfare state was shaped by women's interventions.[14] Gender is, I want to make clear, not the only axis we need to understand, but one among the several (including class, ethnicity, political structures, ideology, economic institutions and, more recently, race) whose consequences are already the subjects of analysis. Gender is embedded in these axes, even as it remains analytically distinguishable.

In what follows, I will, briefly, examine four historically influential and interrelated arenas in which I think gender has helped to shape our conception of power. How, I ask, has gender affected our historical understanding of the formation of subjectivity or identity; class formation; state formation; and for lack of a better word, 'nation building' or the related processes of colonialization and empire creation? I proceed from the inside out.

II

Carr couldn't know, and didn't participate in, the great historian's debate of the modern era as to whether identity and human consciousness are formed in the social arena or in that of language and discourse.[15] At some level he would have been appalled by the post-structural project to destabilize, to find the conflicts within meaning and to reject the search for agency. But I suspect that his concern for the role of human consciousness in history would ultimately have brought him around for there is little doubt about the importance he assigned to both the position of the historian as interpreter and that of the historical actor as the object of investigation. On both counts, Carr was pretty blunt:

> Since Marx and Freud wrote, the historian has no excuse to think of himself as a detached individual standing outside society and outside history. This is the age of self-consciousness: the historian can and should know what he is doing.[16]

The focus of postmodern theory, not merely on identity, but on multiple identities, introduces gender into the formula for assessing consciousness, turning masculinity and femininity into the central tropes through which interpretation is rendered. In some respects, it matters little how far we are willing to push the theory. We need only to acknowledge that language matters; that concepts like manliness at once contain multiple meanings and are imbricated in such notions as 'the family' or 'the public' to see how gender deepens and complicates Carr's assertions. Whether it is constructed through language and discourse, the invention and deployment of symbol systems, or social and cultural positioning, the 'self' that participates in forming the world around us is gendered. The introduction of gender alters some of Carr's most powerful prescriptions. Imagine, for example, reacting through a gendered lens as Carr tells us that 'Modern man is to an unprecedented degree self-conscious, and therefore conscious of history.'[17]

Historians who take the subjective into account have already begun to ask about the political implications of the new facts they discover. I cite two obvious and brilliant examples: Anna Clark's *Struggle for the Breeches*, and Francesca Bray's *Technology and Gender* (a book about late Imperial China).[18] Each explores the relationship between language and the experience of political action. But there are many others that take different forms. Carolyn Steedman delves into the centrality of ideologies of masculinity and femininity not as binary oppositions, but as continuums moulded by historical circumstances, most especially those of class.[19] Sally Alexander and Catherine Hall have been influential on both sides of the Atlantic in exploring the way a racialized gender shapes world views and orders relations within economic institutions.[20] Laura Engelstein and Kathleen Brown have demonstrated how the organization of gender participates in modelling hierarchy, familiarizing individuals with authoritarian patterns of organization and sustaining anti-egalitarian regimes.[21]

The literature of the Western world in the nineteenth century offers no more persuasive example of the reciprocally confirming relationships between consciousness and action than those that emerge from, and are contained by, various kinds of domestic ideology. Taken as a prescriptive model, the injunction to domesticity in its many different forms has played a major role in ordering the world, restraining and shaping the individual expectations of men and women, and provoking both discontent and acquiescence by turns. This is, as Mary Poovey puts it, the ideological work of gender.[22] In that form, it has (as Joy Parr, Jane Lewis and others note) sometimes regulated behaviour, promoting expectations of the breadwinner male and the dependent female.[23] But it has also provoked rebellion as women have sought increasing liberty.

In a second guise, domesticity has provided a powerful and unspoken interpretive framework for historians. Steeped in a seemingly natural gendered order, historians have persistently imposed their own vision of domesticity on the behaviour they seek to analyse: projecting levels of human satisfaction in line with their own images of appropriate domestic arrangements, or describing as sources of action moments that might cause them discontent. We are all familiar, for example, with the patently inaccurate yet, until recently, widely held notions that women have not 'worked' and men have supported families. For years this idea led census takers and historians to overlook women's economic contributions and social reformers to suggest policies that undermined women's efforts to support families. Yet this insertion of the observer's self into the historical record was rendered invisible because the assumptions on which it was based were so commonly shared. In this respect, domestic ideology does double work, inflecting the consciousness of the observer even as it shapes the experience of the historical subject.

Our need to organize the world into public and private spheres reflects a similarly subjective affirmation of our expectations. Shucking that binary has proved terribly difficult, but when we do, we are enabled to see the moments in which households function in an undivided continuum. Household organization can shape and even speed up the proto-industrialization process when women's participation in certain forms of work is encouraged. It can also restrain the industrialization process, for example, when women are sequestered. Scepticism about the ideological quality of the public/private division has yielded a search for new facts that promise to put an end to the dichotomy. In the hands of historians like Earl Lewis and Bonnie Smith, these new facts reveal the ways that men develop identity out of family, and women out of wage work. They demonstrate men's attachment to what Lewis calls the homespace, even as they show women in the public arena of marketplace, workshop, common or church.[24] When we watch public and private dissolve into each other, we are led to ask questions about the political purposes and subjective self-interest inherent in constructing oppositional spheres, like family and employment, or home and politics, in tension with each other. What nexus of power does such restricted vision sustain?

To move on to the second point, there can no longer be much doubt that gender – how the social relations of the sexes are ordered at particular moments in time – participates in class formation. By this I do not mean that either men or women constituted a 'class' in the terms of the 1970s debate on this issue, but rather that gender shares some of the properties of class.[25] Though it is no longer fashionable to refer to class as a central explanatory category, few historians would deny the salience of the social relations of production under particular circumstances and in conjunction with elements like culture, race and ethnicity. Like class, gender is a process, changing over time and in relation to historical circumstance; like class it is ideational and normative, conditioning expectations of individual futures and views of the world.

Because gender is fluid, its participation varies with historical circumstance. Because it constitutes the ground on which identity is built and consciousness formed, it may be more pervasive than class, and is certainly a constitutive element of it. We have learned from the work of Martha Howell and from that of Leonore Davidoff and Catherine Hall, among others, that women and men are differentially implicated in capital formation within families: that the social relations of the sexes (including women's participation in enterprises and their command of skills like reading and weaving in China) affects the pace as well as the manner in which households are established and capital is accumulated.[26] We have also learned that industrial revolutions (which generally depended on the use of female as well as male labour in factories) required renegotiating familial relationships and support systems in order to sustain the economic aspirations of individuals and communities.

More subtly, reframing the economic possibilities of women and men demanded new ideological frameworks. Kathleen Canning has beautifully demonstrated the complexity of this process for nineteenth-century Germany where the transformation of textile manufacturing required men to sever the bonds of manhood to craft and pride in production, and tie them instead to the support of dependants. The shift promoted a new domestic ideology that discouraged the wage labour of married women and fostered male solidarity across class lines. One result was to undermine the development of a class 'for itself'. As the transformation produced a masculinity vested in breadwinning, it sacrificed shopfloor struggles for the sake of job security and expanded incomes.[27]

In the US, where men tied their self-esteem to notions of liberty and freedom vested in the ideal of economic self-sufficiency, fear of competition with women often underlined gendered negotiations. Many nineteenth-century working men (as Mary Ann Clawson notes) developed solidarity and achieved political voice first through craft-related brotherhoods and later through unions; others did so in gender-segregated public houses.[28] And while unmarried women, and some married women as well, utilized economic opportunity to move further towards autonomy and independence, many more tried to make their political voices felt through demands for equal rights.[29] In some instances what should have been a class consciousness unifying women and men in a shared search for economic influence turned instead into a struggle across gender lines as men tried to eliminate women from wage work.[30] Lacking property in their own labour and without a recognized voice in the public arena, women's demands for gender equality could sometimes precede their concern for a diminution of class inequalities.

Within the past decade, historians have begun to explore how masculine culture can divide male workers. I do not mean by this merely the exclusion of women. We have known for some time that everywhere, men attempted to preserve stable images of manhood (as well as jobs) by excluding women from guilds, trade unions, crafts and jobs. Rather, I point to divisions among men based on racial/ethnic stereotypes and the kinds of work performed. In the US Joshua Freeman and Stephen Meyer write about the division as between respectable and rough work.[31] But other divisions (between white- and blue-collar work, for example, are possible). Manly respectable work, arising from craft traditions, was associated with pride, skill and economic security. Those engaged in rough work (the sphere of unskilled labourers) associated manliness with physical strength, courage in the face of dangerous conditions, sexuality and bravado. Each participates in constructing a different world view. Respectable work is closely tied to domesticity, for example, and may well participate in constructing and defending a collective gender identity that fosters restrictions on female labour even as it attempts to reserve the sphere of wage work to men.[32]

Masculinity, as we now know, has been at the core of class formation as well as of workers' resistance, within the workplace. It has also fostered conflicting class loyalties in the political arena. In very different venues Barbara Taylor and Liz Faue, among others, have demonstrated the ways in which male domination (including the iconography and language of organization) has inhibited or encouraged working-class identity by turns.[33] But masculinity is complicated by its racial component. Joe Trotter, Tera Hunter and Glenda Gilmore have revealed how race conspired with gender to create class cleavages.[34] The point is that our new facts (a generation ago, we didn't have the work of Theresa Liu, Barbara Hanawalt, Merry Wiesner, Louise Tilly, and dozens of others) enable us to see how economic transformations are everywhere built on a continuing negotiation of family and household structure and ideologies of manliness and womanliness.[35] In light of our new facts we might be tempted once again to ask Werner Sombart's question, 'Why is there no socialism in America?', for surely we have enough evidence now to assert that at least part of the answer has to lie in the powerful shaping force of gender and racial antagonisms.

III

Moving now to the third point, we've learned something about how gender participates in shoring up state power – indeed, is constitutive of it – and thus contributes to state formation. In terms of what one might call formal politics, women have exerted less influence over the years than men, though, as Susan Pedersen's chapter in this collection argues, issues of manliness formed part of the liberal political agenda of Gladstone's Britain, as they did of Jacksonian America and, in a contrary sense, of revolutionary America. And yet the particular influence of women is not absent during such great moments as the French Revolution of 1789. Women probably precipitated the crisis that ultimately brought Louis and Marie Antoinette back to Paris; their demands to speak publicly, for representation and voice, exposed the

claims to a mythical frontier, rather than its access to vast
of land, sanctioned male struggles towards upward mobility
etitive success.[49] A gendered lens reveals how the individualist
obscured the collective defence and household cooperation
y ensured the survival of individuals and families.

IV

gender history now? It is a way of looking at the past that
ur vision. Using the insights and methods of the postmodern
ot its rejection of the material), it facilitates the exploration of
age and ideology in which behaviour rests. Gender history
e evolving and racialized social relations of the sexes with
anatomy tropes to produce a fuller and richer comprehension
subjective experience that translates ideology into action and
uences for communities, nations and empires. To achieve this
tory, we need facts about women and men as men: we need
history as well as a history of men.
guess that Catherine Morland would not find gender history
less a 'torment'. Her brothers would certainly discover that
s a breadth of explanatory power capable of challenging
interpretations of nation building, national politics and class
In that sense, it fully satisfies Edward Hallett Carr's demand
arochial history. I think he would have been pleased.

references

anks to Charles Budd (Pete) Forcey, who first introduced me to
r.
tation is from Jane Austen, *Northanger Abbey* (London: Penguin, 1995
p. 97.
example, Olwen Hufton, *The Prospect Before Her: A History of Women
rn Europe*, Vol. I (London: HarperCollins, 1995), p. 1.
Northanger Abbey, p. 98.
n Haslam, *The Vices of Integrity: E.H. Carr, 1892–1982* (London: Verso,

Hallett Carr, *What is History?* (New York: Alfred Knopf, 1962), p. 26.
163.

77.
199.
. 96–7.

contradiction in an ideology that espoused the rights of man and yet
insisted that women were not eligible to share those rights.[36]

The economic/ideological nexus is clearer. Faced with a crisis in social
order brought on by rampant industrialization, most nineteenth-century
Western European states tried to shore up their own foundations by
strengthening the walls of the traditional household, and particularly
by paying attention to the male household head's capacity to sustain a
sense of himself as breadwinner. They did this in many ways but chiefly
by regulating the behaviour of family members towards each other, and
policing the boundaries between sexual desire and social behaviour.

To enforce standards for working-class morality, states resorted to a
variety of rules and laws that, for example, regulated the number and
kinds of sexual partners available to men and women; provided
guidelines for disciplining wives; forbade women from withholding
sexual services, and determined the family domicile. Children were held
hostage in this process: their well-being, education, place of residence
and even their legitimacy were governed by parental adherence to new
rules.[37] Married women were denied certain kinds of jobs or entirely
forbidden to earn wages.

States that relied on the labour of women to meet national production
goals resolved the tension between home and family life by regulating
female labour first to accommodate prescriptive ideologies of domesticity
and then to satisfy the needs of male family heads and of children. We
can find these regulations in societies as far apart as Lowell,
Massachusetts, and Meiji Japan. And we can draw parallels between the
housing rules that governed female workers in the silk mills of twentieth-
century Shanghai and those that regulated the families of Calcutta jute
mill operatives.[38] In the twentieth century, protective labour laws became
the preferred vehicle for legitimizing female labour; and ultimately
maternity (and more recently parental) benefits served to affirm the
sexual division of labour.[39] While women's bodies were restrained by
laws that imposed limited hours and maternity leaves, many states
refused to compensate female workers for their lost wages and, at least
until the Second World War, most provided men with differential
benefits and particular messages about family support. These are the
wages of gender.

Mechanisms for regulating the distribution of female labour between
household and family were legion, as were those requiring male support
for the household. Depending on the political and social climate, states
chose to discourage or encourage married women's work by providing or
subsidizing child care or refusing to do so. Some, like France, created

well-developed creches for infants; others, like the US, negated the needs of married women for child care except when it was necessary to serve national needs. Most states denied women who engaged in paid labour the benefits (such as unemployment insurance and seniority rights) routinely granted to men. These differential treatments played a role in every family's decision-making possibilities. A few, like Japan, built powerful economies by appealing to women's patriotic instincts. In the US and elsewhere gender served to regulate the interaction of races as well. Vagrancy laws, for example, dealt with men and women, black and white, in quite different ways. For many Southern black women, they enforced wage work even for those who might have preferred to work in their own families. By making distinctions among women to be regulated, states could and did affirm hierarchies of class and colour. For example, protective labour legislation for women was available only to a small proportion of American women workers.[40] Nation building relied on the ideological as well as the practical statements invested in these strategies.

In many countries seemingly natural gendered understandings legitimized social policies that shored up the loyalties of rebellious peoples. The welfare state differed from place to place, but it seems everywhere to have been built on gendered assumptions and understandings, and designed to maintain particular kinds of family structures. Old age pensions and unemployment insurance in Britain paid attention to family size and the sex of family heads; health insurance and housing policies in Germany were designed to promote women's home roles; changing tax laws and aid to the families of dependent children in the US influenced how very ordinary people thought about marriage and how and when families were formed. By extending the reach of the state into the most intimate areas of personal life, social benefits turned the exercise of gendered behaviour into measures of responsible citizenship.[41]

Turning to our fourth category, it has become impossible to explain the construction and maintenance of nation and empire, as well as the nature of resistance to it, without attention to particular moral codes. Gender participates in at least two modes of analysis: the first postmodern and the second having to do with Enlightenment notions of rights and progress. The postmodern appears most often in efforts to find and interrogate the voices of the subaltern.[42] Attention to these diverse voices has fragmented moral rationales of purpose central to empire building and disrupted the once unified position of the observer. It has placed into the historical equation a new set of facts that remove the exploration of empire from a Euro-centred location to one that focuses on the intersection of colonizer and colonized.

This work suggests that the concepts
themselves shaped by particular forms of s
bounded domestic arrangements. They
literal images meant to reinforce sexual
representation of empire figures in expla
national loyalties in and through deeply r
These include particular images of famil
with the regulation of sexuality.[43] Somet
Victorian values of domestic hierarchy)
formal legislation, shifting sexual boun
patterns of behaviour meant to sharply
the colonizer and thus to provide a ratio
miscegenation laws, sexual purity mov
prostitution – all take their place in the a

In the colonial setting, the work of An
has demonstrated how much the succes
on maintaining a special kind of hetero:
puts it, 'changes in household organizati
and gender-specific control of resources s
Gender constructed then sustained partic
out notions of the passionless European
against the sexual conquest of colonized
ization of colonized men. Colonial powe
further disrupted the lives of people on bo
messages of sexual power through famil
them with military prowess.[46]

In the 'internal colonization' that chai
to the west, gender seems to have playec
here a revaluation of the Enlightenment l
has served the historian well. The solid
different class and ethnic backgrounds f
of struggle that pitted civilization against s
violence that constructed 'white' men a:
Mexicans.[47] Prevailing imagery, which d
empty of women (here equally exclu
householders, and respectable white wor
of masculinity that facilitated conques
resources like gold in the name of extendir
the putative absence of women helped t
political power. It also enabled the spread
of exceptionalism. For example, as A:

America
stretche
and con
mystiqu
that fina

So what
expands
(though
the lang
mingles
other ex
of both
the cons
kind of
a wome

I wou
dull, m
it posse
traditio
formati
for a no

Notes

* Wit
E.H
1. The
[18
2. See
in \
3. Aus
4. Jon
199
5. Edv
6. Ibi
7. Ibi
8. Ibi
9. Ibi
10. Ibi

11. Carl Bridenbaugh, 'The Great Mutation', *American Historical Review*, vol. LXVIII (January, 1963), pp. 322–3.
12. Herbert G. Gutman, *The Black Family in Slavery and Freedom, 1750–1925* (New York: Pantheon, 1976); Eugene D. Genovese, *Roll, Jordan, Roll: The World the Slaves Made* (New York: Vintage, 1976); Nathan Irvin Huggins, *Black Odyssey: The Afro-American Ordeal in Slavery* (New York: Pantheon, 1977).
13. Michel Foucault, *Discipline and Punish: The Birth of the Prison* (New York: Pantheon, 1977).
14. For access to this literature see Sonya Michel and Seth Koven, 'Womanly Duties: Maternalist Politics and the Origins of Welfare States in France, Germany, Great Britain, and the United States, 1880–1920', *American Historical Review*, vol. 95 (October, 1990), pp. 1076–108; and see Linda Gordon (ed.), *Women, the State and Welfare* (Madison, WI: University of Wisconsin Press, 1990); Robyn Muncy, *Creating a Female Dominion in American Reform, 1890–1935* (New York: Oxford University Press, 1991); and Jane Lewis (ed.), *Women's Welfare Women's Rights* (London: Croom Helm, 1983).
15. The most persuasive argument for subjectivity is in Joan Wallach Scott, *Gender and the Politics of History* (New York: Columbia University Press, 1988). For other facets of the debate see especially Victoria E. Bonnell and Lynn Hunt (eds), *Beyond the Cultural Turn: New Directions in the Study of Society and Culture* (Berkeley, CA: University of California Press, 1999); Bryan Palmer, *Descent into Discourse: The Reification of Language and the Writing of Social History* (Philadelphia, PA: Temple University Press, 1990); Patrick Joyce, *Visions of the People* (Cambridge: Cambridge University Press, 1991).
16. Carr, *What is History?*, p. 186.
17. Ibid., p. 129.
18. Anna Clark, *The Struggle for the Breeches: Gender and the Making of the British Working Class* (Berkeley, CA: University of California Press, 1995); Francesca Bray, *Technology and Gender: Fabrics of Power in Late Imperial China* (Berkeley, CA: University of California Press, 1997).
19. Carolyn Steedman, *Landscape for a Good Woman: A Story of Two Lives* (London: Virago, 1986).
20. Sally Alexander, *Becoming a Woman: And Other Essays in 19th and 20th Century Feminist History* (London: Virago, 1994); Catherine Hall, *White, Male and Middle Class: Explorations in Feminism and History* (New York: Routledge, 1988).
21. Laura Engelstein, *The Keys to Happiness, Sex and the Search for Modernity in fin de siecle Russia* (Ithaca, NY: Cornell University Press, 1992); Kathleen M. Brown, *Good Wives, Nasty Wenches, and Anxious Patriarchs: Gender, Race, and Power in Colonial Virginia* (Chapel Hill, NC: Institute of Early American History and Culture, Williamsburg, VA/University of North Carolina Press, 1996).
22. Mary Poovey, *Uneven Developments: The Ideological Work of Gender in Mid-Victorian England* (Chicago, IL: University of Chicago Press, 1988).
23. Joy Parr, *The Gender of Breadwinners: Women, Men, and Change in Two Industrial Towns, 1880–1950* (Toronto: University of Toronto Press, 1990); Jane Lewis (ed.), *Labour and Love: Women's Experience of Home and Family, 1850–1940* (New York: Blackwell, 1986); Mary P. Ryan, *Women in Public: Between Banners and Ballots, 1825–1880* (Baltimore, MD: Johns Hopkins University Press, 1990); Linda Kerber, 'Separate Spheres, Female Worlds, Woman's Place: The

Rhetoric of women's History,' *Journal of American History*, vol. 75 (1988), pp. 9–39.

24. Earl Lewis, *In Their Own Interests: Race, Class, and Power in Twentieth-Century Norfolk, Virginia* (Berkeley, CA: University of California Press, 1991); Bonnie G. Smith, *Ladies of the Leisure Class: The Bourgeoises of Northern France in the Nineteenth Century* (Princeton, NJ: Princeton University Press, 1981).

25. For access to the 1970s debate, see Wally Seccombe, 'Patriarchy Stabilized: The Construction of the Male Breadwinner Wage Norm in Nineteenth-Century Britain', *Social History*, vol. 11 (1986), pp. 53–76.

26. Martha C. Howell, *Women, Production, and Patriarchy in Late Medieval Cities* (Chicago, IL: University of Chicago Press, 1986); and her, *The Marriage Exchange: Property, Social Place, and Gender in Cities of the Low Countries, 1300–1550* (Chicago, IL: University of Chicago Press, 1998); Leonore Davidoff and Catherine Hall, *Family Fortunes: Men and Women of the English Middle Class: 1780–1850* (London: Hutchinson, 1987); Dorothy Ko, *Teachers of the Inner Chambers: Women and Culture in Seventeenth-Century China* (Stanford, CA: Stanford University Press, 1994).

27. For example, see Kathleen Canning, 'The Man Transformed into a Maiden? Languages of Grievance and the Politics of Class in Germany, 1850–1915', *International Labor and Working Class History*, vol. 49 (Spring, 1996), pp. 47–72. On the potential political implications of changing gender subjectivities, see Mary Blewett, 'Deference and Defiance: Labor Politics and the Meanings of Masculinity in the Mid-Nineteenth Century New England Textile Industry', *Gender and History*, vol. 5 (Autumn, 1993), pp. 398–415.

28. Mary Ann Clawson, *Constructing Brotherhood: Class, Gender, and Fraternalism* (Princeton, NJ: Princeton University Press, 1989).

29. Thomas Dublin, *Women at Work: The Transformation of Work and Community in Lowell, Massachusetts, 1826–1860* (New York: Columbia University Press, 1975); Suzanne Lebsock, *The Free Women of Petersburg: Status and Culture in a Southern Town, 1784–1860* (New York: W.W. Norton, 1984).

30. Mary H. Blewett, *Men, Women, and Work: Class, Gender, and Protest in the New England Shoe Industry, 1780–1910* (Urbana: University of Illinois Press, 1988).

31. Stephen Meyer, 'Work, Play, and Power: Masculine Culture on the Automotive Shop Floor, 1930–1960', in Roger Horowitz (ed.), *Boys and Their Toys: Masculinity, Class, and Technology in America* (New York: Routledge, 2001), pp. 13–32; Joshua Freeman, 'Hard Hats, Construction Workers, Manliness and the 1970 Pro-war Demonstrations', *Journal of Social History*, vol. 26 (1983), pp. 725–44; Sonya Rose, 'Respectable Men, Disorderly Others: The Language of Gender and the Lancashire Weavers' Strike of 1878', *Gender and History*, vol. 5 (1993), pp. 382–97.

32. For the use of ideas of masculinity to defend male workspaces, see especially Keith McClelland, 'Some Thoughts on Masculinity and the "Representative Artisan" in Britain, 1850–1915', *Gender and History*, vol. 1 (1989), pp. 164–77; and Ava Baron, 'Questions of Gender: Deskilling and Demasculinization in the US Printing Industry, 1830–1945', *Gender and History*, vol. 1 (1989), pp. 178–99. For the defence of female workspaces, see Judith Bennett, *Ale, Beer and Brewsters in England: Women's Work in a Changing World, 1300–1600* (New York: Oxford University Press, 1996); Katherine Sheldon (ed.),

Courtyards, Markets, City Streets: Urban Women in Africa (Boulder, CO: Westview Press, 1996).

33. Barbara Taylor, *Eve and the New Jerusalem: Socialism and Feminism in the Nineteenth Century* (New York: Pantheon, 1983); Elizabeth Faue, *Community of Suffering and Struggle: Women, Men, and the Labor Movement in Minneapolis, 1915–1945* (Chapel Hill, NC: University of North Carolina Press, 1991); Angela Woollacott, *On Her Their Lives Depend: Munitions Workers in the Great War* (Berkeley, CA: University of California Press, 1994).

34. Joe William Trotter, *Black Milwaukee: the Making of an Industrial Proletariat, 1915–45* (Urbana, IL: University of Illinois Press, 1985); Glenda Elizabeth Gilmore, *Gender and Jim Crow: Women and the Politics of White Supremacy in North Carolina, 1896–1920* (Chapel Hill, NC: University of North Carolina Press, 1996); Tera W. Hunter, *To 'Joy my Freedom: Southern Black Women's Lives and Labors after the Civil War* (Cambridge, MA: Harvard University Press, 1997).

35. Tessie P. Liu, *The Weaver's Knot: the Contradictions of Class Struggle and Family Solidarity in Western France, 1750–1914* (Ithaca, NY: Cornell University Press, 1994); Louise Tilly, *Politics and Class in Milan, 1881–1901* (New York: Oxford University Press, 1992); Barbara Hanawalt, *Of Good and Ill Repute: Gender and Social Control in Medieval England* (New York: Oxford University Press, 1998); Merry E. Wiesner, *Working Women in Renaissance Germany* (New Brunswick, NJ: Rutgers University Press, 1986).

36. See especially Joan Landes, *Women and the Public Sphere in the Age of the French Revolution* (Ithaca, NY: Cornell University Press, 1988); Olwen Hufton, *Women and the Limits of Citizenship in the French Revolution* (Toronto: University of Toronto Press, l992); Joan Wallach Scott, *Only Paradoxes to Offer* (Cambridge, MA: Harvard University Press, 1997).

37. Ellen Ross, *Love and Toil: Motherhood in Outcast London, 1870–1918* (New York: Oxford University Press, 1993); Anna Davin, *Growing up Poor: Home, School, and Street in London, 1870–1914* (London: Rivers Oram Press, 1996); Hendrik Hartog, *Man and Wife in America: A History* (Cambridge, MA: Harvard University Press, 2000).

38. Thomas Dublin, *Transforming Women's Work: New England Lives in the Industrial Revolution* (Ithaca, NY: Cornell University Press, 1994); E. Patricia Tsurumi, *Factory Girls: Women in the Thread Mills of Meiji Japan* (Princeton, NJ: Princeton University Press, 1990); Emily Honig, *Sisters and Strangers: Women in the Shanghai Cotton Mills, 1919–1949* (Stanford, CA: Stanford University Press, 1986); Leela Fernandez, *Producing Workers: The Politics of Gender and Class in the Calcutta Jute Mills* (Philadelphia, PA: University of Pennsylvania Press, 1997).

39. Ulla Wikander, Alice Kessler-Harris and Jane Lewis, *Protecting Women: Labor Legislation in Europe, Australia and the United States* (Urbana, IL: University of Illinois Press, 1995).

40. Linda Kerber, *No Constitutional Right to be Ladies: Women and the Obligations of Citizenship* (New York: Hill and Wang, 1998); Alice Kessler-Harris, *Out to Work: A History of Wage-Earning Women in the United States* (New York: Oxford University Press, 1982).

41. Susan Pedersen, *Family, Dependence, and the Origins of the Welfare State: Britain and France, 1914–1945* (New York: Cambridge University Press, 1993); Alice

Kessler-Harris, *In Pursuit of Equity: Women, Men and the Quest for Economic Citizenship in Twentieth Century America* (New York: Oxford University Press, 2001).

42. Partha Chatterjee, *Nationalist Thought and the Colonial World: A Derivative Discourse* (Minneapolis, MN: University of Minnesota Press, 1998); Spivak Gayatri Chakravorty, *In Other Worlds: Essays in Cultural Politics* (New York: Routledge, 1988).

43. Ann McClintock, *Gender, Nations and Post Colonial Perspectives* (Minneapolis, MN: University of Minnesota Press, 1997); Vron Ware, *Beyond the Pale: White Women, Racism and History* (London: Verso, 1992); Ida Blom, Karen Hagemann and Catherine Hall, *Gendered Nations: Nationalisms and Gender Order in the Long Nineteenth Century* (London: Berg, 2000).

44. For example, Peggy Pascoe, *Relations of Rescue: The Search for Female Moral Authority in the American West, 1874–1939* (New York: Oxford University Press, 1990); Judith Walkowitz, *Prostitution and Victorian Society: Women, Class and the State* (New York: Cambridge University Press, 1980).

45. Ann Laura Stoler, 'Carnal Knowledge and Imperial Power: Gender, Race, and Morality in Colonial Asia', in Joan Scott (ed.), *Feminism and History* (New York: Oxford University Press, 1996), p. 209, and Stoler, *Race and the Education of Desire: Foucault's History of Sexuality and the Colonial Order of Things* (Durham, NC: Duke University Press, 1995); Antoinette Burton, *Burdens of History: British Feminists, Indian Women, and Imperial Culture, 1865–1915* (Chapel Hill, NC: University of North Carolina Press, 1944).

46. Mrinalini Sinha, *Colonial Masculinity: The 'Manly Englishman' and the 'Effeminate Bengali' in the Late Nineteenth Century* (Manchester: Manchester University Press, 1995).

47. Ramon Gutierrez , *When Jesus Came the Corn Mothers Went Away: Marriage, Sexuality and Power in New Mexico* (Stanford, CA: Stanford University Press, 1991); George J. Sanchez, *Becoming Mexican: Ethnicity, Culture and Identity in Chicano Los Angeles: 1900–1945* (New York: Oxford, 1993).

48. Brian Roberts, *American Alchemy: the California Gold Rush and Middle-Class Culture* (Chapel Hill, NC: University of North Carolina, 1999).

49. Annette Kolodny, *The Land Before Her: Fantasy and Experience of the American Frontiers, 1630–1860* (Chapel Hill, NC: University of North Carolina, 1984).

7
What is Intellectual History Now?

Annabel Brett

It is always difficult to explain what one does for a living; still more so when one is asked in so crisp a manner, and with such apparent expectation of definitive response, as in the question 'What is intellectual history now?' I cannot hope to be comprehensive, and my answer will necessarily reflect my own particular specialism and interests. However, I shall attempt to be at least articulate in my reply; and I shall begin by saying that the question seems to me to involve in fact two questions: one, 'What is intellectual history *now*?' (as opposed to then); and two, 'What is *intellectual* history now?' (as opposed to any other kind of history). As we shall see, these two questions cannot be disentangled; for the very same history of intellectual history over the past few decades which has seen such a reinvigoration of the field has at the same time brought into question the distinctive boundaries of that field.

One might, indeed, be happy with a blurring of the distinction between intellectual history and other forms of history. One very distinguished intellectual historian, William J. Bouwsma, recently urged that we prefer the term 'cultural history' over 'intellectual history', in that the latter seems to suggest the existence of some high thing, the 'intellect' or 'intellectual activity', set over and above the baser aspects of living – and thus of an outstanding value – the study of which is itself an exalted intellectual pursuit done only by serious intellectuals. Whereas, he points out, thought or intellectual activity is involved at many levels of human individual and social life, and so it is impossible to skim off an 'intellectual' history of 'ideas' from a broader history of culture.[1] So: intellectual history or sociocultural history? – the question

113

has been posed before;[2] but I am not convinced that one should answer it by submerging the identity of the former in the all-enveloping waters of the latter, nor by acquiescing (at least entirely) in formulations such as 'the "new" intellectual-cultural history'.[3] We may admit that intellectual history, taken pure and *per se*, might have something of an image problem, at least among fellow historians: nothing is more familiar than the claim of some of our colleagues that we study only a limited range of 'high' texts, nor their irony when they tell us that they, unlike us, are not clever enough to do the history of thought and therefore content themselves with more humble enquiries. But I think it is possible to deflect these criticisms while still insisting on the distinctive character of intellectual history: not as some disembodied metahistory of thought, but as a discipline with distinctive *concerns* of its own. For as I shall hope to show, there is a sense in which the history of thought cannot avoid a 'thoughtful' – or, let us say, philosophical – appreciation of its object; and thus intellectual *history* must be in some sense *intellectual* history. I shall try to defend this idea at the end.

Meanwhile, let us address the first of my questions – 'What is intellectual history *now*?' – and start with the point that intellectual history has come a long way from the isolated study of the 'great ideas' of 'great thinkers': that is, a history of human thought or thinking *as distinct from* human action or doings.[4] This sort of history took thinking out of the teleology of individual human agents and generated a history of ideas with a tendency to a teleology all their own. This history had a certain grandeur, but it was unclear in what dimension and in what time these ideas were supposed to exist – unless one were unafraid to posit the timeless present of their Platonic originals; and further problems accordingly came in mapping this story of ideas back onto human story or history in general. On the one hand, a teleology of ideas tended to support a conception of a teleology of history itself. We can see this very plainly in Carr's sixth lecture on 'What is History?' entitled 'The Widening Horizon'. Having had little to say about intellectual history up to this point, he tells us here – in an extraordinary neo-Hegelian flight – that the pivotal figures in the history of modern man are Descartes, Rousseau, Hegel, Marx and Freud, viewed as innovating in the self-consciousness of reason and thereby innovating in history.[5] But, on the other hand, it is unclear whether Carr wants to say that these 'great thinkers' actually moved history on themselves, or whether they are symptomatic of a history which is moving on anyway. Thus the history of modern man is said to 'begin' with Descartes, but Hegel and Marx are the 'representative thinkers' of a transition from the eighteenth century to the modern world.

The work of R.G. Collingwood, about whom Carr had such mixed feelings in his first lecture on 'What is History?', played an important role, at least within the Anglophone historiographical tradition, in the development of a different way of involving human thought in human history. Heir to another Hegelianism through the British idealist tradition, drawing on T.H. Green and F.H. Bradley, Collingwood famously insisted that all history is the history of thought, thus confounding any supposed distinction between the history of thought and the history of deeds.[6] For Collingwood, we cannot understand any human action or production without an understanding of the thought involved in it, and so we cannot write any history which is not a work of interpretation. It is this that alarmed Carr, of course, since it seemed to tip the balance of history too far in the direction of interpretation and consequently to lose that constructive equilibrium with facts which, Carr supposed, was of the essence of history.[7] From the point of view of intellectual history, however, we ought to notice the converse effect; that thought, equally, becomes involved in action and production and consequently in the historical time of historical agents.

We do not, therefore, have to think of intellectual activity as somehow 'above' the rest of human activity in the way that the head is above the body. The basic understanding of thought as involved in action and production has been with us for a long time. None the less, Bouwsma is right to the extent that the way we figure this involvement – the whole way in which we think about human thought – has changed enormously over the decades since Carr took issue with Collingwood. Speaking very roughly, we might identify two major trajectories of that change: one is through the study of language or discourse and its relation to human action and agency; the other is through our increasingly complex conception of the manifold ways in which human beings represent their world and themselves to themselves and to others, and in which these representations inform and are informed by practice. Although originating from diverse historiographical traditions, these two trajectories are not mutually independent, as we shall see. In particular, questions of textuality and its limits have come to play an important role in both.

I

So let me begin with the question of the *language* which had traditionally been taken to 'embody' or to 'express' the thoughts or ideas of thinkers.

This concern was addressed in the early 1960s by a group of scholars working on the history of political thought, who have come to be known collectively as the 'Cambridge School', investigating the relationship between language, thought, agency and time. One direction, explored particularly by Quentin Skinner, took advantage of work which was being done in linguistic theory in the 1950s and 1960s by John Austin and John Searle.[8] Austin, in *How to Do Things with Words*,[9] developed and elaborated by Searle in *Speech Acts*,[10] argued that the function of words is not limited to saying how things are, that is, to an indicative or propositional mode (the 'locutionary' dimension); nor, correspondingly, is making sense of words limited to establishing propositional meaning. Rather, beyond simply saying things, words can in specific contexts be used to *do* things. That is, the speaking is or can be a doing, an action in itself: and thus beyond the 'locutionary' dimension of words, we have to recognize both an 'illocutionary' dimension and a 'perlocutionary' dimension. The 'illocutionary' dimension is what a speaker is doing *in* using certain specific words. The 'perlocutionary' dimension is what a speaker is doing *through* or *by* using specific words. Thus a perlocutionary act, by definition, surpasses or goes beyond the text. But an illocutionary act, also identified by Searle and by Skinner with the notion of an author's *intention* in writing or saying certain words, is contained within the text itself.[11] It is the 'point' of the act (text) from the perspective of the author.[12] This kind of intentionality, Skinner postulated, is recoverable in reading. It contrasts with an author's putative intention *to*, which stands outside the text as part of a psychological portrait and which may well be irrecoverable.

Identification or recovery of a particular utterance as a particular illocutionary act depends on an awareness of its particular speech situation or *context*. We can only know what an author was *doing* in writing a particular text if we know the circumstances of that doing. The result was a method which argues that to understand texts for the specific speech acts that they are, we need to understand the historical context in which they were uttered. As I shall describe in more detail later, 'context' can be multidimensional: a specific political situation, a social or cultural milieu, an institutional context like a courtroom. For our analysis at present, however, what we are concerned with is the historical *linguistic* context (which may be implicated in diverse ways in the other types of context I have mentioned) – what other people were *saying* at the time and the conventions governing that saying. In the background to this idea, in addition to the work of Austin and Searle, stands the work of the later Wittgenstein and his notion, elaborated in the *Philosophical*

Investigations, of the 'language game'.[13] This is the idea that language can be seen as a game governed by certain rules and conventions. These rules dictate what counts as a valid linguistic move and what does not, which is the same as dictating what makes sense and what does not. Without a knowledge of the game and its conventions, particular linguistic acts are completely meaningless (we might imagine not knowing anything about cricket and trying to make sense of the actions of both players and spectators) because we cannot grasp the illocutionary dimension of a text or what the author *intended to do* in writing that text: what was the *point* of the text, in plainer language. Its full sense eludes us.

As will now be clear, one of the fundamental assumptions of intellectual history as a history of utterances within a language (understood as a language game) is that a particular piece of language is no longer seen as the *expression* of thought. The old intellectual history as a history of ideas carried the implication that the idea stood independently of the words that expressed it, such that it could have been expressed in different words, another book. It made the relation of the ideas to the language and the book contingent. Intellectual history as a history of language in use instead sees language usage as constitutive of thought: to use words in a particular way within a particular linguistic horizon just *is* to 'think'. There is no thought behind the words, that is, which can have a history of its own independent of the historically specific activity of language users. This has led some of its practitioners to reject an intellectual history not only in the sense of a history of ideas, but even in the sense of a history of concepts, the German *Begriffsgeschichte*.[14] How someone conceives of something is what linguistic connections and moves they make – no more. There is no supra-linguistic 'concept' available in some abstract dimension for the historian's attention.

Thus a key element of intellectual history practised in this way will be the recovery of past 'ways of speaking', which is a precondition for the adequate characterization of such linguistic moves. The idea of intellectual history as the recovery of specific language games – in other words, the discursive context – is perhaps more associated with the work of J.G.A. Pocock, although the commitment is common to both Pocock and Skinner.[15] When intellectual historians talk of a 'language' in this way, they are not primarily referring to the natural languages – French, English, Latin, and so on – although the existence of different natural languages is undoubtedly an important consideration, as is the history of the practice of translation. Rather, what they are concerned with is the different ways of talking or modes of discourse, what we might call idioms or rhetorics, within natural languages. Although Skinner and Pocock have worked mainly on languages of political thought, the notion can be extended fruitfully to modes of discourse in other domains; for example, natural science or theology. We reconstruct these idioms in the past from groups of texts which all rely on the same standardized formulae and commonplaces; which share the same grammar, vocabulary and rhetoric. In this way we might identify the *language of natural rights*, the *language of Aristotelian science*, and so on.[16] Although this approach is primarily concerned with texts, it does not exclude certain visual vocabularies: the iconography of a certain figure, such as Justice or Fortune, can be treated as part of the range of reference of the term within a particular language or rhetoric; conversely, texts can be used to eludicate iconography.[17]

Languages or discourses conceived in this way are *not* limited to elite productions, a few 'great texts'. The great texts are written in idioms or rhetorics which may be shared with many not-so-great texts of the most varied provenance: occasional pamphlets, cheap novels, newspapers – they are all grist to the intellectual historian's mill. For although the 'great texts' may and will always fascinate, they did not invent the languages in which they speak (albeit they may move them on or subvert them in some way), and hence making sense of what they are about can never be limited to their study alone. Reconstructing those languages involves intellectual historians in other areas of history, political, social or cultural, which form the milieu or the *context* within which that language was deployed. Historians may also – depending on their focus – need to investigate the more minute context of a particular event or series of events within that broader context in order to recover the intentionality of a specific text or series of texts. Thus, an historian of early modern natural science may attempt to situate the early modern philosophical discourse of nature in relation to early modern cultures of collection and curiosity cabinets, of gardening, of courtly display; an historian of political thought will attempt to recover the precise political situation prevailing at the time of a particular text.

The contextual approach to understanding intellectual productions does not posit any simple, one-way relationship between a specific discourse and a specific milieu, nor between a specific text and its specific occasional context. To take an example of the first type, familiar from my own studies: the artificial Latin of the scholastic has to be understood as developed and perpetuated within the specific institutional context of the medieval universities and their formation. This Latin is not a neutral tool of intellectual enquiry, containing as it does within itself a commitment to a specific (Aristotelian) understanding of knowledge and reality. This commitment is itself connected with the demands of academic disciplines, within newly institutionalized structures of teaching and learning, for authoritative theoretical or scientific books. Thus scholastic-Aristotelian form and scholastic-Aristotelian content – what was said *and* the language for saying it – developed together within the context of the formal practices of the universities, the language becoming increasingly technical with the refinement of theory. And as this language became increasingly technical, it also became increasingly unintelligible to outsiders and increasingly the exclusive preserve and practice of a caste of scholars, masters and clerics, a marker of status and of the boundaries of an intellectual community.[18] By the same token, defending those boundaries when they came to be questioned by humanists and by the new science was not simply a matter of language. Among other things it was a matter of professional identity, social prestige – and money.[19]

The relations between specific texts and the specific occasional contexts in which they may be intended as interventions should be understood as equally complex and mutually determining. Any prospective agent is limited not only in what he or she can conceive, but also in what he or she can legitimate or justify, by the shared horizons of expectation implicit in a particular language. Because of the link between public discourse and public action, an agent proposing an innovative course of action would necessarily also need to engage in one of several possible linguistic strategies (the most common of which is attempting to redescribe the proposed action within the normative terminology of the prevailing discourse).[20] Thus in these situations too, language shapes extralinguistic action even while the contrary is also true: the boundary between language and action, the discursive and the non-discursive, is always a *negotiated* one.

I will return to these strategies of negotiation (and control). Meanwhile, I want to focus on an issue which has been raised concerning this methodology insofar as it insists on the centrality of the figure of the language *user* in recovering the meaning of acts of language usage, that is, texts. We remember that the original move was to take intellectual history away from a teleology of great ideas or great thoughts by implicating it in the teleology of individual speakers and writers. It supposes someone who is actually using the words – remember Austin's title, *How to Do Things **with** Words* – as if the words are the instruments of the doer, someone who therefore stands outside language and is not him- or herself linguistically constituted. However, both the centrality of the author or speaker, and the idea that words can be used according to authorial intention, have been subject to extensive challenge from the direction of the European continent (especially France and Germany) in the various challenges known generally under the heading of the 'linguistic turn'.

Essentially, the basic premise of this 'turn' is that language does not reflect an independent reality or world, but instead *constitutes* that reality or world. Although this notion is habitually associated with Continental structuralist and post-structuralist linguistics,[21] it is important that it is also implicit in Wittgenstein's notion of the language game, as his analogy of our language with a city – something that we live *in* – suggests.[22] This intellectual debt means that the methodology of languages and discourse can itself be seen as part of the 'linguistic turn'.[23] The divergence occurs insofar as that methodology still wishes to see language as (at least to some extent) a *resource* of the speaker, something that is at his or her disposal. More 'thoroughgoing' (if that is the word) formulations of the constitutive power of language would argue that language cannot be seen as a tool of ours in any sense, something that we stand behind and that we can use to signal aspects of the world or to act in that world. The hermeneutics of Hans-Georg Gadamer is habitually invoked in the development of this point. Gadamer suggested (influenced ultimately by Heidegger) that language is not something that we use but rather a form of life or a world horizon. Instead of language being at our disposal, language is rather 'behind' 'us', operating and signifying independently of us, beyond our control and indeed controlling us, so that we ourselves become spoken by language rather than speakers of language.[24]

Another challenge to the agency of the language 'user' comes from the work of Michel Foucault. For Foucault, the history of ideas is not a question of intellectual agents responding to particular intellectual or social or political events. Rather, to understand the history of ideas what we have to perceive is a series of blocs of discourse, of talking, which have their own rules of formation and which themselves determine what is there to be talked about and who can do the talking: as Foucault reported of himself,

> my objective in *The order of things* had been to analyse verbal clusters as discursive layers which fall outside the familiar categories of a book, a work, or an author ... I wanted to determine ... the functional conditions of specific discursive practices.[25]

In this history the agent-author is decentred. When we analyse a piece of language, we analyse it in its isolation as an utterance, an element of discourse, without reference to authorial intent:

> in brief, if there exist *things said* – and those things alone – then we should not seek the immediate reason for them in the things which are said there or in the men who have said them, but in the discursive system and in the possibilities or impossibilities of utterance which it provides.[26]

The agency of the author is lost in the structure of discourse of which his or her words form a part and in which he or she inevitably works insofar as he or she is able to discourse about something in the first place. Indeed, authorship or authority becomes instead simply a function of discourse itself.

One might be tempted to think that something of this consequence was always in fact suggested even within the methodology of languages by its insistence upon the importance of linguistic context, for if words only make sense given a specific linguistic context, then it looks as if the context, equally with the author, is an agent of meaning. Moreover, it also looks as if words in context can make that sense – can *do* things – *despite* their author: that what a given author actually succeeded in doing with a particular utterance or text might have been significantly different from what he or she intended to do in speaking or writing.[27] But if this illocutionary force belongs to the text rather than the author, the role of the latter (even in cases where illocutionary act and illocutionary force *do* coincide) then threatens to become purely paratextual.[28] In sum, to the extent to which language games and discursive regimes, the recovery of languages and the archaeology of discourse, share certain common features,[29] the same Foucaldian 'murmur of indifference' seems to arise in both: 'What matter who's speaking?'[30]

Foucaldian archaeology 'kills' the agent-author and therefore that mode of intellectual history which depends on the notion of individual historical agency. But it is not anti-historical, in the sense that it still sees these blocs of discourse or 'regimes of truth' as situated and located in space and time. It is simply that truth itself has a history. However, a second mode of displacement of the subject, associated with the term 'deconstruction', does (at least in its radical variant) threaten to deny any kind of historical determination of meaning. Deconstruction implies in the first place that the author and authorial intention does not determine the meaning of the text. The author is powerless to control the 'free play of the signifier', the surplus of signification produced by signs. Hence, where Austin had recognized occasional situations in which words will miss their mark – the recipient will fail to achieve 'uptake' – Jacques Derrida in response argued that such 'infelicities' are in fact the normal condition of writing.[31] By its very nature, writing *always* exceeds context, and therefore the attempt to fix meaning with reference to context is doomed to failure.

From another but related angle, the deconstructive movement also focused on the relations between texts themselves. The view of supposedly individual texts by supposedly individual authors is replaced by a picture of each text as invaded by other texts to such an extent that its integrity as an autonomous structure of meaning is severely compromised. This mutual complicity of texts is called 'intertextuality'.[32] It is not limited simply to things heretofore identified as 'texts' or 'great texts', but to any writing at all. On the radical forms of deconstruction, there is nothing to say that intertextuality must be limited to any particular historical moment, thus threatening any kind of intellectual history which depends on the notion of *series*. Exposure of this mutual invasiveness of texts has another dimension, however. Part of the conditions for intertextuality, part of the displacement of the author as the agent of meaning, is a focus on the role of the *reader* in determining the meaning of texts. Reading is not seen as a passive absorption or consumption of meaning but a creative act of making or producing meaning.[33] It is, in effect, another act of *writing*: as we read, we write. Again, on radical forms of deconstruction, this creative writing is not limited to an historical moment, for 'we' are doing it in the here and now.

Intellectual history as practised in the Anglophone world can and has responded to these various challenges of the 'linguistic turn' in different ways.[34] First, despite appropriating some of the terminology of 'discourse' and 'archaeology', practitioners of intellectual history have remained resistant to the full-blown Foucaldian idea of the 'episteme', which has been seen as overly monolithic and unable to explain discursive change – that is, the very subject of intellectual *history* – except in terms of 'rupture' or discontinuity.[35] Rather, the discursive past is seen to involve at any particular historical moment the simultaneous existence of plural languages or rhetorics 'in confrontation, contestation and interaction with one another'.[36] These languages can be tied to specific groups with specific social and professional identities, and these groups may therefore have an investment or interest in perpetuating them, defending them or trying to make them dominant. But such groups were very rarely so insulated that they never came into contact with each others' languages:

they could, and did, read and dispute each others' books, for a start. Geographical, social and professional mobility all play their part in this intellectual promiscuity. But beyond the intellectual promiscuity of writers is the promiscuity of verbiage itself. Words do not limit themselves to particular language games: they travel, carrying their semantic baggage with them, undermining the closure of language games and thus of linguistic context.

If this lack of closure is admitted, it follows, first, that we can recognize a certain latitude for the play of the signifier, and exploit, in parallel, certain deconstructive techniques of reading, without abandoning the idea of historical limits on the possibilities of meaning. These limits will be set by an awareness of the conventions of historical languages together with the associated idea of intentionality – be it the intention which we might plausibly attribute to the author, or the intention of the work itself.[37] In practice, the historian will move back and forth between the signification of the words, the place of the text in a conventional milieu, and the possible intentions of the author in writing that text, in an act of interpretation or *making* sense which is necessarily expansive and creative (or 'poetic') but not therefore without historical anchor.[38] It also follows, second, that the use of the definite article, as in 'the' context, is oversimplistic and overdeterministic: there may be plural contexts for any one text, and these contexts may themselves overlap or be related in certain ways. Moreover, a context is by definition something that is shared with other speakers – who on this occasion happen to be the hearers or readers. The speaker or text producer may try in various ways to control the context of his or her utterance or to monopolize the definition of what is 'out of context'; but there is no sure way in which only certain readers (and readings) can be included and certain readers (and readings) not – even if text producers not infrequently may resort to the sword to back certain readings and eliminate others. The publicity of language defies its complete appropriation to the purposes of any individual agent.

Intellectual historians can therefore take on board and, indeed, positively welcome the notion of intertextuality within a broad understanding of intellectual history as the history of language or discourse. Equally, many have welcomed the elision of a sharp distinction between production and consumption of meaning, studying the diffusion of meaning through the various interpretative strategies whereby different readers, adept in different vocabularies, construe text and appropriate meaning. Indeed, it is by stressing in this way the plurality, instability and promiscuity of text, both as written and as read, that intellectual historians may aim to save for the individual author, working within this complex linguistic web, some 'room to manoeuvre', so to speak: some discursive space in which to intervene and possibly to change the course of the conversation; and thus to resurrect the teleology of individual historical agents who are not limited to the discursive realm and are able to *do* things with words, rather than be a mere function of them.[39]

The aim is there: but it is also, I believe, a continuing challenge, as my 'so to speak' bears witness. The problem is exactly *how* we might refer to an author doing something within discourse without, on the one hand, effectively submerging the author in the discourse and, on the other, removing the author to an entirely different, extradiscursive reality – from which any link to the text becomes a matter of psychological speculation or socioeconomic determinism or worse (!). To the extent that this issue remains unresolved, there is (in my view) still more to be done in understanding the dynamics of contextual interpretation and explanation, and therefore in relating intellectual history to the dimensions of human reality postulated in social, economic and political history.

One way of avoiding these residual but fundamental problems of the relation between discursive and non-discursive realms – between text and context, between words and actions – has been to extend the domain of textuality beyond what have traditionally been regarded as 'texts' to cover all forms of cultural activity. I therefore want to turn now to consider my second trajectory of the involvement of thought in action and production, that aspect of intellectual history which concerns itself with representations and practices.

Thinking about the ways in which people have thought has not been limited to thinking about the languages which carry their constructions of the real. Another way of handling the question, strongly indebted to the mid-twentieth-century French School of social history, concerns itself in various ways with what we might loosely term the 'mental world' of human beings, individually and collectively. The basic idea is very familiar: that the world (both social and natural) which people inhabit is not *the* world, whatever that might be, but the world as it presents itself to them through the mediation of a particular structure of cognition. An all-encompassing description such as this is necessarily very vague: I mean it to cover what Lucien Febvre originally termed the *outillage mental*, or mental toolkit for constructing the world, and more broadly the concept of *mentalité* which went on to be central to sociocultural analysis among historians of the *Annales* School and those influenced by them.[40] Both *outillage mental* and *mentalité* were taken to cover not only linguistic equipment or even intellectual or conceptual framework, but also states of perception and affectivity or feeling;[41] indeed, the 'social history of ideas', insofar as it concentrated on the collective mentality as a cultural baseline, was decidedly not focused on the 'high' texts of an intellectual elite but rather on the structure of popular beliefs.

As Roger Chartier argues, despite the subtlety of Febvre's original formulation, the 'history of mentalities' – relying as it did on the quantitative techniques of analysis which characterised the *Annales* School of social history – tended towards a reductive interpretation of texts together with an overly monolithic understanding of the conceptual/perceptual framework of any particular society or social group.[42] More recent historians of the *Annales* School, Jacques Le Goff and Chartier himself, have preferred to speak of *l'imaginaire social*, the 'social imaginary', or of collective representations. In Chartier's handling, representation is a more flexible and subtle concept involving a triple aspect: the intellectual configurations by which reality is constructed by different groups, the practices that symbolically present or exhibit status or rank or a particular way of being in the world, and the institutionalized forms in which social groupings are perpetuated in visible form.[43] Such a conception allows room not only for a monolithic 'mental world' but also for the dynamic and contested process whereby different social groups produce and consume, publish and appropriate representations or images of themselves and others, defining in the process their own identity and that of others.

The term 'representations' brings us finally to consider the type of literary and cultural analysis that goes under the name of 'new historicism' or the poetics of culture. The work of the cultural anthropologist Clifford Geertz was and continues to be enormously influential in suggesting that we should read cultural practices like texts in the sense of 'a collectively maintained symbolic structure' having a certain meaning within a shared public system of signification. Geertz's argument, that 'the culture of a people is an ensemble of texts, themselves ensembles',[44] opened the door to a whole new type of intellectual history, bringing objects and practices hitherto overlooked or apportioned to another type of history into the domain of textuality. Geertz's most famous example was the Balinese cockfight, but public spectacles, rituals, and games of all sorts, as well as less overtly theatrical activities such as sheep raids, present themselves on this analysis for 'reading'. New historicism, following on Geertz's work (among other sources of inspiration[45]), could thereby open up the 'artful' or 'representational' character not just of works of 'art' (taken as literature, painting and so on) but of more everyday acts and practices.[46] It could therefore construct an intertextual reading of the relation between texts and what had hitherto been thought of as 'contextual'.[47] A good example might be Jonathan Sawday's reading of the Renaissance practice of anatomy in relation to (among other texts) the courtly *blason* in his study *The Body Emblazoned*.[48] This reading of texts in the light of culture, exploring the intertextuality of representations, has proved a fruitful field of enquiry, bringing intellectual history in its new, post-theoretical form together with certain types of cultural history, literary history, art history and in general all histories which understand themselves as histories of representations. This is so much so that it is often hard to say where intellectual history ends and these other types of cultural study begin.

Nevertheless, for all the stimulation of this way of thinking, historians have expressed some reservations about the extension of textuality. For it creates an effect similar to the 'linguistic turn' in the theory of language, that is, the occlusion of the possibility of access to an extratextual domain. Both world and subject are constructed in terms of cultural symbols (textualized) and all history thus becomes an intertextual reading.[49] Geertz himself alerted to the dangers of 'turning cultural analysis into a kind of sociological aestheticism',[50] and Gallagher and Greenblatt insist in their turn that, although 'representations ... cease to have a settled relationship of symbolic distance from matter and particularly from human bodies', the functions, passions, illness, life and death of bodies 'cannot simply be reduced to those representations'.[51] But as Gabrielle Spiegel comments, 'it is difficult to discover in what the materiality of the material domain consists'.[52] The threatened result is not merely the loss of any explanatory or causal hierarchy, but 'the sense of social agency, of men and women struggling with the contingencies and complexities of their lives in terms of the fates that history deals out to them and transforming the worlds they inherit and pass on to future generations'.[53] Perhaps, therefore, we have simply arrived again, by a different route, at that central burden that history cannot evade: the story of bodily human beings, the story of the real.

II

I have given a very schematic outline by way of response to the first of my initial questions, 'What is intellectual history *now*?' In broad terms, we have seen that intellectual history as it stands encompasses both the history of discourses and the history of representations, with no necessary barrier – indeed, rather the possibility of fruitful interchange – between them. But in the light of this long detour, I want finally to turn to the second of my initial questions, 'What is *intellectual* history now?' What is it that is distinctive to intellectual history, that stops it from being simply a form of cultural history? We have seen that modern intellectual history cannot be divorced – and nor does it want to be – from cultural history and indeed from social and political history, for in all its forms it accepts the mutual involvement of the conceptual and the material dimensions of human being. But it is possible to argue nevertheless that intellectual history retains its own distinctive focus. For what intellectual historians are interested in is not simply the ways in which people spoke, or their visual imaginary, and how these related to their social, cultural and political context or to other dimensions of their self-representation. It is also – and primarily, I would say – interested in those ways of speaking as ways in which people in the past *made sense* of their world: and therefore it must concern itself with the internal coherence and logic of the structures of mental reference or the languages which it studies. It is here, I think, that texts, and most especially the 'great texts', as the most complex explorations of the limits of language or conceptual frame at a given time, will always have a certain pride of place in what Dominick LaCapra has described as a dialogical enquiry between past and present.[54] This is the properly *philosophical* dimension of the practice of intellectual history, the boundary line which it shares with philosophy rather than any other kind of history.

This boundary line with philosophy is blurred just like the others. However, this fluidity is not necessarily in the direction of philosophy as traditionally understood. The very notion of 'intellectual history' betrays the figure of *sophia* and the erotics of knowledge as the thirst after the eternally true, the eternally desirable. The intellectual realm is a human, historical creation: understanding it is understanding the materials out of which it is made, the languages and the imagination we have inherited. In this sense, to do intellectual history just *is* to do philosophy. If philosophy has a further task, it is not to gain a better insight into reality, but, analogously to poetry, to stretch our imagination and our language and thus to help create a new world for living in.[55] We might add that doing intellectual history can itself be understood as poetic in that sense, for intellectual history does not merely unravel the structure of what we have inherited but can also unearth what we have lost: ways of speaking and ways of seeing the world, once current, now exotic and (perhaps) full of possibility.

I do not, therefore, wish to close by appearing to substitute for Carr's deliberately optimistic vision of the widening horizon of rational consciousness a picture of intellectual historians ruefully picking over the remains of verbiage in a disconsolate attempt to make sense of it all.[56] Rather it is that in trying to unravel the mental worlds of the past, we give ourselves the opportunity to re-weave our own.

Notes and references

1. W.J. Bouwsma, *The Waning of the Renaissance 1550–1640* (New Haven, CT, and London: Yale University Press, 2000), p. ix.
2. By Roger Chartier, in a wonderfully lucid and thoughtful overview of the problems involved. See R. Chartier, 'Intellectual History or Sociological History? The French Trajectories', in D. LaCapra and S.L. Kaplan (eds), *Modern European Intellectual History: Reappraisals and New Perspectives* (Ithaca, NY: Cornell University Press, 1982).
3. Cf. N.J. Christie, 'From Intellectual to Cultural History: The Comparative Catalyst', in D.R. Woolf (ed.), *Intellectual History: New Perspectives* (Lewiston; Queenston; Lampeter: Edwin Mellen, 1989), p. 82.
4. A point very familiar by now, thanks to the seminal work of Quentin Skinner. For its original incisive and sparkling formulation see Q.R.D. Skinner, 'Meaning and Understanding in the History of Ideas', *History and Theory*, vol. 8 (1969), pp. 393–408, reprinted in J. Tully (ed.), *Meaning and Context: Quentin Skinner and His Critics* (Cambridge: Polity Press, 1988); see also J.A.W. Gunn, 'After Sabine, After Lovejoy: The Languages of Political Thought', in Woolf, *Intellectual History*.
5. E.H. Carr, *What is History?* (2nd edn) (London: Penguin, 1987), pp. 134–5.
6. For a good treatment of Collingwood within this tradition see D. Boucher, *Texts in Context: Revisionist Methods for Studying the History of Ideas* (The Hague: Martinus Nijhoff, 1985), pp. 39–71.
7. Carr, *What is History?*, pp. 21–7.
8. See, especially, Skinner, 'Meaning and Understanding', and Q.R.D. Skinner, 'Motives, Intentions and the Interpretation of Texts', *New Literary History*, vol. 3 (1972), pp. 393–408, reprinted in Tully, *Meaning and Context*.
9. J.L. Austin, *How to Do Things with Words* (2nd edn) (Oxford: Oxford University Press, 1975).
10. J.R. Searle, *Speech Acts: An Essay in the Philosophy of Language* (Cambridge: Cambridge University Press, 1969).
11. In developing this focus on authorial intention as the condition of an illocutionary act, Skinner deliberately departed from Austin, who had insisted on the successful 'uptake' of the act on the part of the recipient as a condition for the completion of an illocutionary act. For Skinner, a speaker or text producer can perform an illocutionary act whether or not that act was received as the speaker had intended. See Q.R.D. Skinner, 'A Reply to My Critics', in Tully, *Meaning and Context*, pp. 261–4.
12. I stress 'from the perspective of the author', as it is necessary to differentiate it from the 'point' that a text may have of itself: cf. Tully, *Meaning and Context*, p. 10. Skinner, 'A Reply', distinguishes between the illocutionary act, which

must be an intentional act on the part of the author – the author's 'point' in writing – and the illocutionary force of a particular text – let us say its 'pointedness'. Skinner acknowledges here that illocutionary act and illocutionary force may not coincide; this will be important later on. See below, p. 121.

13. L. Wittgenstein, *Philosophical Investigations* (3rd edn) (English text only) (Oxford: Blackwell, 1968): the term is introduced at p. 5. See also the analogy, so suggestive for intellectual history, of our language as an ancient city, with additions from many periods (p. 8).
14. For a discussion of this issue see J.G.A. Pocock, 'Concepts and Discourses: A Difference in Culture? Comments on a Paper by Melvin Richter', in H. Lehmann and M. Richter (eds), *The Meaning of Historical Terms and Concepts: New Studies in Begriffsgeschichte* (Washington, DC: German Historical Institute, 1996), pp. 47–58, and M. Richter, 'Reconstructing the History of Political Languages: Pocock, Skinner and the *Geschichtliche Grundbegriffe*', *History and Theory*, vol. 29 (1990), pp. 38–70.
15. For a clear statement of this sort of method see J.G.A. Pocock, 'The Concept of a Language and the *Métier d'Historien*: Some Considerations on Practice', in A.R.D. Pagden (ed.), *The Languages of Political Theory in Early Modern Europe* (Cambridge: Cambridge University Press, 1987).
16. Pocock, in 'The Concept of a Language', lists: the language of medieval scholastic, of Renaissance emblematic, of biblical exegesis, of common law, of civil law, of classical republicanism, of commonwealth radicalism (acknowledging that the list is necessarily biased by his own studies).
17. See, for example, Skinner's study of the Lorenzetti frescoes in the Palazzo Pubblico of Siena: Q.R.D. Skinner, 'Ambrogio Lorenzetti: The Artist as Political Philosopher', *Proceedings of the British Academy*, vol. 72 (1986), pp. 1–86.
18. For these points see L. Giard, 'Du Latin médiéval au pluriel des langues: Le tournant de la Renaissance', *Histoire, épistémologie, langage*, vol. 6 (1984), pp. 35–55, especially pp. 40–1.
19. M. Biagioli, 'The Anthropology of Incommensurability', *Studies in the History and Philosophy of Science*, vol. 21 (1990), pp. 183–209, especially p. 203.
20. For an analysis of the relation of ideology to political action see Skinner, 'Motives, Intentions'; J. Tully, 'The Pen is a Mighty Sword: Quentin Skinner's Analysis of Politics', in Tully, *Meaning and Context*, pp. 10–16, 22–5.
21. E.g. in Spiegel, 'History, Historicism and the Social Logic of the Text in the Middle Ages', *Speculum* (1990), reprinted in K. Jenkins (ed.), *The Postmodern History Reader* (London: Routledge, 1997), pp. 180–283.
22. Cf. note 13 above; see also M. Jay, 'Should Intellectual History Take a Linguistic Turn? Reflections on the Habermas–Gadamer Debate', in LaCapra and Kaplan, *Modern European Intellectual History*, pp. 86–110, at pp. 87–8.
23. Skinner, 'A Reply', p. 276, points out that his own argument 'leaves the traditional figure of the author in extremely poor health'.
24. For a discussion of Gadamer's hermeneutics and its debt to Heidegger see Jay, 'Should Intellectual History Take a Linguistic Turn?'.
25. M. Foucault, 'What is an Author?', in D.F. Bouchard (ed.), *Language, Counter-Memory, Practice: Selected Essays and Interviews by Michel Foucault* (Ithaca, NY: Cornell University Press, 1977), pp. 113–38, at p. 113.
26. M. Foucault, *L'archéologie du savoir* (Paris: Gallimard, 1969), p. 70: 'bref, que s'il y a des choses dites – et celles-là seulement –, il ne faut pas en demander

la raison immédiate aux choses qui s'y trouvent dites ou aux hommes qui les ont dites, mais au système de la discursivité, aux possibilités et aux impossibilités énonciatives qu'il ménage'.

27. Cf. p. 116 above, and note 12 above.
28. I mean 'paratext' in Gerard Genette's later sense of all the material which surrounds the text and affects how it is read (preface, titles, epigraphs, illustrations, notes, and so on). See G. Genette, *Paratexts: Thresholds of Interpretation* (trans. J.E. Lewin) (Cambridge: Cambridge University Press, 1997).
29. Cf. Pocock, 'The Concept of a Language', p. 25, who speaks of the 'historian-archaeologist'.
30. Foucault, 'What is an Author?', p. 138.
31. See Derrida's response to Austin: J. Derrida, 'Signature Event Context', in his *Margins of Philosophy* (trans. A. Bass) (Chicago, IL: University of Chicago Press; Brighton: Harvester, 1982), pp. 307–30.
32. For an introduction to the various definitions of intertextuality and the issues involved see M. Worton and J. Still (eds), *Intertextuality: Theories and Practices* (Manchester: Manchester University Press, 1990).
33. In another context Michel de Certeau has analysed how consumption itself can be a form of production through strategies of appropriation and assimilation. See M. de Certeau, *The Practice of Everyday Life* (trans. S. Rendall) (Berkeley, CA; Los Angeles; London: University of California Press, 1984), pp. xi–xxiv.
34. For a thoughtful discussion of the possibilities for intellectual history 'after the linguistic turn' see J.E. Toews, 'Intellectual History After the Linguistic Turn: The Autonomy of Meaning and the Irreducibility of Experience', *American Historical Review*, vol. 92 (1987), pp. 879–907.
35. I. Maclean, in 'Foucault's Renaissance Episteme Reassessed: An Aristotelian Counterblast', *Journal of the History of Ideas* (1998), pp. 149–66, discusses how Foucault's idea of the Renaissance episteme is both misguidedly formulated and also, more profoundly, fails to take account of the resources available within Renaissance discourse for a reflexive awareness of their own modes of cognition.
36. Pocock, 'Concepts and Discourses', p. 47.
37. Umberto Eco has developed the idea of an intention of the work, *intentio operis*, in his secod Tanner lecture of 1990. See U. Eco, *Interpretation and Overinterpretation* (Cambridge: Cambridge University Press, 1992); especially p. 64: 'To recognise the *intentio operis* is to recognise a semiotic strategy. Sometimes the semiotic strategy is detectable on the grounds of established stylistic conventions ... How to prove a conjecture about the *intentio operis*? The only way is to check it upon the text as a coherent whole.' Eco goes on to discuss the relations between this *intentio operis* and the intentio of both *lector* and *auctor*.
38. It seems to me that this is preferable to making a radical separation between 'meaning' in the sense of what the author meant, and 'meaning' in the sense of the signification of the text, leaving the first – the recovery of intention – to the historian and the second to the literary critic or the philosopher, as argued, for example, in M.P. Thompson, 'Reception Theory and the Interpretation of Historical Meaning', *History and Theory*, vol. 32 (1993), pp. 228–72. For one thing, the intentionality or 'pointedness' of the text itself

(see note 12 above) lies in between these two poles, mediating between them. For another, it then becomes quite unclear why someone interested in what the text means should have any concern for what the author may have meant. I suggest rather that the task of the intellectual historian is both historical *and* critical-philosophical (see further below, p. 127).

39. For this humanist commitment, see A.R.D. Pagden, 'Introduction', in his *The Languages of Political Theory*, p. 2.

40. See Chartier, 'Intellectual History or Sociocultural History?, pp. 18–32; R. Chartier, *Cultural History: Between Practices and Representations* (trans. L.G. Cochrane) (Cambridge: Polity Press in association with Blackwell, 1988), pp. 20–48; P. Burke, *Varieties of Cultural History* (Cambridge: Polity Press, 1997), pp. 162–82.

41. As defined by Febvre, *outillage mental* includes the state of the language, its lexicon, its syntax, the scientific language and instruments, and also the 'sensitive supports of thought' represented by the system of perception (Chartier, 'Intellectual History or Sociocultural History?', p. 19); as defined by Mandrou, *mentalité* includes 'what is conceived and felt, the field of intelligence and of emotion (*affectivité*)' (ibid., p. 23).

42. Ibid., pp. 29–32.

43. Chartier, *Cultural History*, pp. 9–10.

44. C. Geertz, *The Interpretation of Cultures* (New York: Basic Books, 1973), p. 452.

45. For a helpful diagnosis of their own enterprise, and its origins and effects, by two of the leading 'new historicist' scholars, see C. Gallagher and S. Greenblatt, *Practicing New Historicism* (Chicago, Il: University of Chicago Press, 2000), pp. 1–19.

46. Cf. S. Greenblatt, *Renaissance Self-Fashioning from More to Shakespeare* (Chicago, Il: University of Chicago Press, 1988), pp. 4–5.

47. For a critical discussion of this intellectual move see Spiegel, 'History, Historicism', pp. 185–92.

48. J. Sawday, *The Body Emblazoned: Dissection and the Human Body in Renaissance Culture* (London: Routledge, 1995), pp. 196–212.

49. The conference laughed at the idea of 'pan-representationalism' – that the only true (and possible) object of historical study is representation – but one can see how the idea can take hold.

50. Geertz, *The Interpretation of Cultures*, p. 30.

51. Gallagher and Greenblatt, *Practicing New Historicism*, p. 15.

52. Spiegel, 'History, Historicism', p. 192.

53. Ibid., p. 195.

54. For this dialogic aspect of intellectual history, and the continuing importance of the 'great texts' therein, see D. LaCapra, 'Rethinking Intellectual History and Reading Texts', in LaCapra and Kaplan, *Modern European Intellectual History*, especially pp. 83–5.

55. See R. Rorty, *Contingency, Irony and Solidarity* (Cambridge: Cambridge University Press, 1989), for the development of these views of what follows from accepting the radical 'contingency of language'.

56. I refer, of course, to Umberto Eco's marvellous allegory of language in the closing pages of *The Name of the Rose* (London: Picador, 1984; trans. W. Weaver), p. 500.

8
What is Imperial History Now?

Linda Colley

Let me begin with some autobiography. My first formal introduction to imperial history was as a student at Bristol University in the early 1970s. The subject was personified there by a very considerable specialist on British colonial Africa who was often to be seen dressed in a khaki safari suit. From observing him, his students and his course schedules, I jumped to certain conclusions about imperial history. These reflected in large part the woeful extent of my own undergraduate ignorance. But I was also reacting to certain characteristics of *British* imperial history as a discipline at that stage which tended, I suspect, to put many of my generation and later generations off the subject, and caused us to misapprehend what it was potentially about.

So what were my student impressions of imperial history? First, that it was thoroughly compartmentalized. British imperial history as taught at Bristol appeared to have little or no connection in terms of subject matter or approach with anything else I learnt about the past there. British history, imperial history, American history and European history, the mainstays of the Department, all tended indeed to operate along parallel tracks, though this compartmentalization was (and is) scarcely peculiar to Bristol. The second thing I concluded was that – even more than other varieties of the discipline – imperial history seemed a comprehensively masculine enterprise. It was taught by chaps of course. Virtually everything at Bristol was then. But it was also studied overwhelmingly by chaps, and appeared to be centrally concerned with what chaps in the past, mainly of the pale variety, did to, or for, yet more chaps who were often not pale. Partly as a consequence of all this,

I decided that imperial history was too alien, too specific and – I confess – too fusty for my taste. It seemed to me then to be history with a matte rather than a high gloss finish, preoccupied very expertly with the study of treaties and their makers, diplomacy, administration, agriculture and trade, and only occasionally relieved by the odd war, railway construction, or bauxite mine.[1]

These reactions on my part were perhaps understandable given the circumstances of the time, and not uncommon, but in retrospect they were very foolish. For in regard to this subject, the appropriate question is less: 'What is imperial history?', than 'What isn't imperial history?' As Dane Kennedy and others have pointed out, in recent decades, this branch of history, broadly defined, has been transformed and taken off in all sorts of new directions. Imperial history, in terms of the scholarly study of empires, their ideologies, workings and effects, is now far more cross-disciplinary and much more diverse in terms of subject matter and methodologies. Archaeologists, art historians, cartographers, feminist historians, area studies people, historians of medicine, intellectual historians, literary scholars, post-colonialists and more have all contributed their particular perceptions and agendas, though many of these scholars would not describe themselves as imperial historians. This has resulted in a wealth of new information and insights, and made possible not just entirely new avenues of study, but also means whereby older, often very valuable work can be revisited and reassessed.[2] In part because there are now so many different kinds of writing around the phenomenon of empire, imperial history has become much more controversial and far more overtly politicized. It has also become more fashionable. In the United States, at least, it is now difficult to secure a university post teaching British history unless you affirm a willingness to teach imperial history as well.

Yet, as this last development suggests, the recent take-off of interest in and diversity of imperial histories has not always been accompanied by a comparable gain in understanding of or clarity about what this subject rightly involves. The demand that British historians in particular be able to practise imperial history reflects an (all too common) assumption that imperial history is peculiarly and necessarily to do with the history of the British empire. This may be a natural view for Americans to adopt, but it is still wrong. Imperial history includes but is not exclusively or essentially about what the British did in the past, any more than it is primarily about what other Western Europeans did in the past. Imperial history, the study of empire over time, properly involves looking at far more than just Western history, and at more than what has happened in the last 500 years. Indeed, the study of empire involves looking at more than simply the past. We may be living in post-colonial times, but we are not yet living in post-imperial times. The whole point, attraction, essence and challenge of imperial history is that – while not identical to global history – rightly understood, it comes extremely close to it. What I wish to do in this chapter, therefore, is not so much to celebrate the more diverse imperial history that has already emerged (though I do celebrate it), as to suggest some ways in which we might profitably advance still further and more thoughtfully. In response to the question 'What is imperial history?', I wish to focus on three answers, while emphasizing that this is by no means an exhaustive list of possibilities.

To begin with, I shall argue, imperial history involves a recognition that different kinds of empire, together with different kinds of monarchy, have been the most ubiquitous and persistent forms of power and government in the global past and present. Consequently, the imperial historian needs to adopt a comparative perspective and be mistress of the *longue durée*. Second, and leading on from this, imperial history is quintessentially about what has been called connexity. Those practising it must be sensitive to and willing to investigate the manifold, often paradoxical connections that have operated between different territories and peoples over time, and acknowledge as well the full diversity of power systems and actors involved. I will discuss this second point with particular reference to Britain's empire, but it applies to all empires at all times. Third, and last, because of its massive scope and intrinsic contentiousness, imperial history is an immensely challenging discipline. I want to conclude this chapter by suggesting indeed that, in the current state of British academe, pursuing this subject with an appropriate degree of breadth, rigour and audacity is extremely hard. Yet there are few subjects more indispensable for forging a proper understanding both of this country and the world in general.

I

First of all, then, there is the importance of the comparative dimension and the *longue durée*. As Eric Hobsbawm has remarked, because empire has often possessed pejorative overtones as a word and as an idea, different states and polemicists have repeatedly chosen to represent it as something practised by others, but not by their own kind and tribe. Evil empire is always something done by somebody else.[3] Thus in the seventeenth and eighteenth centuries, both the English and the Dutch argued that oppressive territorial empire was the preserve of states with large armies, like Ancient Rome or Catholic Spain, whereas their own brand of overseas activity was quintessentially maritime and commercial, and consequently far more benign. It should go without saying that this was a highly selective analysis. The British and Dutch empires *were* maritime and strongly commercial, but they were concerned with far more than trade. They always had a military dimension, and they increasingly involved territorial invasion and colonization.[4] Such casuistical and self-serving redefinitions of empire employed so as to condemn certain powers, while letting others off the hook, have recurred throughout the centuries. In 1899, the American Vice President of the Anti-Imperialist League, Carl Schurz, told a Chicago audience that there was a 'vital difference between the expansion of the [American] Republic and its free institutions over contiguous territories ... and imperialism which reaches out for distant lands to be ruled as subject provinces'. This remains a widespread view, particularly in the US. Yet as revisionist frontier historians like Patricia Limerick have argued, and as Mexicans, Canadians and Native Americans have always known, nineteenth-century American westwards expansion contained many imperialist features and needs to be examined in tandem with contemporaneous European imperialisms.[5]

Similar forms of amnesia and selectiveness can obstruct scholarly and political understanding today. When Edward Said argued in 1988 that 'modern European imperialism ... [was] a constitutively and a radically different type of overseas domination from all earlier forms', he too was expressing a widespread view that is in part correct. Yet unless the European maritime empires that have monopolized Said's concentration and censure are properly compared with those non-European empires he omits from his books – the Chinese empire, the Mughal empire in India, the Safavid empire of Iran and, crucially, the Ottoman empire, which lasted longer than most Western European empires – then assertions of the latter's constitutive and radical difference will remain merely that: assertions.[6] By the same token, we need to recognize that when later twentieth-century politicians and propagandists in the United States attacked the then Soviet Union and occasionally China as evil empires, and were attacked in return by Soviet and Chinese politicians and propagandists as exponents of malign Western imperialism, these actors were at once acting in accordance with long-established rhetorical and casuistical strategies, and giving voice to partial truths. Beneath their carapace of mass democracy and nationalism, the US, Russia and China do in fact retain many of the characteristics – and many of the problems – of empires, which historically is scarcely to be wondered at.

The only way that imperial historians can protect their scholarly vision from these kinds of self-serving and partisan blinkers, is by cultivating an awareness of the different forms of empire that have existed over the centuries in different parts of the world. Such a broad-angled vision is essential for positive reasons too. Unless we approach the history of empires comparatively, we cannot appreciate how much the different imperial systems themselves regularly learnt from and borrowed from each other. When the British moved into India, they adopted – while also adapting – many of the fiscal, administrative and ritual devices of the previous Mughal imperial system. The Roman empire, of course, served as a model for virtually all of its Western successors. It was no accident that the new American republic promptly acquired a senate, a capitol, and an eagle for its emblem. These were all conscious borrowings from Ancient Rome, another great republic that became an empire, and reflected the Founding Fathers' interest in the United States in turn becoming what Alexander Hamilton called 'an empire in many respects the most interesting in the world'.[7]

The real and bogus knowledge that different empires possessed of each other proved formative in other respects. At one level, it could aid legitimization and confidence among the imperializers themselves. European states were able to construct their own overseas empires, strengthened by an awareness – which a study of the Greek and Roman classics bestowed on all their male elites – that empires had always existed, and moreover, and according to the likes of Caesar and Tacitus, had often proved benevolent and civilizing.[8] But the recognition that empires were ubiquitous and had always existed in some form also aided mass acceptance of them. For obvious political reasons, scholars tend now to dwell on examples of mass resistance to empires, yet, for much of global history, it was the degree of mass acquiescence in empire that was actually more striking, and one of the reasons for this was that the existence of various imperial systems covering most of the globe was – often – simply taken for granted. This said, an awareness at grass-roots level of other empires might also empower. When the British moved into Canada after 1759, they had to deal with indigenous peoples who had grown accustomed for almost two centuries to the techniques of French imperial rule. Over subsequent decades, British imperial administrators were compelled to become more attentive to matters like gift-giving, the award of medals, ceremonial and diplomatic forms, and so on, because indigenous leaders repeatedly lectured them on their deficiencies in regard to these matters by comparison with their French predecessors.[9]

So this is one positive reason why imperial history must involve a comparative perspective: because people in the past, both the makers of empires and those they sought to rule, often possessed a comparative perspective too. Adopting this kind of approach is also vital because different empires rose, changed and fell in close relation and in response to each other. As Dominic Lieven has recently documented, you cannot understand the fortunes and dimensions of the Hapsburg and Russian empires over time without some appreciation of how these were affected by the flux of the neighbouring Ottoman empire.[10] The extension of British territorial influence in India after 1750 was intimately connected, in ways that are still hotly disputed, with the protracted weakening of the Mughal empire. The rise of American informal empire in different parts of the world since the early twentieth century has to be examined in tandem with the retreat of British imperial power, and so on. This is and always has been an interconnected world, and part of the task of imperial historians is to show how and why this was so.

However, imperial historians need to illuminate the divergences between different imperial systems and not just their borrowings from, linkages with and similarities to each other. Protestant and Catholic European empires possessed many points in common, but they were also sometimes characterized by rather disparate attitudes to issues such as missionary work and intermarriage between whites and indigenous peoples. Maritime empires and contiguous, land-based empires sometimes exhibited very similar motives, aggression, and techniques of rule, but there were also major and recurring differences between them. Most obviously, and as J.R. Seeley perceived, maritime empires were usually more short-lived and vulnerable than contiguous empires. It was always easier to construct and consolidate rule over one single continuous stretch of territory than to be dependent on ships and have to project imperial authority over vast oceans and seas.[11] This was why the Russian empire, the Ottoman empire and above all the Chinese empire proved far more durable than, say, the British, Spanish or Portuguese empires.

Of course, no single scholar can hope to acquire expertise about the overall history of a single empire, whichever one it may be, still less accumulate detailed and expert knowledge of all empires over all time. Unlike the phenomenon of empire, individual human beings, even the cleverest and most industrious of them, last only a very short time. None the less, while omniscience is beyond us, a willingness to adopt a comparative dimension in regard to specific areas of study should not be. It is unwise and usually just plain wrong to make dramatic assertions about the characteristics and consequences of a particular empire unless you have checked out other empires first. Let me give you an example. In recent years, some historians and literary scholars have argued very powerfully that Britain's massive imperial expansion after 1750 informed and still informs its attitudes to race to a pernicious degree.[12] To an extent, this argument seems to me to be a feasible one. Yet – assuming that there are some connections between empire and racial attitudes – Britain's experience surely needs testing against that of other empires, *and indeed against other states which lacked empires*. Why is it, for instance, that Germany, which invested in overseas empire far more belatedly, and to a much lesser extent than Britain, none the less exhibited in the twentieth century, and *arguably* still exhibits now, a greater volume of domestic racial violence and explicitly racial politics than Britain?[13] I do not know the answer, but those interested in the study of race and imperialism should be asking this as well as other comparative questions.

II

Let me move on now to my second theme: that imperial history is vitally about connexity, the identification and investigation of the manifold connections that existed over time between different sectors of the world and different peoples. Approaching the British empire (and any other empire) in this fashion – as an 'entire interactive system, one vast inter-connected world', to quote Philip Morgan – imposes massive challenges on historians. On the one hand, it is no longer sufficient, and it never was, for British imperial historians to concentrate on the impact of successive English, Welsh, Scottish and Irish diasporas on the peoples and lands they invaded. It is not enough, as one very able Dutch imperial historian insisted as early as the 1930s, to put the white man at the centre of things and tell the story of global contacts and invasions over-whelmingly 'from the deck of the ship, the rampart of the fortress, the high gallery of the trading house', or indeed from the perspective of the libraries and studies of European writers.[14] We always need to consider as well how those on the receiving end of British and other European imperial attentions impacted on and influenced what happened, just as we need to investigate the effects of empire on these islands themselves and on other European states. Imperial history should not be a one-sided, one-directional story invariably privileging only one set of voices. On that, I think, we may all agree.

However, and this is sometimes forgotten, investigating connexity in the context of the British empire challenges more than just historians of Britain. British scholars need to acquire a multilateral understanding of what empire was and what it did, and an awareness too of the autonomous pasts of the societies impacted on by Britain: yes indeed. But, by the same token, historians of Asia, North America, the Caribbean, Africa and the Pacific need to develop an up-to-date, variegated and nuanced appreciation of the *British* dimension in empire. They need an informed sense of just what kind of power and society Britain really was at particular times, as distinct from what it appeared to be or what it is still generally thought of as being. Understanding the interconnections spun around British empire, in other words, is a huge, multifaceted and strictly mutual task, and not just a challenge for the former imperial power alone. I wish briefly to develop these points, particularly the latter which has been neglected.

Many of us would agree with David Armitage in lamenting 'the persistent reluctance of British historians to incorporate the Empire into the history of Britain', not least because unless you make connections between sites of overseas empire and the metropolis in this way, and recognize how the former impacted on the latter and not merely vice versa, then whole areas of the British past cannot be rounded out or rendered fully comprehensible.[15] Consider something as basic as tax and revenue. There are real and well-documented connections between fiscal policy and attempts to reduce smuggling in this country in the 1770s and 1780s, on the one hand, and the activities and flux of Chinese and Indian tea-growers and traders, on the other. And both of these things were further connected to the commercial grievances of American colonists and to the timing and format of the Boston Tea Party. Here indeed was one vast, interconnected imperial world.[16] In much the same way, it was the scale of non-European warfare (and non-European resistance) – and not just the battle with Napoleon in Europe – that made the wars of 1793–1815 hideously expensive for British tax-payers. This contributed to the campaigns of British middle-class activists after 1815 to reduce if not abolish the income tax, and in particular to cut expenditure on the armed forces.[17] And these retrenchment campaigns in turn impacted not just on incomes and livelihoods in Manchester, Glasgow, Belfast and Cardiff, but also in Bengal, Madras and Bombay. Increasingly (though the events of 1857 changed things somewhat), much of the burden of defending the British empire, in terms both of paying taxes and supplying manpower, was passed on to the inhabitants of the Indian sub-continent. As the more cynical version of the famous music hall song had it:

> We don't want to fight,
> But, by Jingo, if we do,
> We'll stay at home and sing our songs
> And send the mild Hindoo.[18]

Incorporating the imperial dimension in British history not only amplifies and usefully complicates the story, but also sometimes transforms it and the questions that can be asked about it. Consider one of the oldest chestnuts in the book. Even now, histories of Britain still regularly assert that, after the seventeenth century, the armed forces here were effectively depoliticized and subordinated to the civil power. I have doubts about this Whiggish version of events even in regard to domestic history, but its insufficiency appears stark once one looks at the British Army in an imperial context. Individual military men, like Arthur Wellesley in India or James Murray in Canada, acted out largely autonomous political roles (sometimes in defiance of the politicians in London) as well as fighting wars. Moreover, such imperial warlords sometimes also possessed political power and connections in the metropolis itself. As Lewis Namier and John Brooke long ago demonstrated, army and navy men formed the biggest category of MPs in successive eighteenth- and early nineteenth-century parliaments; and the proportion of peers with military backgrounds was also considerable.[19] These facts are normally cited without much comment and without any attempt to qualify the notion that Britain's armed forces were apolitical. Yet there were surely connections between the expansion of Britain's empire overseas and the simultaneous prominence of the military in its political life at home. It would be nice to know what these were.[20]

Recognizing the importance of connexity in regard to empire should not, however, be an exclusive business; very much the reverse. Imperial history, properly pursued, must involve the insertion of non-European forces and perceptions into our reconstructions of British history: yes, absolutely. But this need not and must not involve ignoring other influences. Eurocentrism, for instance, is sometimes condemned (understandably enough) without always acknowledging its real impact and significance in the past. Yet, for the British, matters European were generally at least as important and as preoccupying as matters extra-European and imperial. Indeed, these things were often interconnected. There are several aspects that need touching on in this regard. To begin with, imperial historians need to pay more attention than they have generally done thus far to Britain's empire within Europe. Gibraltar, Minorca, Malta, Corfu and Cyprus were never primarily zones of settlement, any more than they were major markets or suppliers of raw materials, but in naval, strategic and overall commercial terms, such bases were vital; in some ways the keys to Britain's entire global system. As this suggests, in response to the more specific question 'What is *British* imperial history?', we badly need to incorporate the Mediterranean as part of the answer, and not merely the Atlantic, the Pacific and the Indian Ocean.[21]

In addition, and coming back to my insistence on the importance of global interconnections, we need to bear in mind the absolute link between Britain's power vis-à-vis the rest of Europe, and such imperial power as it was able to exert at different points in time in different parts of the extra-European world. As long as Britain was engaged in major wars and rivalry with continental powers, its imperial efforts were compromised or rendered paranoid in style. Thus, very dramatically, it lost the Thirteen Colonies after 1776 in large part because its arch-rival France declared war on Britain and lent the Americans massive military and above all naval aid. By the same token, once Britain finally defeated France in 1815 and established European hegemony, it was able thereafter to tighten the screws in imperial terms. The fact that, in the early nineteenth century, Britain, the other Western European powers, the United States and Russia together claimed authority over some 35 per cent of the world's territory, whereas by the early twentieth century these powers laid claim to over 80 per cent of the world, was directly connected to the fact that – in the intervening period – these states were generally at peace with each other, and consequently far freer than they had been before to intervene in other, more vulnerable geographical zones.[22] Conversely, once Britain and the other main European powers involved themselves after 1914 in what were effectively two vast, successive continental civil wars, the pace of decolonization was enormously quickened. So, while connexity in the context of British imperial history means being sensitive to non-European voices and influences, this needs to be combined with a proper consideration as well of the pan-European dimension.

III

To summarize then: tracing the bewildering array of global interconnections is indispensable to British and to other varieties of imperial history, but by definition this must be done eclectically and not selectively. And this brings me neatly to my next and related point: that understanding British empire requires a comprehensive and clear-sighted understanding of the British themselves. As C.A. Bayly has suggested, treatments of the British as imperializers by Indian, or indeed American or Caribbean or Australian or African, scholars can at times be schizoid in quality. On the one hand, and for perfectly understandable reasons, the British are often derided and their formative contribution to these vast regions of the world minimized or denied. Yet the British are also regularly wheeled on like an old, stuffed pantomime horse whenever major turning-points in these regions' pasts which are deemed deplorable are to be explained, and attributed in this context with truly extraordinary degrees of power and influence.[23] And this tendency is not confined to writings. Think of Mel Gibson's film *The Patriot* where, at one and the same time, British redcoat officers in the American revolutionary war are represented as almost too stupid or naively malevolent to find the door, yet are simultaneously shown as possessing vast, disciplined legions on an almost Nuremberg and quite inauthentic scale. Here is a classic example of what might be styled the schizoid post-colonial gaze, at once diminishing the former imperial power and simultaneously exaggerating its coercive force. Of course, all nations need usable pasts, and it is to be expected that post-colonial societies will choose in their popular culture and political myths to misperceive and/or demean the British, just as the British once misperceived and/or demeaned them. But as historians – whatever we may think of this or any other empire – we need to cut seriously deeper and attempt to see the British and their fluctuating imperial power for what they actually were.

Consider in this regard the issue of British smallness. The power and reach of the British empire can easily be overestimated by too much reliance on one of its most successful pieces of propaganda: that all-too-famous map – much reproduced in the Victorian and Edwardian eras, and a standard feature of textbooks ever since – which exhibits vast stretches of the world all shaded a common pink or red. Even more than most maps do, this one deceives. It deceives because it suggests that the British empire constituted a uniform monolith, a single imperial project, which was never the case. It deceives, too, because it gives the entirely erroneous impression that the only substantial empire existing at the time was Britain's own. But the most effective and devious deception involved in this famous map is the way it distracts the eye from the smallness of the metropolitan power itself. The United Kingdom's marked physical limits are adroitly obscured in a global spread of pinkness. It is all too easy, looking at this piece of cartographic sleight of hand, to be beguiled into the familiar misconception that size matters more than anything else, and that the unique scale of Britain's empire at its apex was straightforwardly accompanied by a unique degree of power. Yet, insofar as size did matter in relation to imperial power, what needs to be noticed is not just the massive extent of the territory that Britain presumed to claim, but also its own puny domestic dimensions.[24]

And remember just how puny those dimensions are, especially when compared with today's great powers. The United States is 3000 miles from sea to shining sea, and – like China – covers almost 3.7 million square miles. The Russian Federation was recently estimated as over 6 million square miles in extent; while present-day India – which Britain sought to rule before 1947 – comprises some 1.2 million square miles. By contrast, Great Britain and Ireland together comprise less than 125,000 square miles. The island of Britain itself is smaller than Madagascar. You could fit it into Texas twice over with room to spare. Of course geopolitical size has never been the sole or even the prime determinant of a state's power, and there were other small European states in addition to Britain that spawned mighty empires. None the less, the extent of the disparity between Britain's physical smallness, on the one hand, and the eventual scale of its empire, on the other, was unique. At the start of the twentieth century, the French empire was some twenty times the size of France itself, but the British empire was 125 times the size of Britain.[25]

We need to factor these astounding statistics into any assessment of British imperial power, especially as British smallness was not merely a function of geographical size. For most of its imperial history, Britain was far smaller in population than its main Catholic rivals for empire, France and Spain. As Adam Smith pointed out, Britain's regular army, as distinct from its navy, was also limited, given the scale of its imperial activities. In 1715, when Britain already claimed authority over half a million men and women in North America, large parts of the West Indies, coastal settlements in India, and also outposts in the Mediterranean, its army was no bigger than the King of Sardinia's. In 1850, in many ways the apex of its global power, Britain's home-produced army was still conspicuously modest by comparison with that of Russia, or France, or even Prussia.[26] And early modern and nineteenth-century Britain had to contend with yet another aspect of smallness. Today, English is the world language, and television, CNN, Hollywood, popular music and the net are all available to spread American ideas, interpretations of events, and cultural forms across the globe. But for much of Britain's imperial phase, English was still a minority language, and not even spoken by all the inhabitants of Scotland, Wales or Ireland. So Britain's ability to deploy its written and spoken language as a tool of empire and global influence was far more circumscribed than is the case with the United States today.

This is why practising connexity in the sense of feeding accurate British domestic information into histories of the imperial system it constructed is indispensable. We have to be sensitive not just to the ways in which this state undeniably succeeded in exerting power globally, but also to the ways in which its own domestic dimensions – the smallness of its home resources, the limits of its population, its badly overstretched army and its minority language – necessarily qualified and restricted its imperial power at different times and in different places. The extent to which Britain was able so presumptuously to construct this global edifice from its own small base, and to get away with it for so long, was really very peculiar: and we should never lose sight of that intrinsic peculiarity or cease sceptically and broadly to investigate it.[27]

In this connection, the tendency of some recent and often very deservedly influential scholarly writings about empire to sideline material factors, and concentrate instead on matters of epistemology and race, has sometimes proved unhelpful and obscuring. Let me be clear: the greater interest in exploring the cultural histories of empire and the retreat from the excessive economic determinism that sometimes afflicted imperial histories are healthy developments that I support completely. But the impression is sometimes conveyed and/or received that if you can only demonstrate Britain's, or France's, or Spain's capacity to accumulate real or bogus information about other peoples, and demonstrate too these powers' racism (which is usually not hard), then you have somehow accounted satisfactorily for the existence and persistence of their respective empires. You have not. As Kenan Malik has argued in regard to the British empire, it is easy enough to find evidence of racial epithets and racial ideologies in the British past, but the British were not witchdoctors. They could not use racist language and ideas magically and automatically to summon up global dominion.[28] Race could be used to legitimize dominion and often was: but it does not supply a comprehensive explanation for both the peculiar scale and the limitations of British imperial power. As always, we need to practise connexity and examine a broad diversity of forces and factors, not just concentrate on one.

IV

So let me conclude. One of the problems of addressing oneself to the question 'What is imperial [or any other] history?', is that it is easy to seem over-prescriptive and dogmatic. It bears repeating that the approaches to imperial history that I have outlined in what has necessarily been a brief chapter are emphatically and manifestly not exhaustive. If ever there was a field of history where 'let a thousand flowers bloom' was a necessary and desirable injunction, it is this one. I remain convinced, however, that – whatever one's specialization within this vast subject area in terms of country, chronology, methodology, or particular empire or focus of interest – it is essential to practise an element of comparative history over the *longue durée*, and to be sensitive to multiple connections. A broad-angled and eclectic vision is not an option in this field. It is indispensable; what it is all about. And this leads me to my final point: namely, that imperial history, properly conducted, is an extraordinarily demanding discipline. It is, heaven knows, hard enough to keep up with the latest scholarly work in regard to one discrete aspect of one country's past. To evolve a workmanlike knowledge of the histories and controversies of a wide range of conflicting states and societies over a broad span of time is hideously difficult, and yet it must be attempted if imperial history is to be further developed and opened up appropriately as a subject.

The difficulty is particularly acute this side of the Atlantic for reasons that scarcely need to be laboured. When even specialized and national libraries are obliged by budgetary considerations to cut back on foreign-language books, periodicals and history texts not judged sufficiently mainstream (by which is meant not British history); when graduate students (and their supervisors) are prevented by time and money constraints from learning new languages or from visiting archives in other parts of the world; when academics are put under incessant pressure to publish, and consequently urged in the direction of manageable, precise monographs on customary topics, rather than being encouraged to investigate new, big, exciting, cross-cultural subjects, then the prospects for a revitalized, generously interpreted imperial history cannot be good. And yet it matters, and not just for academics. When E.H. Carr wrote the classic we celebrate and commemorate in this volume, he complained of the parochialism of British history which 'weighs like a dead hand on our curriculum'. This parochialism is arguably still more of a problem today. Yet, as Carr warned, 'by our inability or unwillingness to understand ... [we risk] isolating ourselves from what is really going on in the world'.[29] Imperial history has a universal significance. But, as far as this country is concerned, it supplies an obvious way to jigsaw British history into global history, to see ourselves as others saw us and still see us, to examine the myriad ways, many of them unhappy, in which different regions of the world, and different peoples, have come together over time, collided and coalesced. As such, the ultimate answer to the question 'What is imperial history?' is really very simple. It is indispensable.

Notes and references

1. I stress that these were undergraduate perceptions forged in the late 1960s and early 1970s. Major rewritings of British and other imperial histories were in fact already underway by this point – one thinks of R. Robinson and J. Gallagher with A. Denny, *Africa and the Victorians* (London: Macmillan, 1961) – but it took time for such revisionist work to impact fully on history teaching in the universities, never mind on ideas outside them.
2. On these points, see Dane Kennedy, 'Imperial History and Post-Colonial Theory', *Journal of Imperial and Commonwealth History*, vol. 24 (1996), pp. 345–63; and his 'The Boundaries of Oxford's Empire', *International History Review*, vol. 23 (2001), pp. 604–22.

3. Eric Hobsbawm, *The Age of Empire, 1875–1914* (London: Weidenfeld and Nicolson, 1987), p. 60.

4. See David Armitage, *The Ideological Origins of the British Empire* (Cambridge: Cambridge University Press, 2000), especially pp. 100–45.

5. Frederic Bancroft (ed.), *Speeches, Correspondence and Political Papers of Carl Schurz*, 6 vols (New York: G.P. Putnam's, 1913), vol. VI, pp. 119–20. For an excellent sample of recent revisionist work on American westward expansion, see William Cronon, George Miles and Jay Gitlin (eds), *Under an Open Sky: Rethinking America's Western Past* (New York: W.W. Norton, 1992).

6. Edward Said, *Yeats and Decolonization* (Belfast: Field Day, 1988), p. 6. Two recent works that place the Ottoman empire in a broader European and imperial context are Donald Quataert, *The Ottoman Empire, 1700–1922* (Cambridge: Cambridge University Press, 2000), and Dominic Lieven, *Empire: The Russian Empire and its Rivals* (London: John Murray, 2000).

7. Hamilton is quoted in Lieven, *Empire*, p. 17.

8. Though critics of empire also drew on versions of the Roman past to argue that imperialism necessarily resulted in corruption, loss of liberty and decay: see Anthony Pagden, *Lords of all the World: Ideologies of Empire in Spain, Britain and France c.1500–c.1800* (London: Yale University Press, 1995).

9. See Richard White, *The Middle Ground: Indians, Empires, and Republics in the Great Lakes Region, 1650–1815* (Cambridge: Cambridge University Press, 1991). This is an excellent example of what may be achieved by examining different imperial systems in tandem.

10. See Lieven, *Empire*.

11. *The Expansion of England* (London: Macmillan, 1883).

12. Dane Kennedy lists a sample of these in the articles cited in note 2 above.

13. Though, as Professor Richard Evans informs me, it is possible that – as far as present-day racist politics is concerned – German outbursts are simply better-reported than the British variety.

14. J.C. Van Leur quoted in Henk Wesseling, 'Overseas History', in Peter Burke (ed.), *New Perspectives on Historical Writing* (Cambridge: Polity Press, 1992), p. 74; Philip D. Morgan, 'Encounters between British and "Indigenous" Peoples, c.1500–c.1800', in Martin Daunton and Rick Halpern (eds), *Empire and Others: British Encounters with Indigenous People 1600–1850* (London: University College London Press, 1999), p. 68.

15. Armitage, *Ideological Origins*, p. 13.

16. I am grateful to Dr Emma Rothschild of King's College, Cambridge, for information on this point.

17. J.E. Cookson, 'Political Arithmetic and War in Britain, 1793–1815', *War & Society*, vol. I (1983), pp. 37–60; and Philip Harling and Peter Mandler, 'From "Fiscal-Military" State to Laissez-faire State, 1760–1850', *Journal of British Studies*, vol. 32 (1993), pp. 44–70.

18. Quoted in Michael W. Doyle, *Empires* (Ithaca, NY: Cornell University Press, 1986), p. 287.

19. See their *History of Parliament: The House of Commons 1754–1790*, 3 vols (London: HMSO, 1964), vol. I, pp. 138–45; and R.G. Thorne (ed.), *The History of Parliament: The House of Commons 1790–1820*, 5 vols (London: Secker & Warburg, 1986), vol. I, pp. 306–13.

20. For a useful introduction to this issue, see Hew Strachan, *The Politics of the British Army* (Oxford: Clarendon Press, 1997).

21. On this point, see Part One of my *Captives: Britain, Empire, and the World 1600–1850* (London: Jonathan Cape, 2002).

22. James D. Tracy (ed.), *The Political Economy of Merchant Empires* (Cambridge: Cambridge University Press, 1991), p. 163.

23. C.A. Bayly, 'Returning the British to South Asian History: The Limits of Colonial Hegemony', *South Asia*, vol. XVII (1994), pp. 1–25.

24. I develop these arguments in *Captives*.

25. Norman Davies, *Europe: A History* (Oxford: Oxford University Press, 1996), pp. 1068–9.

26. J.A. Houlding, *Fit for Service: The Training of the British Army 1715–1795* (Oxford: Oxford University Press, 1981), pp. 7–8; Miles Taylor, 'The 1848 Revolutions and the British Empire', *Past & Present*, vol. 166 (2000), pp. 150–1.

27. There are some wise remarks on this point (and many others) in A.G. Hopkins, 'Back to the Future: From National History to Imperial History', *Past & Present*, vol. 164 (1999), pp. 198–243.

28. Kenan Malik, *The Meaning of Race: Race, History and Culture in Western Society* (London: Macmillan, 1996), pp. 231–2.

29. *What is History?* (London: Macmillan, 1961), pp. 145, 147.

9
Epilogue: What is History *Now*?

Felipe Fernández-Armesto

E.H. Carr 'would envy', he said, a historian unchanged in his outlook after fifty years of work.[1] Although only forty years have elapsed since the publication of *What is History?* they have been, as a nineteenth-century dowager might say, forty interesting years, crowded with novelty. Like other academic disciplines – perhaps, in some respects, more than most – history has both stimulated and reflected enormous changes in modern Western societies. An egalitarian revolution has narrowed gaps between classes, sexes, generations, ranks and almost all categories of social differentiation, except for the gap between rich and poor, which, with impressive tenacity, has continued to widen. In some cases, maybe, as cause – and certainly in consequence – historians have been able to cross those gaps with increasing ease, penetrating parts of society which earlier histories hardly reached, discovering the histories of formerly underprivileged or outcast minorities, including women and children, workers and criminals, the sick and the insane. Thanks, meanwhile, to the cultural and demographic revolution which has bestowed pluralism and multi-culturalism on most of the West – the retreat of white empires, the counter-colonization of metropolitan homelands by the former 'victim-peoples' and subject-peoples of colonialism – historians have felt freed and equipped to attempt some of the new explorations Carr foresaw and welcomed: studying the history of peoples formerly said to be 'without history';[2] embracing global history, including non-European subjects in comparative histories; broaching the histories of once apparently marginal ethnicities; drawing on the experience of a world in rapid transition to open new chapters in the study of identity. The battle

Carr joined to bring 'non-Western' history to the Cambridge faculty could not be so fiercely fought, or so tenaciously resisted, today (though the resistance of inertia is still obvious in some universities); nor would anyone repeat Hugh Trevor-Roper's opinion of 1963 that 'undergraduates, seduced by ... journalistic fashion, demand that they should be taught the history of black Africa ... But at present there is none or very little ... And darkness is not a subject for history.'[3]

Alongside these social revolutions, what we loosely call 'postmodernism' has also modified the practice of history, mounting an epistemological challenge which once seemed formidable. Like another contributor to the present volume, I wrote a memoir of encounter with it at a time when it seemed to threaten to subvert historians' dearest traditional quests: for truth and for the language in which to express it.[4] For a moment, historians feared that librarians of the future would consign history to the same shelves as fiction. This would not, in my opinion, have been a bad thing: my books would have joined the company of good literature. Postmodernism, however, proved to be a paper tiger of fearful asymmetry. British university history departments now have token postmodernists, as once they had token women and token blacks. But even as the tide receded, postmodernism left a rich residue on the shore, encouraging historical beachcombing. 'Virtual' histories, histories of the counter-factual, the ambiguous, the implicit, the liminal, the transgressive, the self-reflexive, the semiotic, the representational, the unconscious and the dreamed have become fascinating and irresistible or, at least, interesting and acceptable to almost everybody.

I

History, in short, has multiplied; indeed, it has exploded. The work of professional historians has never been as multifarious. Two further changes have helped. The revolution in information technology has speeded up scholarly output, created and expanded networks of collaboration, and generated enormous databases for work in 'cliometrics' and textual analysis. Above all, the numbers of professional historians have exploded with the expansion of higher education. The results have been mixed. They include the curse of over-specialization: historians dig ever deeper, narrower furrows in ever more desiccated soil until the furrows collapse and they are buried under their own aridity. Yet on the other hand, whenever one climbs out of one's furrow, there is now so much more of the field to survey: so much enriching new work, which can change one's perspective or broaden one's framework of comparison.

There is simply so much more to learn from. The amount of output, of course, is now frankly unmanageable. Even a quite narrow specialist is unlikely to be aware of – much less to read – everything of relevance. The consequent sense of uncertainty contributes, no doubt, to postmodern bewilderment and encourages inordinate scepticism about our command of the facts of the past. Inevitably, the growth of output means the growth of rubbish. But it means the increased availability of good work, too. I no longer know what it is like to be young, but it is bliss to be alive in such a dawn as ours, when to be an historian is to be part of an unprecedentedly productive community of fellow scholars, and when there is more interesting and improving historical work available than ever before.

Readers will sense a 'But' in the offing. We have learned so much in the past forty years: so much scepticism, so much science. And we have forgotten so much. We have forgotten how to defend successfully history's privileged place in the school curriculum. We have forgotten how to keep fully in touch with history teachers in pre-university education and how to feed their work with awareness of the refreshing and enlivening effects of new research: I say this not *de haut en bas* but as a trench warrior who has crossed no man's land and who has spent long spells as a schoolteacher. Any professional historian who has marked A level papers or similar examinations will know what I mean.

Deeper in the public arena, we seem to have forgotten how to influence debate and policy on the leading issues of the day. I can think of many instances, in recent years, of government policy formulated – with varying degrees of disaster – in glaring ignorance of the past. I can think of only one case of a policy influenced by new historical research. Unfortunately, it is a case which supplies little encouragement: the willingness of the early Thatcher government in the UK to embrace high unemployment as 'a price worth paying' for low inflation was evidently influenced by the revisionist work of Sydney Pollard and others of his circle on the British economy in the 1930s. I do not insist that historians' business is to influence policy; I maintain only that it is interesting that once they did so and that now they no longer do. The reading room formerly set aside for members of the legislature of the US in the Library of Congress was decorated in 1896, sumptuously but with only two paintings, which face one another from over the enormous fireplaces at either end of the room, dominating it and reminding congressmen of their duties. They represent, respectively, law and history. It is hard to imagine history occupying a similar place in an iconographic scheme of similar intent today.

Finally, we have forgotten how to perform in the public arena. This is important because an answer to the question 'What is history now?' must include what history is for everybody who is interested in it, not just those lucky enough to devote themselves to it professionally. The historians with whom Carr contended were the leading public intellectuals of their day whose controversies were aired on the wireless and reported in the press. For reasons I shall come to shortly, we shall, in present circumstances, not see the like of Isaiah Berlin, Hugh Trevor-Roper and A.J.P. Taylor again. Today, the past is genuinely popular: indeed, there has probably never been so much public interest in it and taste for it, depite, or perhaps because of, the shrinkage of history in the curriculum. The past of popular taste is not, however, on the whole, the past professional scholars disclose. The big growth areas today are what are misnamed 'family history' – that is, private genealogical research – 'heritage' and 'infotainment'. These were areas unvisited and unanticipated by Carr. Before returning to them, I propose to look back over the most conspicuous elements of the subject covered in *What Is History?* and ask how they ought to be modified in answer to the question 'What is history now?'

Important but neglected is Carr's choice of title. Today, contributors take part happily in a work called *What is History Now?* because the addition of the last word has a transforming effect on the sentence. It implies that in a moment's time history may be something else, as indeed it will. The question is formulated in a way which alludes to the essential mercuriality of the subject. To ask 'What is history?' is another, less attractive question. I would not call it a rhetorical question, because it is not rhetorical in form. But it is rhetorical in the sense that it does anticipate and invite a certain type of answer, of the kind, 'History is *x*' or 'History is *y*', thereby excluding the answer, 'History is *p*' or 'History is *q*.' It is an implicitly prescriptive and proscriptive question. And indeed, Carr's book, though broad-minded by the standards of its day, did pick fodder for the tumbrils. Carr condemned counter-factual work, moralizing, and what he called theology and literature. Today, I think, most of us would want to be more generous and embrace *nihil humanum alienum* or even the all-encompassing, *todo es historia* – the title of the periodical of a Latin American Academy of History – as our motto. Everything that we do or think, everything that we imagine about the future passes instantly into the past and becomes a proper subject for historical enquiry.

There are two further ways in which we should probably now admit that history is genuinely all-encompassing, without qualification. First, it includes all people. I do not mean that it includes all people merely as objects of study, though the extension of the range to include all sorts and conditions is very welcome, but also as participants. History is the most open and accessible of academic disciplines. Everybody can do it – indeed everybody does do it, because everybody has experience of the past and all people have privileged access to the sources of their own stories. It requires no special training, except in modest skills which any literate person can easily and quickly pick up without help. There are good reasons for being a graduate student in history, but the acquisition of peculiar professional competence, or of esoteric or heiratic knowledge, is not one of them. My favorite history books include works by scientists, lawyers and nuns. E.H. Carr himself, who never had a degree or an appointment in history, exemplifies the point. This is one of the many reasons why historians should avoid jargon – the refuge of scoundrels who want to make their work unintelligible to non-initiates. Communicability is a hallmark of good historical writing. Others – I should add, since I do not wish to imply that because history is open to everybody, everybody is equally good at it – are faithful to the sources in the presentation of a version of the past which is convincingly imagined and vividly evoked.

As well as including all people, history should include all disciplines. If I remember correctly, my reason for becoming a historian was the sheer voracity of my interests. Unable to choose between the disciplines which attracted me, I fixed on the one which included a little of all the others. History is fodder for Buridan's ass. Some disciplines, of course, are more helpful than others. Anthropology, as we have all come to recognize since Carr wrote, is highly relevant, because the past even of one's own society is another culture, where 'they do things differently'. Studies of literature and art should be followed by historians, first, because the creative work of the past is a precious source for the images and sentiments which informed thought and behaviour, and second, because texts and material evidence have to be interpreted with the help of all the critical techniques which allied disciplines can make available. Archaeology is an ineluctable source of evidence for historians. It is a poor historian who knows no philosophy or economics or theology. I have never been attracted to sociology: I associate the discipline with over-generalization and Procrustean habits of modelling; yet I found some classic sociological theory of enormous help in my recent work, devoted to understanding new kinds of intercommunal relationships forged in early modern colonial societies.[5] Linguistics is important not because of the impact of the 'linguistic turn' in the humanities so much as because change in language is a barometer of other kinds of historical change. The insights of psychology can make a huge difference, not only for the obvious kinds of psycho-history practised by historical biographers, but also in the effort to understand collective mentalities and relations between social groups. To take an example from my own field, I suspect that the ever perplexing problem of how the Spanish empire worked in the sixteenth-century New World will become more intelligible when we start thinking psychologically about the relationships between the young, often orphaned native aristocracy and the newly arrived clerical and conquistador elites, who took on quasi-fatherly roles.[6] Interdisciplinarity echoes through the present volume: pursuing one's specialism in the conviction that it is permeable, and that it overlaps with others, and that it is very much the richer for it.

Above all – among disciplines which belong in the historian's toolkit – though Carr insisted that history was a science, I do not think he appreciated, as we are beginning to do today, the degree to which historians have to be scientifically educated. This is not only a matter of appreciating analogies between historical processes and changes in the natural world, or of applying particular sciences to the study of the past, as, for instance, in helping to resolve problems of chronology connected with bits of material evidence, or in applying genetics to the study of migrations in the manner startlingly pioneered by Luigi Cavalli-Sforza.[7] More important still is the recognition that history can no longer remain encamped in one of 'two cultures'. Human beings are obviously part of the animal continuum. We are enmeshed in the ecosystems of which we are part, and nothing, in my submission, in human history makes complete sense without reference to the rest of nature.[8] That is why historical ecology, or environmental history, deserves a growing place in the curriculum. It is also why, on a more frivolous level, when people ask me 'What is your period?', I always say 'From primeval slime to the future', and when they ask me 'What is your field?', I say 'I only do one planet.' History now has to be scientifically informed in order to encompass the natural environment. In order to study historical ecology, I had to resume my own scientific education at the age of forty, having given it up, in the manner formerly approved by English schools, at the age of fourteen. I regard young historians now as greatly privileged, because normally, by the time they get to university, they have done at least a little bit of science.

II

It is impossible to answer the question 'What is history now?' without raising the question 'What is history for?' Although Carr did not ask this question explicitly, he answered it implicitly in the course of the book. His answer still has sympathizers, who demand from history that it explain the present, and mould the future, serving a political or social agenda, which in Carr's case was connected with his notion of progress. I do not want to stop historians studying with those objectives in mind, if they so wish, as long as they are candid and clear about what they are doing, so that no one is misled. But it does contradict one of our dearest historians' shibboleths, which is that we study the past for its own sake. And I share our ancient reluctance to pin the historical project to any particular purpose, though it is a dispiriting thing to say to people who have to fill in research funding applications. There are, in my submission, only two reasons for studying anything: to enhance life and to prepare for death. The study of history enhances life because it conjures in the mind a vivid context for the appreciation and understanding of encounters with people and with artefacts, with streets and texts, with landscapes and ruins. And it prepares you for death by cultivating what Carr called 'imaginative understanding', which some contributors to this volume have called 'empathy' or other names of which Carr would disapprove.[9] By broadening the mind, by exercising the ability to understand the other, history has a moral effect on the person that studies it. It can make you a better person. But other disciplines can also have effects of these sorts. Our best peculiar justification for history is to say that it needs no justification. Because it is everything, it is inescapable. You can say of it what Mallory said of Everest.

After the title, the next thing to strike readers of Carr's book in its day was his doctrine of the historical fact which seemed – as Alice Kessler-Harris recalls – subversive and elusive because of its challenge to conventional assumptions about historical objectivity. Carr's doctrine is much criticized: it is vitiated by circularity of argument, because it represents the historical fact as a fact used by historians, and historians as people who use historical facts. His one great example of a 'fact about the past' in the course of transmutation into a 'historical fact' has turned out, under Richard Evans's scrutiny, probably not to have been a fact at all, but a memoirist's faulty recollection.[10] Yet Carr was right about the nature of facts in a way for which he has got insufficient credit. He realized that there was a genuinely objective, true account of the past out there, waiting to be found, but what he called the 'process' of selection and interpretation necessarily removed the work of the historian from that truth and compromised the objectivity with which it was presented. That is surely right. The truth is out there. We are not equipped to get at it.

But Carr overlooked three points on which we can now take his scepticism further. First, we can say that the facts that we do know objectively, and with certainty, are facts only about the sources. For a work called *What is History?*, his book seems amazingly innocent of sources, whereas everything in the present volume, and everything in modern historical scholarship, is saturated in reference to sources. Our facts are not those of the past in general, but of the sources in particular: we can know only what the sources say, not – of course – the further realities which lie beyond them, because the sources are the only part of the past that is directly accessible to our senses. The further realities we can know only as contingencies: if such and such a source is reliable, we can say, then what it says is true. For these reasons, the past we study as historians is not the past 'as it really was'. Rather, it is what it felt like to be in it. The growing bibliography of the history of passions, sentiments, sensibilities, anxieties and the like is a measurable recognition of this.

Second, the objectivity which we are committed to seeking, but which we can never attain, lies at the sum total of all possible subjectivities, those subjectivities so glitteringly arrayed in Miri Rubin's contribution to this volume. That is why historical enquiry should always shift perspective. By changing perspective, we compile multiple perspectives and approach the objectivity which lies at the sum of all of them. Undeterred by the suspicions of the politically correct, I always tell my pupils that history is a muse glimpsed bathing between leaves: the more you shift your point of view, the more is revealed. This is nothing to do with relativism, which on the whole I dismiss. And my final reason for endorsing and extending Carr's scepticism is itself a matter of hard, verifiable, scientific fact: the demonstrable deficiency of human memory. It is astonishing to me how little interest historians take in memory, because so many of the sources on which we rely pass through the medium of memory before they get to us. Some of us are aware that it is socially or culturally constructed. Some of us give our students Halbwachs to read on social or so-called collective memory and reflect on his maxim that 'the past is not preserved but is reconstructed on the basis of the present'.[11]

Yet the problems of memory go much further than that: to the roots of individual memories, on which social memory depends and of which most historical sources are composed. We know very little about it except that it is usually bad. There has been an enormous amount of work in recent years by psychologists and anthropologists, but above all by neurophysiologists, which combines to undermine our faith in memory even further. In the work of a psychologist such as Alan Baddeley, it resembles a trick mechanism for evading awkward facts, as much as a trap for capturing them.[12] We practise convenient oblivion. We retrieve memories through rosy filters. The memory is the massage. Among anthropologists, in work well-represented by a paper by Jack Goody,[13] it is increasingly recognized that non-literate cultures' orally transmitted memories are not fossilized, word for word, in bardic retrieval systems, but are substantially re-created, reinvented with every retelling. Memory is wired to be warped. It is not a highway for time travel: the past it takes you to never really happened quite in the way you think. Recall is a siren call. Surprisingly, perhaps, this is just what one would expect from the results of experimental work of recent years by cognitive scientists working with literate subjects. Memories are 'recorded' or registered in an environment of hectic neural activity in which synapses fire and proteins are generated: in the judgement of the leading authority, Daniel Schachter, it is practically impossible to suppose that memories are recorded unchanged:

> Memories are never exact replicas of external reality. Psychophysical studies and electrical recordings from the brain have shown that incoming sensory information is not received passively. ... In this sense all memories are 'created' rather than simply 'received'. No memory or mental image exactly replicates the constellation of nerve impulses associated with the initial sensation. Past experience, encoded in the strength of synaptic connections throughout the activated neural networks, modifies the incoming information.[14]

This is, for historians, equivalent to the uncertainty principle for phycisists. The environment in which memories are retrieved introduces more levels of uncertainty, while often at the same time deluding the memorist into 'a conviction of accuracy which the empirical data does not support'.[15] So memory is always removed from reality, though, for reasons we still do not know, it works better in some cases than others. Unless and until we understand how differences between good and bad memory arise, caution and scepticism are our best recourse.

Apart from the passages on the fact, Carr's doctrine of causation is the most striking part of his book. Nowadays I am a regular visitor to the London School of Economics but I only visited it for the first time a few months ago. I was staggered to find emblazoned on the wall, inside the main entrance, in letters of gold, a quotation from another text which, like that of E.H. Carr, I knew all too well in my youth: Virgil's *Aeneid*. The writing on the wall reads *Felix qui potuit rerum cognoscere causas*. I can remember reading that line when I was, I suppose, about sixteen and thinking to myself what a good joke of Virgil's this was. For Virgil's world resembles the cosmos of chaos theory, where causes are untraceable and effects untrackable. The fates spin away offstage, directing history towards a preordained goal. Meanwhile, however, the random interventions of shifty people and capricious gods keep twisting and snapping the thread. What makes the *Aeneid* a good story is that it is impossible to know what is going to happen next. You cannot know the causes of things; therefore you cannot predict their outcome. Yet this irony of Virgil's has been transformed on the walls of the LSE into a solemn pronouncement which is taken all too literally. And it is the same kind of pronouncement that you find resonating in the work of Carr, in which history is one damn cause after another and these vast chains of causation link the whole narrative together. History stretches connectedly, like a brontosaurus's backbone.

Implicitly, recent historiography seems to recognize the inadmissability of this way of picturing the past. Most of the long-term chains of causes inherited from the historiography of previous generations turn out, on close examination, to be composed of brittle links. Historians now are whittling vast schemes to fragments. To understand the fall of Rome, no one now feels the need to go back to Augustus or even the Antonines. The Reformation happened because of the way things were in the sixteenth century, not the way they had been in the Middle Ages. The English Civil War is now thought by most specialists to be best understood in the context of the generation or so immediately preceding its outbreak. The origins of the American and French Revolutions and the First World War have been chopped short by similar blades. These examples could be multiplied. Cleopatra's nose resembles a butterfly's wings. Most of the rest of Carr's main themes – the attempts to ostracize the individual, proscribe the unique, outlaw moralising, appropriate science and reify progress – now seem old-fashioned; but they were probably already rearguard actions in their day and can be set aside as matters unlikely to sustain present controversy. It will be more profitable to devote the last lines at my disposal to changes unanticipated by Carr which make history now different from the discipline he described.

III

Part of the recent explosive growth in history, which I began by celebrating, has been in popular taste and demand, to which professional historians have contributed little and responded hardly at all. Private genealogical research is clearly very important. The conference at which the present volume took shape was tremendously impressed to hear from Elizabeth Hallam-Smith that 70 per cent of researchers at the Public Record Office are engaged in this. Yet as far as I know no academic institution has taken much interest in the phenomenon. Globally, we have more or less abrogated institutional participation in this area of popular historiography to the Church of Jesus Christ of the Latter-Day Saints, whose cult of the baptism of the dead has aroused church members to heroic feats of work in tracing their ancestors. We cannot dismiss this subject as of no interest, and the amateur genealogists as mere antiquarians. Antiquarianism is the foundation of historical knowledge and genealogical research can fire bricks with which to build historical edifices.

Alongside so-called 'family history', the sector known as 'heritage' is now many people's main point of contact with history, thanks to the attenuation of history in the school curriculum. Some of this is in the hands of scholarly museum curators and *fonctionnaires*. Much of it, however, is at the mercy of theme-park economics, dire and dumbed-down. Historians contribute relatively little guidance. As a source of historical 'infotainment', even the reach of 'heritage' is puny compared with that of television. In Carr's day, it was easy for professional historians to control the presentation and output of history on television, for the charismatic lecturer wrote or extemporized his own script and determined the choice of images, if any. A.J.P. Taylor lectured for television as for the classroom without modification of style. Kenneth Clark literally called the shots. Jacob Bronowski's director rarely knew, until the cameras were rolling, what the presenter was going to say.[16]

Those days are irrecoverably past. I know that there are some good telehistory programmes, despite the circumstances I am about to describe. David Starkey, Simon Schama and other presenters of immense power and talent may be better at manipulating the television professionals than most of us are. In *Ad Familiares*, Paul Cartledge has struck an optimistic note in recent correspondence about his own excellent contributions to television. During the conference at which this volume took shape, he and Richard Evans both expressed broad satisfaction with the current treatment of history on television. I think that optimism is misplaced. I recommend pessimism to everybody. It is the only way to indemnify oneself against disappointment. But more importantly, I want to leave a strongly pessimistic message about this in order to help ensure that the worst does not happen. The function of pessimism is to arm resistance against disaster.

Most television history still has professional presenters or voice-overs reading scripts uninfluenced by historians. Academics play bit-parts, stamped as boring by the convention which has them seated in studies, staring off-screen, as if they could not be trusted to address the cameras. Their contributions are edited to fit a version of the past written by the production team, with their own ratings-driven agendas. Although it is a relatively young art form, television already has its own conventions and clichés, its tired, fossilized ways of packaging images and stifling ideas. My own experiences in working on telehistory make me wise and wary. Although I demand clauses in my contracts, which give me nominal control over my own material and specify that nothing that I write can be changed without my permission, editorial control necessarily remains with the producers. The directors drive the narratives because they select the images; the commissioning editors drive it downward and dumbward, because most of them seem to hold their audiences in intellectual contempt. The sheer pressure of working with a creative team – which is one of the joys of making television programmes – imposes concessions, some of which are made for reasons which contribute nothing to the integrity or validity of the programme. One has to defer to colleagues, as in any collaborative venture, and that sometimes means deferring to judgements which are unrestrained by the discipline of the sources.

I discovered when I was working on the *Millennium* television series, which was based on one of my books and for which I wrote or co-wrote most of the scripts, that television cares passionately about the logistics of programme making and almost not at all about the content. The really important thing is to get the camera crew to the right place at the right time, with the right weather and, in certain exotic locations, with grease applied to the right political palms, when there is no currency crisis or political coup or famine. And, by comparison with these important considerations, nothing else matters much. With a deficient script, you still have a programme. With botched logistics, you have nothing.

A problematic blessing is that television teams are full of wonderfully creative people: forty creative intellects, in the case of the *Millennium* series, all threatening to cancel each other out. One of my jobs on the series was to draw up lists of images that the camera crews had to film in the different locations. They nearly always came back with a completely different range of images, because of the interventions of logistic problems or adventitious enthusiasms. On one occasion a crew came back without filming anything on their list, and without images from the period to which the programme was supposed to relate. I said, 'Why have you done this?' 'Unfortunately,' the director replied, 'all those mosques you listed were ruined and shabby.' I pointed out that, with our enormous videographics staff and budget, we could have reconstructed the original glories of the mosques on screen, and it would have been wonderful for the audience. And he said, 'Ah yes, I know that, but I didn't want to give those blighters in Video-graphics that satisfaction.'

On the basis of experiences like these, I do not believe that at the moment we have the right relationship with the enormously powerful and influential medium of television. This is symptomatic of a more general crisis, which separates the historical profession from the public. Yet why should I repine? If, as I insisted above, history is something everybody can do, then television directors can do it and their audiences can do it; baptizers of the dead and self-appointed heritage-guardians can do it. Historians are unnecessary. My answer to that is that although anybody can do it, people privileged by their profession to do it all the time and to be paid for it – people with privileged access to the sources – do have a certain obligation of guidance, even of leadership. At the moment, I think, at the very least, we are facing a lost opportunity and perhaps, at worst, a failed responsibility.

Notes and references

1. E.H. Carr, *What is History?* (Harmondsworth, 1964), p. 42.
2. E. Wolf, *Europe and the People without History* (London, 1982).
3. H.R. Trevor-Roper, *The Rise of Christian Europe* (London, 1965), p. 9.
4. F. Fernández-Armesto, *Truth: A History* (London, 1997); R.J. Evans, *In Defence of History* (London, 1997).
5. F. Fernández-Armesto, 'The Stranger-Effect in Early Modern Asia', *Itinerario*, vol. xxiv, no. 2 (2000), pp. 84–103.
6. F. Fernández-Armesto, *Continuity and Discontinuity in the Sixteenth-Century New World*. The James Ford Bell Lectures, no. 39 (Minneapolis, 2001), p. 18.
7. L. Cavalli-Sforza, *History and the Geography of Human Genes* (Princeton, 1994).
8. F. Fernández-Armesto, *Civilizations: Culture, Ambition and the Transformation of Nature* (New York, 2001), p. 4.
9. Carr, *What is History?*, pp. 24, 97.
10. Evans, *In Defence of History*, pp. 76–8.

11. M. Halbwachs, 'The Social Frameworks of Memory', *On Collective Memory* (Chicago, 1992), pp. 96–124. See also P. Burke, 'History as Social Memory', in T. Butler (ed.), *Memory: History, Culture and the Mind* (Oxford, 1989), pp. 97–113.
12. A. Baddeley, *The Psychology of Memory* (London, 1992). See also D. Rubin (ed.), *Autobiographical Memory* (Cambridge, 1986); J. Prager, *Presenting the Past: Psychoanalysis and the Sociology of Misremembering* (Cambridge, MA, 1998).
13. J. Goody, 'Memory in Oral Tradition', in *The Power of the Written Tradition* (Washington, DC, 2000), pp. 26–46.
14. D.L. Schachter (ed.), *Memory Distortion: How Minds, Brains and Societies Recontruct the Past* (Cambridge, MA, 1995), p. x.
15. Prager, *Presenting the Past*, p. 185; Schachter, *Memory Distortion*, pp. 17–18.
16. Rita Bronowski, personal communication.

Notes on Contributors

David Cannadine is Director of the Institute for Historical Research at the University of London, having returned to England from a Chair in History at Columbia University. His many books include *The Pleasures of the Past*, *History in our Time*, *The Rise and Fall of Class in Britain* and *Ornamentalism: How the British Saw their Empire*. He edits the journals *Historical Research* and *Reviews in History*.

Richard J. Evans is Professor of Modern History at the University of Cambridge, and fellow of Gonville and Caius College. He is the author of ten books including *In Defence of History* and, most recently, a controversial study of the Irving Trial, *Telling Lies about Hitler*.

Paul Cartledge, Professor of Ancient History at the University of Cambridge, and Fellow of Clare College, is the author of three books on Sparta and one on Aristophanes, and has edited three collections of essays on Greek and Athenian history. His most recent books are *The Greeks*, *Democritus and Atomistic Politics*, and *The Greeks: Crucible of Civilization*, a companion volume to a major US television series. He has edited the *Cambridge Illustrated History of Ancient Greece*, and co-edits the series 'Key Themes in Ancient History' and 'Classical Inter/Faces'.

Annabel Brett is a Fellow of Gonville and Caius College, Cambridge. Her publications include *Liberty, Right and Nature* and an edited collection of essays *On the Power of Emperors and Popes*.

Linda Colley is Leverhulme Research Professor in History at the London School of Economics and Political Science. Formerly Richard M. Colgate Professor of History at Yale University, she has also taught at the University of Cambridge. Among her many publications, the bestselling *Britons: Forging a Nation, 1707–1837* won the Wolfson Prize.

Susan Pedersen is Professor of History at Harvard University. Her publications include *Family Policy and the Origins of the Welfare State: Britain and France, 1914–45*, and *After the Victorians: Private Conscience and Public Duty in Modern Britain* edited with Peter Mandler.

Olwen Hufton is Leverhulme Research Professor at the University of Oxford and a fellow of Merton College. She is also a Fellow of the British Academy and the Royal Historical Society. Her many publications include *Europe: Privilege and Protest 1730–1789, Women and the Limits of Citizenship in the French Revolution* and *The Prospect Before Her: A History of Women in Western Europe, I: 1500–1800*.

Miri Rubin is Professor of European History and Director of Research at Queen Mary, University of London. She has previously held academic positions at Cambridge, Princeton and Oxford. Her publications include *Corpus Christi: The Eucharist in Late Medieval Culture* and *Gentile Tales*, and she co-edited *Framing Medieval Bodies*. She is currently writing the late medieval volume of *The New Penguin History of Britain*.

Alice Kessler Harris is Professor of History at Columbia University. She has published extensively on women's labour history, in which the latest of her four published books is *In Pursuit of Equity: How Gender Shaped American Economic Citizenship*. She is co-editor of *Protecting Women: Labor Legislation in Europe, Australia, and the United States, 1880–1920* (1995), and *U.S. History as Women's History* (1995).

Felipe Fernández-Armesto is Professor of History at Queen Mary, University of London. His many books include *Civilizations: Culture, Ambition and the Transformation of Nature, Millennium: A History of the last Thousand Years*, and *Truth: A History and a Guide for the Perplexed*.

Index

Compiled by Sue Carlton